CIVIC SERVICE

CIVIC SERVICE

WHAT DIFFERENCE DOES IT MAKE?

JAMES L. PERRY AND **ANN MARIE THOMSON**

M.E.Sharpe
Armonk, New York
London, England

Copyright © 2004 by M.E. Sharpe, Inc.

All rights reserved. No part of this book may be reproduced in any form
without written permission from the publisher, M.E. Sharpe, Inc.,
80 Business Park Drive, Armonk, New York 10504.

Library of Congress Cataloging-in-Publication Data

Perry, James L.
    Civic service : what difference does it make? / James L. Perry and Ann Marie Thomson.
        p. cm.
    Includes bibliographical references and index.
    ISBN 0-7656-1275-5
    1. Labor service—United States. 2. National service—United States. 3. Volunteers—
United States. I. Thomson, Ann Marie, 1954– II. Title.

HD4870.U6P47 2003
361.3'7'0973—dc21   2003050596

Printed in the United States of America

The paper used in this publication meets the minimum requirements of
American National Standard for Information Sciences
Permanence of Paper for Printed Library Materials,
ANSI Z 39.48-1984.

∞

BM (c)   10   9   8   7   6   5   4   3   2   1

Contents

III. Research Synthesis Findings

IV. Summing Up and Taking Stock

V. Appendices

Tables and Figures

Tables

Figures

Acknowledgments

This book is a joint effort between professor and former student, mentor and mentored, but foremost two students of civic service. It originated during the senior author's sabbatical at the Corporation for National and Community Service (CNCS) in 1999–2000. Bill Bentley, then head of the Corporation's Department of Evaluation and Effective Practices (DEEP) and now senior vice president at the Points of Light Foundation, arranged an Intergovernmental Personnel Act mobility assignment. Although a synthesis of national service research was high on the list of tasks developed prior to the sabbatical, no one could have anticipated either the demands of the range of tasks or the enormous effort required to complete this synthesis. We are both pleased to finally be at the end of this journey.

Many former colleagues at CNCS contributed to this project in a variety of ways. Bill Bentley not only initiated the project that led to the book and commented on early drafts of chapters, but he has also persistently asked, "How is the synthesis coming?" whenever we saw him. This persistence comes as no surprise to those who know Bill and, for us, it is one of his endearing traits. Lance Potter, director of evaluation, Chuck Helfer, his deputy, and other staff in the Office of Evaluation were helpful in sharing their views with us and, on occasion, pointing us to the only copies of long-forgotten studies. We especially thank David Rymph, director of research and acting DEEP director after Bill's departure. David was a continuous source of support both during and after the sabbatical.

Two CNCS chief executive officers played less direct but nonetheless important roles in the development of this book. Harris Wofford was CEO during the time the junior author served as a National Service Fellow in 1998–99 and during the senior author's sabbatical. Harris was a gracious, accessible, and supportive host during these experiences. His more than forty years of commitment to our civic service institutions is an inspiration to us both. Before serving as CNCS CEO from 2001–03, Les Lenkowsky was a colleague and collaborator at Indiana University. We owe much to Les for his intellectual stimulation and friendship.

We would like to thank Harry Briggs, executive editor at M.E. Sharpe, for his timely efforts to bring this book to press. He has been encouraging at every step of the way. Editors Elizabeth Granda and Henrietta Toth capably steered the manuscript from typescript to final form.

Moving this manuscript to press also benefited enormously from talent in Indianapolis and Bloomington. Whitney Simic and Trevor Nagle provided research assistance at various stages along the way. Dawn Olilla accepted the demanding but essential task of converting endnotes to final form. She performed admirably. We owe a deep debt to Katherine Murray, a talented editor and believer in civic service, who began working with us at the developmental stage of this book. She has been a constant source of insight and affirmation.

We take full responsibility for errors of omission and commission.

James L. Perry   Ann Marie Thomson
Indianapolis   Bloomington

Introduction

This book comes in the wake of September 11, 2001. Calls for a renewed ethic of service to country and community characterize the current public ethos. In his 2001 inaugural address, President George W. Bush articulated the ethos as a challenge to Americans to be "citizens, not spectators [building] communities of service and a nation of character."[1] In a June 2002 letter to Congress, all fifty United States governors echoed President Bush's challenge. "As Governors," they wrote,

> we have long been involved in and concerned with volunteer efforts in our respective states. We have seen the progress of young people inspired by older students, the importance of trained hands helping after a disaster, and the pride of a senior sharing his or her time with a child in need of mentoring. Since the events of September 11, our citizens have responded and done even more to meet the critical needs in our communities. We recognize the value of national service as a tool in meeting important needs in our states. We have seen national service at work and want to continue and expand service in our communities, states, and country.[2]

Civic service has not always enjoyed such strong public support. Yet, as Part I of this book will demonstrate, service remains an enduring part of the American psyche—both as an ideal (rooted in the abstract moral and political philosophies of classic liberalism and civic republicanism) and as a historical reality (rooted in institutional legacies left behind in the ebb and flow of popular support). Furthermore, as the remaining chapters will demonstrate, a review of service-related research demonstrates that a distinct field of civic service does exist—rich with a variety of studies yielding potentially valuable information from both scientific and anecdotal sources.

In the wake of the current public ethos, this book arrives at an important point in the history of civic service. Despite its long legacy as both an ideal and as a historical reality in the United States, and despite the burgeoning number of studies in the field, civic service remains poorly understood. "We do not know very well," writes civic service scholar Michael Sherraden, "how to understand service as an institution, nor do we have an adequate theoretical empirical foundation to guide policy and program development."[3] Perhaps this is because so few attempts have been made to build cumulative knowledge from the rich array of single studies on civic service.

The primary purpose of this book is to fill a void left by the noncumulative nature of research findings to date. As one of the most comprehensive attempts to synthesize what we know about civic service, this book seeks to build integrative knowledge and identify how that knowledge can be used in research and practice. Three questions drive the current volume:

- What are the attributes of the research that have been conducted about civic service?
- What are the summative effects of civic service on servers, recipients of service, institutions, and communities?
- What does the research say about civic service implementation?

We invite you to join us as we explore these three broad questions. In the following pages, we will synthesize what we know so far about civic service, identify the implications of this knowledge for research and practice, and make several contingent inferences about civic service and its outcomes in the form of propositions that can be tested in future service-related research.

Defining Civic Service

Not surprisingly, several authors of the seminal works on civic service claim that "any definition [of civic service] is necessarily somewhat arbitrary"[4] and that, as a general term, *civic service* "has had different meanings at different times."[5] A comprehensive review of service-related research since 1990 substantiates these claims. In its recent report, the Grantmaker Forum on Community and National Service argues convincingly that the literature on service since 1990 demonstrates no agreed-upon understanding of the meaning of service.[6] Some people believe

> that true service can only be unpaid voluntary action. Others feel that service includes stipended community service through national programs like AmeriCorps. Similarly, some feel that mandatory service is valuable and rewarding, while others feel it is an oxymoron. [Moreover], it is unclear where the boundaries lie between volunteerism and service.[7]

If the meaning of service lies primarily in volunteerism, as some believe, then service is necessarily a private, even intimate, individual response to a particular need. Most proponents of this view believe any intrusion of the public (government) in this essentially private realm should be resisted. If, on the other hand, the meaning of service lies in a response to the historical social and economic problems of a particular era, then service is necessarily public, institutional, and formal in nature.

From an institutional perspective, the meaning of service lies in its instrumental value. Service is nearly always seen as a means to achieve particular ends—public and private. Examples include inculcating civic virtue, meeting unmet social needs, achieving economic and social stability, and building strong communities.[8] This view of service champions a strong public sector role in an otherwise private activity—although that role need not be a national government role. As Michael Sherraden points out, more and more service opportunities occur at state and local levels through loosely affiliated intersectoral programs and nongovernmental organizations.[9]

The historical evolution of civic service suggests increasing popular support for this latter view. In either case, however, whether service is seen as a private expression of gratitude or as a means to solve social problems, the concept persists in the American psyche because its meaning lies in the uneasy tension between moral individualism and civic obligation. Given the historical ebb and flow of popular support for institutional, formal programs of civic service, developing a conceptual definition of service proves difficult, but not impossible, if we are willing to allow it to be a growing, evolving definition.

A definition of this sort, while it must acknowledge the essentially private nature of volunteerism, must also emphasize its essentially public nature rooted in the persistent, rhetorically powerful belief that citizenship demands some kind of self-sacrifice for the sake of the demos. From this perspective, Sherraden and Eberly's 1982 definition of civic service still stands as one of the best in the service-related literature. "As a general term," they write,

> [service] refers to a period of service given by the individual to the nation or community [that] embodies two complementary ideas: one, that some service to the larger society is part of individual citizenship responsibility; and two, that society should be structured in ways which provide citizens with opportunities to make meaningful contributions . . .[10]

The value of this definition lies in its emphasis on both the private (individual citizenship responsibility) and public (structuring society to provide citizens service opportunities) nature of service. Besides this inherent private/public nature, several of the seminal scholars of civic service further categorize the public nature of service into military and civic service.

Sherraden, for example, argues that civic service—as an alternative to military service—represents an equally important and viable social institution with a different, but complementary role to play in society.[11] Civic service according to Sherraden, fills a gap that military service cannot fill by providing an alternative for large numbers of young people (who may be either disinclined to join the military or not needed because changes in the military require smaller armies) to fulfill civic obligation so necessary for a healthy democracy.

Sherraden extends this line of reasoning further by asserting that civic service fills yet another gap created by the failure of the private sector (markets) to build institutions for social cohesion, social capital, and the expression of civic ideals. We are only now realizing, he writes, the importance of such institutions for a healthy society; civic service provides the means for "re-stating the role of government and re-honoring public life and public affairs" through the building of institutions that "respond to basic human and environmental challenges and create vital social and economic institutions."[12]

This institutional perspective on civic service represents an increasingly accepted view among national service scholars and practitioners and one that we espouse. We define civic service in terms of the following key dimensions: (1) a significant commitment beyond oneself, (2) with minimal monetary reward, (3) for a defined but prolonged length of time, (4) that contributes to the benefit of local, national, and/or global communities, (5) through formal organizational structures and programs. These key dimensions emphasize the public and institutional nature of service as distinct from solely private voluntary activity. It is important to note that these dimensions closely follow the definition developed by Michael Sherraden for the Global Service Institute at Washington University, St. Louis.[13]

For the purposes of this synthesis, we find that the Global Service Institute's definition provides a common ground upon which to examine the large (and growing) body of service-related research that currently exists. Like Sherraden, we view civic service as an emergent institution. We also share his belief that the time is ripe for expanding our understanding of service beyond the private voluntary acts of individual citizens; rather, to view civic service as an important social institution necessary for the health of a nation (or the world, for that matter). In analyzing this research, we hope to extract knowledge that will prove useful for understanding how and what kinds of civic service constitute opportunities for citizens to make meaningful contributions to society.

Why This Study?

In their 1986 book, *National Service: What Would It Mean?*, Richard Danzig and Peter Szanton criticize debates on civic service for being so general as to preclude any serious analysis of particular forms of service.[14] The purpose of this current volume on civic service is to move the debate beyond this level of generality by gathering and analyzing the many evaluations of civic service programs that have been conducted and identifying the policy implications of these evaluations for the future of civic service. To date, few attempts have been made to examine this body of research using research synthesis. Furthermore, what we do know is frequently presented as best practices based on anecdotal evidence rather than on systematic reviews of the growing body of literature in the field of service.[15]

Research synthesis is important if we are to examine more closely the claims made about national civic service. The writings of William James, Morris Janowitz, Charles Moskos, William F. Buckley, and others attest to the great expectations that this form of service engenders.[16] National civic service is perceived as a social policy tool with the transformative power to instill civic virtue, create a shared politics of meaning, and provide avenues for civic obligation that will heal individuals, communities, and the nation. Many of the previous claims about service relied on policy arguments grounded in either analogies or scenarios projecting the impacts of that service. Danzig and Szanton's excellent analysis of four models of civic service is a case in point.[17] Military service has been the primary analogy used to gauge the benefits and costs of national civic service in studies done to date.[18]

Analogies and scenarios are useful devices for exploring policy options, but they have limitations. Foremost among the limitations is that they are prospective—that is, forward-looking and predicated on assumptions about how a program will work—rather than retrospective, looking back on what the program does, indeed, deliver.[19] This study takes a retrospective look at civic service. We use the tools of research synthesis, which involves the systematic analysis of research findings.[20] Although by the standards of other fields and the general sophistication of research synthesis methods, the synthesis in this study will be relatively rudimentary, it is the most systematic and comprehensive synthesis conducted on civic service research to date.

At the beginning of the twenty-first century, the field of civic service faces significant challenges and opportunities. One major challenge, write James Perry and Mark Imperial, is

> integrating the new understandings and practices associated with service into our traditional understanding of volunteerism. Practices such as mandatory service, stipended service, and using service as an integral tool for solving difficult public problems signal the emergence of a field of citizen service with boundaries different from those that defined voluntary action research during the 20th century.[21]

These boundaries have increasingly expanded into the public realm in the last decade. Both the National and Community Service Act of 1990 and the National and Community Service Trust Act of 1993 demonstrate the strong bipartisan support for publicly funded programs that provide opportunities for citizens to serve their communities. Moreover, program advocates and administrators of civic service programs are increasingly sophisticated in the implementation of national service policy, creating a strong network of practitioners eager to champion civic service as a valued social institution.

The rapid expansion of research on civic service since the 1990s further underscores a growing interest in the scholarly community equal to that of practitioners and policy makers. Scholars of civic service increasingly recognize the need for an interdisciplinary research infrastructure that allows for the accumulation of knowledge in contrast to the lack of interdisciplinary dialogue that currently characterizes the civic service field; invariably, single studies that do not build on each other hold limited value.[22]

Each of these trends suggests that the field is ripe for a comprehensive assessment of what we currently know (and do not know) about civic service. Research synthesis is a valuable tool for researchers, practitioners, and policy makers who seek cumulative evidence about cause-effect relationships involving service and its design, implementation, and outcomes. As an integrative research tool, research syntheses

> attempt to integrate empirical research for the purpose of creating generalizations. Implicit in this definition is the notion that seeking generalizations also involves seeking the limits and modifiers of generalizations.[23]

Throughout this book, we seek to identify similarities, differences, and patterns across a comprehensive number of studies on civic service in order to develop contingent generalizations about civic service, its outcomes, and mediating factors that may (or may not) enhance the likelihood of the positive outcomes frequently attributed to civic service.

This book can be used by practitioners, researchers, and policy makers:

- to step back and reflect on the larger picture that is civic service,
- to foster cross-fertilization of research findings and encourage interdisciplinary dialogue in hopes of organizing the individual pieces of the puzzle into the larger "explanatory puzzle,"[24]
- to specify theories of change that identify key factors affecting the relationship between civic service and its outcomes,
- to explore the contextual factors that impact civic service policy implementation,

- to inform policy makers about what works (and does not work) in achieving civic service policy goals, and
- to identify areas in need of future research that will further illuminate our understanding of the explanatory puzzle we will construct in the following pages.

Overview

We organize this book into four parts. Parts I and II provide an overview of national civic service and of the synthesis presented in this volume. In Part I, Ideological and Historical Context, we examine civic service as an ideal rooted in the tension between classic liberalism and civic republicanism. We then examine the historical evolution of civic service by evaluating four distinct policy cycles. In Part II, Evidence and Methods, we provide an overview of the synthesis of civic service research, discussing the current state of the civic service field, the nature of the evidence about service and its impacts, and the difficulties of establishing benchmarks for high-quality research. We then present an operational definition of civic service and discuss the methodology used in our analysis.

In Part III, Research Synthesis Findings, we present the findings of this research synthesis regarding civic service outcomes and implementation. We examine what the 100–plus studies collected in this synthesis have to say about the relationship between service and outcomes. Four analytic categories of outcomes associated with civic service are scrutinized; these are the impacts of service on (1) the server, (2) the beneficiaries, (3) the institutions, and (4) the community. We then examine what these studies have to say about the implementation of civic service policy. In the spirit of Pressman and Wildavsky's classic study of implementation,[25] we review what the evaluations and applied research suggest are the critical implementation issues for civic service.

Part IV, Summing Up and Taking Stock, includes a summary and concluding discussion of the implications of these findings for policy and research. We first summarize what is known as a result of the synthesis, presenting propositions that emerge from our analysis. We conclude with a discussion of the policy implications implicit in evaluation findings and identify questions that emerge from the synthesis that have yet to be answered.

Terms and Definitions

Throughout this book we use several terms, sometimes interchangeably, such as *national service, community service, national civic service,* and *citizen service*. Earlier in this introduction we made the case for an evolving definition of civic service. As Part I will demonstrate, the meaning of service changed throughout the twentieth century, as popular support changed with the historical, social, and economic context of a particular era. Consequently, what earlier twentieth-century scholars called national service can now be understood as two distinct forms of service, military and civic service. Furthermore, the latter years of the twentieth century brought devolution and consequently an increased emphasis on service as a form of community problem solving—hence, community service in contrast to national service.

Although each of these terms emphasizes a particular aspect of service, overall they have their root in the tradition of civic mindedness. Charles Moskos describes this civic tradition best in his 1988 book, *A Call to Civic Service*. National service (and we would add, community service), he writes, means

> the performance of citizen duties that allow individuals to have a sense of the civic whole—a whole that is more important than any single person or category of persons. It is upon some such norms of fulfillment of a civic obligation, upon some concept of serving societal needs outside the marketplace, upon some sense of participation in a public life with other citizens that the idea of national service builds.[26]

Civic service embodies a complex view of service that enriches both our private and public understandings of volunteerism. We believe civic service is evolving into a valued social institution that allows for private initiative (individual citizens expressing their citizenship responsibilities) through publicly supported programs. These formal programs seek to meet unmet social needs that neither the market nor the government can meet alone. Underlying this understanding of civic service as a social institution is the belief that complex social problems require the concerted efforts of both the public and private sectors of society.

In the following pages, we will explore the evolution of civic service and, through research synthesis, begin to put pieces of this important puzzle together. We seek to challenge practitioners and scholars to pause briefly and reflect on the cumulative knowledge represented in these pages in order to illuminate where we need to go from here. Now that we have drawn the map for the path ahead, let's get started.

I

Ideological and
Historical Context

1

The Ideal

So long as antimilitarists propose no substitute for war's
disciplinary function, no moral equivalent of war. . . so long
they fail to realize the full inwardness of the situation.
[A] permanently successful peace-economy cannot be a
simple pleasure-economy. [We] must still subject ourselves
collectively to those severities which answer to our real
position upon this only partly hospitable globe. . . . Martial
virtues must be the enduring cement; intrepidity, contempt of
softness, surrender of private interest, obedience to command,
must still remain the rock upon which states are built. . . . The
martial type of character can be bred without war. . . . The only
thing needed henceforward is to inflame the civic temper as
past history has inflamed the military temper.
—*William James*

Civic service, in its ideal form, is most frequently viewed as a means of
educating citizens about the civic virtue so necessary for democratic citizenship. For William James, writing at the beginning of the twentieth century,
civic virtue is embodied in the martial values of "intrepidity, contempt of
softness, surrender of private interest, [and] obedience to command."[1] Mandatory conscription into national service provided a peaceful way to instill
civic virtue in America's youth.

But this requisite civic virtue, although it represents a potential of human nature, is neither inevitable nor assured. For America's founders, the
development of civic virtue was the responsibility of individuals, not government, whose only role was to "elicit rather than to command appropriate
actions from virtuous people."[2] Though their political philosophy rested on
belief in the "necessary relationship between the realization of the ideal of
the Republic and citizen virtue," the founders, writes scholar David K. Hart,
"took the bolder and riskier path of moral individualism, understanding that

virtue had no meaning if it was not achieved through the voluntary efforts of a free people."[3]

This tension between reliance on the private nature of moral individualism and the public nature of an active citizenry defines the heart of American politics and may explain the sometimes dramatic swings in support for civic service. In his book *The Democratic Wish: Popular Participation and the Limits of American Government*, James Morone argues that, at its core, American politics is characterized by a certain dread and yearning; Americans dread losing their individual liberties through public power while they simultaneously yearn for "an alternative faith in direct communal democracy."[4] The historical development of civic service as an ideal mirrors American political development and embodies this same dread and yearning.

Political development in the United States, Morone argues, results from the cyclical expression of two competing political ideologies that mark the "the soul of American politics," one rooted in classic liberal democracy, the other in classic republicanism.[5] Classic liberalism—with its emphasis on the individual, limited representative government, private interest, and primacy of the private realm—finds its roots in the moral individualism of America's founders. Classic republicanism's roots, on the other hand, rest in an equally strong belief that without civic obligation to the whole, the ideal of the republic will never be realized.

For Morone, the classic republicanism belief in a shared politics of meaning (which transcends narrow individual interests) is a powerful "democratic wish" that periodically asserts itself as a strong rhetorical and ideological device to reform status quo institutions rooted in a liberal political equilibrium of private interests.[6] But the power of this wish is inherently self-limiting because the dread of too much public power threatens individual freedoms, leading to a reassertion of classic liberal values. In this way, Morone concludes, both ideologies conspire to create weak government as a result of the dread and yearning so ingrained in the American psyche.

The development of a civic service ethos follows a similar developmental pattern, illustrating Americans' fear of centralized power while longing for a democracy of "virtuous citizens."[7] As an expression of the democratic wish, popular support for civic service mirrors reform movements of the past, a reaction to classic liberalism's focus on individual rights at the expense of civic duty. Civic service from this perspective is frequently viewed as simultaneously changing politically indifferent citizens into virtuous ones and transforming society into more intimate, private communities of actively engaged citizens.

Nowhere is "civic-service-as-democratic-wish" more popularly described than in President Bill Clinton's 1993 announcement of the new civic service initiative, AmeriCorps. Civic service, he claimed, is nothing less than the American way to change America. It is rooted in the concept of community: the simple idea that every one of us, no matter how many privileges with which we are born, can still be enriched by the contributions of the least of us.[8]

But the often vociferous debate in Congress and the national press over President Clinton's AmeriCorps program demonstrates just how powerful the dread of government intrusion in the private lives of Americans can be.[9] The evolution of civic service in America, rooted as it is in the great democratic ideals of civic virtue expressed through citizenship, is without doubt also rooted in the American founders' fundamental belief that, "responsibility for the development of that virtue belonged to individuals, free from authoritarian or paternalistic institutions (whether public, private, or religious) that would force them into some predefined and artificial character."[10] Like the development of American politics, the development of support for civic service embodies inner tensions between seemingly conflicting relationships— liberty and obligation, individual rights and public duty, dread of the power of government to create "artificial character" by mandating civic virtue and yearning for a naturally virtuous citizenship rooted in community.

The late Morris Janowitz, a leading theorist on civic service, provides a complementary perspective that helps to clarify our understanding of the ideal of civic service as caught between the swings of classic liberalism and classic republicanism. From this perspective, civic service may act as a self-regulating force between these two powerful ideologies. Janowitz links the ideal of civic service to the concept of social control which involves a society's capacity to regulate itself according to principles valued by society (civic virtue, for example). As a form of social control, civic service has the potential to motivate society to pursue civic republicanism's ideals and, at the same time, minimize coercive control (the dread of classic liberalism) because, as Janowitz points out, social control is "directly linked to the notion of voluntaristic action [and] to articulated human purpose and actions."[11]

In an expansion of this theme, Janowitz links civic service to the development of citizenship in *The Reconstruction of Patriotism*. Janowitz, more sanguine than Morone in his view of political institutions, sees citizenship as having played a persistent and positive role, however, "incomplete and distorted," in the development and maintenance of democratic institutions over time partly because it rests on "voluntarism [that is] motivated by a sense of moral responsibility for the collective well-being." For Janowitz, the strength of democratic citizenship depends not only on existing forms of political participation (such as voting) but on "forms of local self-help currently associated with the idea of community or national service [because] participation in these activities gives the idea of [civic] obligation concrete meanings.[12]

Charles Moskos, writing five years later, provides yet another perspective on civic service as an ideal. His is a less idealistic understanding of "civic-service-as-democratic-wish" than President Clinton's, but like Janowitz, Moskos insists there is a place for civic service in a classic liberal democrary.. "While we must be wary of nostalgia for civic perfections that never existed," he writes,

> we must confront openly the question of how to revive citizenship in a technological and bureaucratic society. Words like fraternity and community are so soaked in sentimentalism as to become almost useless as guides to the real possibility of democratic citizenship in tomorrow's America. Modern life has changed the possible forms of civic solidarity, but not the necessity for it.[13]

Moskos concludes his seminal work on civic service by relying both on civic republicanism's emphasis on norms of civic obligation and on liberalism's primary tenet that any intrusion of government into otherwise private realms (like the development of civic virtue) must be justified. For national service programs to work, he argues, they "must perform tasks neither the market nor government can provide";[14] they must also evoke a new understanding of civic solidarity and democratic citizenship.[15] If government is to involve itself in educating the citizenry in civic virtue through civic service (albeit indirectly), it must do so on the grounds that it can achieve this purpose at less cost than by other means.[16] In the more pedestrian language of political rhetoric, Moskos writes,

> National service conceives a much more balanced approach to citizenship [than civic republicanism or classic liberalism]. "Ask what your country can do for you," it urges, "*and* what you do can do for your country."[17]

Perhaps because the ideal of civic service is often expressed as democratic wish, it remains (until most recently), as Danzig and Szanton claim, "an issue whose time seems never to come."[18] Yet, as Morone argues, reform rhetoric embodied in the democratic wish provides a powerful incentive for change.[19] The history of civic service, according to Moskos, lends some support for institutional changes over time. Although the history of civic service demonstrates a cyclical pattern in which "a slow inflow of national service support is followed by a rapid ebb," he writes, "[at] each upswing in the cycle, the level of support for national service is established at a higher level."[20]

In its contemporary form, a major shift in the cyclical pattern seems to have occurred.[21] This shift is most clearly evident in concern for the institutionalization of the ideal rather than in the nature of service itself. Advocates of civic service have increasingly used (though not without struggle) the ideal of "civic-service-as-democratic-wish" to create a politically savvy and growing constituency for civic service programs. They have done so by successfully linking the private ethos of voluntarism (characteristic of classic liberalism) with civic republicanism's sense of obligation and citizenship.

Moreover, the rhetorical power of the democratic wish is strengthened by a growing recognition that the postindustrial society in which we find ourselves is increasingly marked by economic, political, and social interdependence. Many of the problems we currently face (nationally and globally) require new types of working relationships between government and community. Scholars refer to these new working relationships as networks—"webs of public, not-for-profit, and business organizations in crosscutting configurations."[22] In a world increasingly characterized by interdependence and the need to respond to ever more complex social problems, elements of classic republicanism (expressed in the democratic wish) may attenuate the power of classic liberalism's emphasis on individualism.

These complex social issues, "wicked problems,"[23] are precisely the kinds of problems civic service programs seek to address. It is not surprising, as the next chapter will demonstrate, that civic service programs today are necessarily intersectoral and multiorganizational in nature. By bringing together constituencies found in both the public and private spheres of society, these civic service networks may act as a primary factor in building civic service as a viable social institution

Conclusion

Today, civic service stands at a crossroads. As an ideal, it remains the antidote to many of the ills created by classic liberalism's emphasis on individual rights and private interests. Arguments abound demonstrating liberalism's failure to create civic virtue and the potential for civic service to fill that role.[24] At the beginning of the twenty-first century, however, it is not entirely clear that the new institutions of civic service emerging since the 1900s can meet the idealistic demands civic republicanism places on them.

Civic service today faces different challenges than those articulated by William James at the turn of the nineteenth century. Current challenges rest in the difficulties inherent in institution building and the risk of returning to what Morone calls "the political stalemate of American liberalism," where the "reassertion of a liberal political equilibrium (around a new political status quo)" results in the perpetuation of weak government that is "ill-geared to contemporary problems."[25]

Part of the challenge implicit in building civic service institutions rests in the capacity for critical self-reflection even as institutions are created and evolve. In the spirit of the reinventing government movement—where program evaluation and continuous improvement are paramount—evaluations of civic service programs abound, especially since the 1990s. In the last decade, these program evaluations have resulted in a long list of best practices, to the benefit of hundreds of organizational networks that implement civic service policy across the United States. How to incorporate this learning into the institution-building process remains unclear, however. This book intends to strengthen our capacity to use knowledge we currently have on civic service for the benefit of the field, both in practice and research.

Examining how civic service has *actually* evolved over time is an important starting point if we are to learn how to build institutions that embody the democratic wish articulated by William James (and others who have championed his call, like William F. Buckley Jr.). In the end, however, the most useful way to learn is to gather the best cumulative evidence we can about the relationship between civic service goals (that embody the democratic wish) and civic service outcomes. Ultimately, if "civic-service-as-democratic-wish" is to move beyond the merely rhetorical, we need to first determine the extent to which outcomes match the claims made about civic service.

In the following pages, we will examine the impacts of service, not only on those who serve but also on the people, institutions, and communities that civic service programs target for positive change. It is in synthesizing the evidence for the goal-outcome relationship, and identifying factors that affect the relationship, that we can begin to learn about creating social institutions of civic service that bring the democratic wish closer to reality. But, first, we turn to a historical overview of civic service as it evolved throughout the twentieth century.

2

Policy Evolution

If civic service is merely an ideal, it is nonetheless a resilient one that has been periodically expressed through American public opinion in response to economic and social conditions. Rhetorically, the ideal of civic service, like the "democratic wish," is expressed in the language of reform, a response to classic liberalism's focus on liberty and individual rights at the expense of obligation and citizen duty.

Historically, however, the ideal has been expressed in more concrete ways—as a means to revive the economy devastated by the Great Depression in the early twentieth century, address issues of poverty and urban unrest in the 1960s, provide youth with meaningful educational and work opportunities in natural resource conservation, and build local communities through problem-solving strategies. From an institution-building perspective, each of these historical expressions has provided what Morone calls "democratic moments" that result in the creation of new political institutions around a new political status quo.[1] Some of these institutions, like the Civilian Conservation Corps, no longer exist, while others, like the Peace Corps, continue to operate with broad popular support.

This chapter provides a historical context in which to understand the gradual transformation of the ideal of civic service into concrete administrative structures and programs. Unlike the steady, successful institutionalization of the great democratic ideals of liberty and individual rights, the historical expression of the ideal of civic service tends to follow an episodic and cyclical pattern. Barry Checkoway, professor of social work at the University of Michigan, describes this history in terms of cyclical "windows of opportunity" that periodically occur and are measured by "what is left behind after the cycle concludes."[2] A historical account of civic service from an institution-building perspective suggests that since the beginning of the twentieth century, four distinct cycles of civic service policy have occurred.

Policy Cycle One: Civilian Conservation Corps

The economic crash in 1929 and the subsequent years of the Great Depression served as the impetus for developing the first large-scale civic service program in the United States. With large segments of the American population unemployed—nearly 14 million by 1933—and social conditions worsening nationwide, the pressure for innovative governmental relief mounted.[3] In March 1933, newly elected president Franklin D. Roosevelt launched the Civilian Conservation Corps (CCC). Established as a prescriptive tool for economic recovery during the New Deal, the CCC undertook numerous conservation projects in rural regions of the country. Essentially, the CCC combined what Roosevelt saw as the two primary policy issues of this New Deal administration: the economy and conservation of natural resources.[4] During the nine years of the program's existence, the CCC employed over 3 million young men.[5]

The organizational structure behind the CCC was innovative for its time, reflecting the extraordinary circumstances of the Depression. The CCC was initially administered cooperatively under the Departments of War, Labor, Agriculture, and the Interior. The army, whose primary responsibility was providing for the general welfare of program participants, shouldered the bulk of the effort. By having the army provide housing, food, medical attention, and supplies, the CCC demonstrated the possibility of utilizing military expertise in the administration of civil projects and programs. For their part, the Department of Labor administered the selection of enrollees, and the Departments of Agriculture and the Interior carried out the planning and implementation of specific work projects. Although conservation projects varied by region, the foci included erosion control, reforestation, the restoration of public lands, and the development of general waterway and flood infrastructures.

Despite its ingrained administrative complexity, the CCC was judged a tremendous success, both as an income redistribution program and in natural resource preservation. The program provided each participant a salary of $30 a month. Of this amount, $25 was redirected to the participant's family. Individuals agreed to six-month service obligations for up to a maximum of two years. Participation levels in the CCC grew to a peak level of 500,000 volunteers in 1936, after which efforts to balance the federal budget forced a reduction to 300,000 volunteers over the remainder of the 1930s. The advent of American involvement in World War II signaled the end of both the feasibility and the necessity of the CCC. The need for specialized economic recovery programs disappeared almost overnight with the growing military demand for young men. Hence, by 1942, the supply of capable young men had dried up and the CCC ceased to exist.[6]

Regardless of its short life, the CCC resulted in a number of exceptional achievements. These include planting 2 billion trees, building 126,000 miles of roads, and protecting 40 million acres of farmland from erosion. In addition, Morris Janowitz notes that the CCC "evolved as a sociopolitical movement" characterized by CCC participants who "felt engaged in an enterprise of practical and moral worth [and who] developed a collective consciousness—not to be exaggerated, but one that was realistic." The productivity of CCC participants in meeting the relatively simple, focused goal of conservation and the evolution of the CCC into "an institution with its own collective spirit" account for the CCC being the most popular of all New Deal programs.[7]

Policy Cycle Two: Fighting Poverty

The end of World War II brought with it a rebound in the numbers of young men in the American workforce. The economic prosperity of the late 1940s and 1950s required little in the way of income redistribution, which had spawned programs such as the CCC in the prewar decade. By the early 1960s, American idealism was reignited by President John F. Kennedy's promise of a New Frontier. The most notable and long-lasting byproduct of this era was Kennedy's establishment of the Peace Corps in 1961. American society embraced the spirit of the program, through which over 160,000 participants have volunteered in the past forty years. In fact, the early success of the Peace Corps in rallying support for public service contributed significantly to the development of later service programs.

Despite Kennedy's assassination in 1963, the advent of Johnson's Great Society and the War on Poverty brought together the forces necessary to initiate new domestic civic service programs in the wake of public approval for the Peace Corps. The Johnson administration quickly developed a flurry of new service programs, all directed toward poverty relief. These programs included Volunteers in Service to America (VISTA), the Foster Grandparent Program and Teacher Corps. The goal was to enact changes in the ways institutions addressed issues of poverty and community empowerment.

VISTA was established by the Johnson administration under the Economic Opportunity Act of 1964. The program addressed poverty-related issues by providing material resources and organizational expertise to communities through the placement of volunteers in government agencies. The overall goal was to enhance the self-reliance of local communities in combating urban and rural poverty. VISTA's underlying logic rested in civic republicanism's ideal of communal democracy, popular participation, and the value of providing work opportunities to all members of society, especially those most affected by poverty. The means to improve community conditions lay in the program's ability to empower individuals to address their own community problems. For more than thirty-five years, over 140,000 Americans have participated as VISTA volunteers. Promotion of VISTA as the domestic Peace Corps helped sell the program to the public.

The Foster Grandparent Program (FGP) also emerged from the Johnson administration. It was designed to engage low-income elderly persons in community service and to "provide social, psychological, and educational benefits to children with developmental disabilities and other special needs through development of a person-to-person relationship between foster grandparents and foster grandchild."[8]As with VISTA, the FGP evolved administratively from its origins within the Department of Health, Education, and Welfare (HEW) and the Office of Economic Opportunity. Administrative control was transferred to HEW's Administration on Aging in 1969 to ACTION, a new federal agency for service programs, in 1971, and finally to the Corporation for National and Community Service in 1993. The FGP is now part of the Corporation's National Senior Service Corps.

To participate in the FGP, volunteers must meet both age (at least sixty years old) and low-income requirements. Modest stipends and insurance are provided to FGP volunteers as an incentive for continued participation in the program. FGP volunteers work in hospitals with injured or ill children, provide tutelage to children with a variety of educational or special needs, and mentor adolescents and youth in correctional facilities. The majority of the work projects in recent years have focused on educational interactions between participating senior citizens and students with exceptional needs. The development of long-term relationships is seen as one of the ultimate goals of the FGP.

Similar to Johnson's Foster Grandparent Program, the Senior Companion Program (SCP) initially was authorized and established by Congress under the Domestic Volunteer Services Act of 1973 primarily as a way to provide volunteer opportunities to low-income elderly citizens. The program also sought to benefit adults with special needs by pairing them with program participants. Although specific programmatic details of the SCP differ from state to state, the overarching goals remain constant nationally. By pairing volunteers age sixty or older with elderly beneficiaries in need of assistance in daily living, the SCP is able to address both objectives of the program. Senior Companions typically receive modest compensation for their assistance to individuals both in and out of assisted living institutions. The provision of such compensation is administered through federal grants to community networks.

Another example of public service programs promulgated during the 1960s is the Teacher Corps. Also developed as a poverty-fighting program, the

Teacher Corps, according to some, represented an "unprecedented attempt to mobilize temporary networks of organizations."[9] The purpose of the Teacher Corps was threefold: (1) to provide increased educational opportunities to children from low-income households; (2) to promote the growth of teaching careers in low-income areas through the use of work-study opportunities; and (3) to increase the quality of teacher training programs through the cooperative involvement of colleges and universities, local schools, and departments of education. The driving force behind the Teacher Corps program was a societal belief that teaching in low-income environments requires different teaching skills than are necessary in middle- and upper-class schools.[10] Teacher Corps interns were provided with eight weeks of initial training, followed by two years of experience teaching in lower-income schools. Subsequently, interns participated in a two-year master's program designed to acclimate individuals fully into the teaching profession.

Despite high public support for civic service programs during the 1960s and early 1970s, political attention turned to other issues with the beginning of the Nixon administration. The idealism marking the Kennedy and early Johnson years had been transformed into cynicism, primarily over the United States' involvement in Vietnam. Such cynicism brought with it a decline in support for civic service programs.

Policy Cycle Three: Conservation and Youth Corps

The general decline in popular support for government during the Nixon administration led to a subtle change in the emphases of civic service programs. Although self-sufficiency remained a core value of civic service in the 1970s and 1980s, the model of change shifted. Rather than seek to alter institutions, as VISTA and the Teacher Corps had, new programs sought to change individuals. In this sense, new programs were designed akin to the CCC of the 1930s. The auspices changed from primarily highly centralized, federally administered programs to more decentralized, cooperative programs. New programs combined federal resources with local administration centered on community or regional needs and objectives. The foci of many of these programs became youth-oriented. Examples include the Youth Conservation Corps, the California Conservation Corps, and the many urban youth corps that sprang up in communities nationwide.

The Youth Conservation Corps (YCC), like the CCC, came about as a result of dual objectives: to respond to the nation's environmental problems and to strengthen the nation's focus on the social, physical, and economic needs of individuals. As in the 1930s, the federal government in the 1970s and 1980s paid increasing attention to the state of the nation's environment and the need to develop and conserve natural resources. The environmental movement's increasingly sophisticated grassroots organizing efforts raised awareness of environmental problems during this time such that environmental issues found their way onto the political agenda. In April 1970, Wisconsin senator Gaylord Nelson founded Earth Day, a national day of observance focusing on the nation's environmental problems, which involved over 20 million demonstrators from thousands of schools and communities.[11]

In establishing the YCC in 1970, Congress emphasized building ties between the environment and "the youth, upon whom will fall the ultimate responsibility for maintaining and managing these resources for American people."[12] Young adults, it was hoped, would gain a respect for environmental protection and conservation that would help to sustain the national park system, national forests, and other public lands and waterways.

Initially a summer work program for teenagers, the YCC gave rise to the short-lived Young Adult Conservation Corps (YACC), which expanded the objectives to year-round work for young adults between the ages of 16 and 23. The downfall of the YACC program came in part because the goal of conservation took priority over skills development of participants, resulting in low participant morale. Although originally designed as a one-year service program, the average tenure of participants was only four months.[13] Program continuity consequently suffered. In the end, the YACC lasted only until 1982 (when the Reagan administration did not renew the program). The YCC, however, continues to provide summer employment opportunities to youth.

The late 1970s and early 1980s witnessed a rise in the number of states that, recognizing the relevance of federal service programs, attempted to replicate these conservation programs. In 1976, California governor Jerry Brown signed legislation establishing the California Conservation Corps. The goal was to carry out extensive natural resource development and maintenance while simultaneously providing "meaningful educational and work opportunities" to the state's youth population. Similarly, the objective of individual development was pursued through rigorous programmatic requirements, including daily mandatory participation in physical fitness training and various planned educational and recreational activities. In addition to developing work skills, however, the California Conservation Corps stressed character development through leadership and supervision, and "concern for developing in youth a feeling of corps spirit, the value of service to community and pride in achievement."[14]

Where the California Conservation Corps differs from previous service programs is that it was, and still is, funded entirely by the state of California.[15] A similar movement occurred in the growth of municipal youth corps during this same time period. Examples of cities and counties with strong urban corps initially included Marin County in California, Milwaukee, and New York, but expanded throughout the 1980s to numerous metropolitan areas. Many of the urban corps developed in the late 1980s as a result of the Urban Corps Expansion Project (UCEP) were based on a model similar to those in California.[16]

Decentralization and devolution of previously federally funded initiatives drove the decisions of metropolitan leaders to establish programs that would provide civic opportunities to low-income youth. This emphasis on devolution is not surprising, given the general mood of the 1980s, demonstrated in Ronald Reagan's efforts to shrink the size and breadth of the federal government. In fact, the Reagan administration's downsizing of federal support for many civic service programs, including the YCC, represented a decline from the high-water mark of the early 1980s.

This ebb did not last, however. In her monograph *Ten Years of Youth in Service to America*, Shirley Sagawa, long-standing advocate for civic service, writes that by the end of the 1980s, a resurgence of interest in civic service occurred in part because youth service offered

> a strategy for achieving several diverse goals [such as increasing] academic performance [through] experiential, hands-on education, [teaching] life skills, [developing] problem solving abilities, [preparing] young people for the world of work, [getting] things done that would not otherwise be addressed by existing public programs or the private sector, [bridging] gaps in understanding among people of different backgrounds, [developing] active citizens who are engaged in the community, [and helping] young people learn that with rights come responsibilities.[17]

One innovative program that emerged during this time that embodied these diverse goals was City Year. Launched in Boston in 1988 (with funding provided entirely from the private sector), City Year adopted three primary objectives: to instill civic engagement in youth, break down social and racial barriers, and provide meaningful community service to urban youth. In addition to mandating service in a variety of human services areas, City Year required civic participation through such methods as mandatory voter registration and certification in first aid and cardio-pulmonary resuscitation. Since its founding, City Year has expanded into thirteen cities or states nationwide.[18]

Popular support for civic service was further fueled in the early 1990s by President Bush's imagery of volunteerism as igniting a thousand points of light across America. This imagery, made more concrete by President Bush's daily practice of selecting an exemplary volunteer to be a "daily point of light," helped to place civic service on the political agenda with enough bipartisan support for Congress to pass the National and Community Service Act of 1990.[19] Introduced by Senator Edward M. Kennedy and signed into law by President Bush, this law created the Commission for National and Community Service and provided funding for a new, nonpartisan, nonprofit organization called the Points of Light Foundation. Its mission is to "engage more people more effectively in volunteer service to help solve serious social problems." Service increasingly became a strategy for social problem solving.[20]

Policy Cycle Four: Service as a Problem-Solving Strategy

With the election of Bill Clinton to the presidency in 1992, political pressure to expand and develop civic service programs intensified. Many Americans, rallied by Vice President Gore's "reinventing government" message and the tail of the economic recession of the late 1980s and early 1990s, embraced the push for civic service programs that would promote individual self-development and contribute to a strengthened national community. The driving force behind this resurgence was an attempt to deal with the difficulties faced by all levels of government as the country slogged through economic recession. Fiscal shortages demanded innovative solutions to growing national and local social problems. One such approach was to develop service programs that would both aid existing governmental agencies and fill the gaps in coverage between agencies, providing much needed problem solving at federal, state, and local levels of government.

Under Democratic leadership both in the White House and the legislature, Congress passed the National and Community Service Trust Act of 1993. This law expanded on the 1990 law by creating a new umbrella agency, the Corporation for National and Community Service (CNCS), to house all domestic civic service programs in the United States.[21] No other program more clearly demonstrates the new institutional developments created under this new law as AmeriCorps, President Clinton's signature civic service program. In their book *Common Interest, Common Good*, two of AmeriCorps' chief visionaries, Shirley Sagawa and Eli Segal, write about their vision for AmeriCorps:

> The legislation that we and our colleagues put together challenged much of the conventional wisdom applied to federal social policy. In contrast to many programs that caused local groups to compete with one another for resources, we hoped to create incentives for community organizations to work together.[22]

Adopting the label "domestic Peace Corps" (which also had been applied to VISTA nearly thirty years earlier), AmeriCorps provides full- and part-time community service opportunities to individuals in four programmatic areas: education, public safety, environment, and human needs. In exchange for serving in AmeriCorps, participants may receive a modest stipend and health insurance and are eligible for an educational award after completion of service. Funding for the AmeriCorps program is provided through matching grants to state community service commissions and national nonprofits that dispense monies to state and local nonprofit organizations.

The statutory statement of purpose for AmeriCorps is expansive. The scope of its architects' ambitions and the ideologies that drive them created immediate controversy over the AmeriCorps program in the early years of the decade. Critics took a classic liberalism stance, arguing that AmeriCorps was a perversion of volunteerism and an extension of big government into realms previously reserved for private nonprofits. Supporters tended to take a classic republicanism stance, agreeing with President Clinton's vision that civic service represented "one of the few remaining remedies [left] for the fragmentation and polarization that threaten our country."[23] This vision found its rationale in the belief that community building occurs best when "people, [community-based organizations], and their government work at the grass roots in genuine partnership."[24]

At the national level, hints of the "democratic wish" emerged as the underlying rationale for the program. Personal acts of service were seen as having the potential to change individual lives by bringing together diverse groups of people to solve social problems. Through their common public tasks, individuals would develop civic consciousness, which would manifest itself in a more active citizenry, healthier communities, and, ultimately, a strong democratic system.[25] Furthermore, the devolved nature of these programs suggested that development of civic consciousness would occur from the bottom up as AmeriCorps members worked to solve local problems through local community-based organizations.

Similarly, the public spirit of the early Clinton years led to the establishment of another program, Experience Corps, in 1996. Administered by two 1960s civic service programs now housed at the Corporation for National and Community Service—the Foster Grandparent Program and the Retired Senior Volunteer Program—Experience Corps addresses the needs of poor urban elementary students by mobilizing the talents and skills of elderly citizens. The move throughout the 1990s in the direction of Experience Corps and AmeriCorps demonstrates the growing reliance on cooperative public-private service ventures. In this most recent policy cycle, the dwindling availability of federal and state governments to fully support public service initiatives has been met with increased nongovernmental and nonprofit participation, both in the funding and the administration of civic service programs.

Generalizations About the Evolution of Service in America

Making broad generalizations regarding the evolution of civic service in American society is difficult. Certain characteristics can be identified with each of the distinct policy cycles, yet seemingly unique characteristics can also be traced from one era of public service to another. Over time, a multitude of civic service interventions have emerged, leaving a field strewn with occasional institutional legacies. Undoubtedly, the ideal of civic service, expressed historically, served a variety of purposes throughout the twentieth century, ranging from civic education to problem-solving strategies for meeting the needs of local communities burdened by fragmentation and poverty.

In Policy Cycle One, the CCC became a principle means of combating the economic hardships of the Great Depression. Although the CCC is often held up as a model for civic service, the circumstances surrounding its creation and operation set it apart from virtually all other civic service programs outside military service. Undoubtedly, the dismal economic conditions of the Great Depression produced a unique opportunity for the federal government to employ millions of young workers, not merely to ameliorate the poverty of CCC participants and their families but to directly address national economic and labor policies. The manpower available to the government for undertaking extensive conservation projects was staggering until World War II diminished the number of available working men and the CCC no longer filled the need that it had during the Great Depression.

In Policy Cycle Two, civic service was again used as a way to combat poverty, but for different reasons. American society in the 1930s was in the midst of economic collapse and demanded recovery programs. In the 1960s, Johnson's Great Society and the War on Poverty programs were the result of a reignited idealism throughout the country rather than a response to economic needs. The economic self-sufficiency focus of the 1930s remained a core value of civic service, but the idealism of the 1960s expressed itself in terms of community empowerment and institutional change.

Policy Cycles Three and Four also witnessed changes in the focus of civic service programs. In Policy Cycle Three, economic self-sufficiency and institutional change remained important, but proponents of civic service saw its potential to change individuals, not only through skills development but through the development of civic consciousness and environmental awareness. During this time, in the 1970s and 1980s, the model shifted focus from institutional change to individual change.

Policy Cycle Four has witnessed the continuation of the economic themes, but the emphasis is now not only on changing individuals but also on creating new institutional forms—joint ventures of governmental, nongovernmental, and nonprofit organizations. When all four policy cycles are examined over the twentieth century, they share an institutional legacy rooted in the economic and social conditions of the time, but with different mixes of intended outcomes, targeted participants, and servers.

Can civic service in American society be viewed as an evolutionary idea, morphing with the changing tides of economic conditions and public preference? After all, programs generally have survived across each of the policy cycles. Even though Policy Cycle One's principal program, the CCC, did not formally last beyond the initial years of World War II, the theme of conservation persisted and emerged in the Youth Conservation Corps of Policy Cycle Three. Programs such as the Peace Corps and VISTA have lasted across policy cycles, albeit often under changing administrative control. For example, initial program management for VISTA was placed with the Office of Economic Opportunity, but was transferred to ACTION in 1971 and finally absorbed into CNCS's AmeriCorps in 1993. Similarly, the Senior Companion Program was originally authorized by HEW's Administration on Aging, but is now administered by the CNCS's Senior Service Corps.

An examination of the evolution of civic service in the twentieth century suggests that weak evolutionary links exist across the four policy cycles. Some institutional and program learning has indeed taken place as the institutional development of civic service has evolved over the past seven decades. It is likewise probable that civic service will continue to develop in the new millennium in new ways and with new foci while remaining similar to those programs and institutions that emerged in the twentieth century.

The beginning of the twenty-first century marks a challenging time for civic service. The focus of Policy Cycle Four on local responses to local needs through intersectoral partnerships has continued into George W. Bush's administration. AmeriCorps has weathered the attacks of its strongest critics in Congress. Congressional representatives and governors have viewed firsthand the results of AmeriCorps programs in their local districts and a growing group of alumni and beneficiaries have created a potent lobbying force in support of civic service programs.

Furthermore, innovations are occurring at the state and local levels as a result of the learning that has occurred in implementing civic service policy. Civic service program advocates, administrators, and state policy makers demonstrate an increasing professionalism and sophistication in the support, management, and governance of civic service programs. State Community Service Commissions, for example, have formed the American Association of State Service Commissions, whose mission is to "advance service and volunteerism in the states through a national peer network of state commissioners and staff that promotes and is representative of all streams of national and community services."[26] Working with the CNCS, the association has greatly improved communication among states by coordinating peer-to-peer interaction and fostering collaborative individual and institutional relationships. Dissemination of information has also greatly increased through the availability of multiple Internet sites on civic service, such as the CNCS's clearinghouse for the sharing of best practices.[27]

New foci are also emerging. The terrorist attacks that damaged the Pentagon and leveled the World Trade Center in New York City on September 11, 2001 have created a renewed commitment to service through a number of bipartisan initiatives. On December 10, 2001, for example, Senators Evan Bayh (D) and John McCain (R) jointly introduced the Call to Service Act of 2001 (S. 1792), which would, among other initiatives, link AmeriCorps to the new department of Homeland Security, greatly expand senior service opportunities, and establish a commission on Military Recruitment and National Service. This commission would be jointly appointed by the secretaries of defense and state to "shrink the civilian-military gap and develop ways to bring in a larger pool of college graduates."[28]

In the House, the Citizen Service Act of 2002 (H.R. 4854) represents another bipartisan effort to institutionalize civic service by reforming and extending for five more years the CNCS and its programs. This act, although it is not identical to President Bush's vision for citizen service legislation, follows many of the principles and reforms identified by the White House.[29] Included in the president's vision are a number of innovative approaches to civic service, such as linking civic service programs with smaller, grassroots, community and faith-based organizations assumed to represent an as yet untapped resource for meeting local needs and piloting a program that would allow individuals to choose organizations they want to serve from a variety of options.[30]

Concerns for homeland security after September 11 are prominent in President Bush's national service policies. On January 31, 2002, the President officially announced the creation of the USA Freedom Corps, a coordinating council housed in the White House and chaired by the president. This initiative set goals for two existing national service organizations—the Peace Corps and CNCS—and creates a Citizen Corps designed to support local homeland security. Some of the initiatives included under the Citizen Corps are a Medical Reserve Corps and Volunteer Police Service.[31]

Conclusion

The institutional evolution of civic service has not been steady, but it has remained an ideal that has reached a level of public support sufficient to keep civic service on the political agenda for some time to come.[32] In 1990, William F. Buckley Jr. compared the promotion of civic service to the environmental and racial tolerance movements, each of which eventually resulted in a sea change in national attitudes.[33] For Buckley, the promotion of civic service means "[engaging] in the subtle business of trying to shape the national ethos." This subtle business, he writes, involves facing the "negative case for civic service" and learning the lessons of misspent federal philanthropy; in the end, however, the overwhelming positive case for civic service lies in "the absolutely secure conviction that the man or woman who helps someone who needs help is better off for the experience."[34]

Our examination of the history of civic service as it has evolved through the four policy cycles suggests that a sea change may have occurred in the national ethos regarding service. The mantra of the AmeriCorps program, "getting things done," and the accompanying emphasis on results-oriented service; the growth in professionalism of national, state, and local administrators; and the belief (as Buckley articulates so well) of conservatives and liberals alike in the ideal of helping someone who needs help may have provided the impetus necessary to create the change advocates of civic service seek, though it is unlikely that the intensity of that change can ever reach the ethos briefly engendered during the World War II years. Controversy over mismanagement of the AmeriCorps education trust fund as this book goes to press has reignited hostility among some in Congress toward the CNCS. Nevertheless, the chorus of popular and editorial support for AmeriCorps and consistently strong advocacy by governors, mayors, and senators like Evan Bayh and John McCain lead us to believe a sea change may well have occurred. If that change has, indeed, occurred, then the greatest challenge for civic service in the twenty-first century may lie in building the capacity to evaluate carefully the impacts of service on individuals, institutions, and local communities. Building that capacity begins with evaluating where we have been and where we currently are. It is this challenge, made all the more salient given the recent Congressional scrutiny of the CNCS, that drives the remainder of this book.

II

Evidence and Methods

3

The Nature of the Evidence

> From the moment we are introduced to science we are told it
> is a cooperative, cumulative enterprise. Like the artisans
> who construct a building from blueprints, bricks, and mortar,
> scientists contribute to a common edifice called knowledge.
> Theorists provide the blueprints, and researchers collect the
> data that are the bricks. . . . Research synthesists are the
> bricklayers and hod carriers of the science guild. It is their
> job to stack the bricks according to plan and apply the
> mortar that holds the structure together.
> —*Harris Cooper and Larry V. Hedges,*
> *The Handbook of Research Synthesis*

If we extend this analogy further, a necessary first step in the building process involves carefully assessing the general condition of the bricks before
stacking them and the mortar before applying it to the bricks. In Part II, we
take this first and necessary step. Cooper and Hedges prepare us by asserting
that research synthesists should know that, in reality, "several sets of theory-
blueprints often exist, with no a priori criteria for selecting among them
[and that] the data-bricks are not all six-sided and right-angled [but] come
in a baffling array of sizes and shapes."[1] As you will discover in the following pages, this reality is no less true for the field of civic service. The
purpose of this chapter is to identify the substance of the bricks and mortar
at our disposal in order to construct as credible an edifice of integrative
knowledge as we can.

To that end, we organize this chapter into five component parts. First, we
reflect briefly on where we have been. We then discuss where we are going
in the remaining pages of this book. Third, we begin the detailed work of
examining the quality of the bricks and mortar. We review the sources and
quality of existing service-related research and identify the problems we face
as we begin to build a clearer, more comprehensive understanding of civic
service in the United States today. Fourth, we discuss our approach to

addressing the problems that characterize the widely varying primary studies on civic service. And last, we conclude by offering ways to make use of the research despite some of its flaws.

In the introduction to their book on research synthesis, Cooper and Hedges acknowledge that "scientific sub-literatures are cluttered with repeated studies of the same phenomena [either] because investigators are unaware of what others are doing, [are] skeptical about the results of past studies, and/or because they wish to extend [previous] findings."[2] Even under flawed conditions, however, research synthesis is a worthy challenge. Indeed, systematically reviewing and synthesizing the evidence on civic service and its outcomes is not just a formidable task: in the interests of creating usable knowledge for practice and of building theory in a nascent but quickly growing field of research, it is absolutely critical if we are to construct a credible edifice of knowledge from all the single studies that currently dot the civic service landscape.

Where We Have Been and Where We Are Going

If we continue the construction analogy that began this chapter, our journey starts with scanning the general landscape upon which we seek to build. In Part I, we explored the philosophical origins of civic service (expressed as an ideal rooted in civic republicanism) and the historical evolution of this ideal throughout twentieth-century America. In the process, we discovered an inherent tension between two perspectives that coexist in the American psyche regarding civic service. On the one hand, civic service is frequently viewed as a private, intimate, voluntary response to individual need. On the other hand, civic service is also viewed as a public, formal, institutional response to social, economic, and political forces beyond the private domain.

We also discovered the dread and yearning characteristic of the American psyche regarding the role of government in the lives of private citizens and communities. We argue that this dread and yearning partly explain the wavelike pattern so characteristic of the historical evolution of civic service through four policy cycles; instead of evolving in a linear fashion, civic service has evolved episodically according to swings in popular support determined by unique historical factors of particular eras.

Nevertheless, we believe that by the end of the twentieth century, popular support for civic service had reached enough force to create a sea change in national attitudes toward service. The current policy debates on civic service seem to be less on government's ill-advised role in stimulating private voluntarism and more on addressing increasingly complex social problems that require the joint efforts of private citizens, organizations, and governments to adequately solve.

September 11 has only strengthened popular support for civic service, as evidenced by the Call to Service Act of 2001 and the Citizen Service Act of 2002 introduced in the months following the terrorist attacks of that day. Our scan of the landscape suggests that this synthesis comes at a historically important moment in the evolution of civic service as policy makers, practitioners, and researchers all seek to gain a clearer understanding of civic service as a potentially important social institution for the twenty-first century.

Having scanned the landscape, we spend the remainder of this book examining the nature and quality of materials with which we have to work and constructing cumulative knowledge about the relationship between civic service and its outcomes. We will discover that the nature of the evidence we currently have on civic service is flawed, but not hopelessly so. We openly discuss these flaws not only for the sake of research integrity, but also to set the stage for understanding the context in which we make generalizations as a result of the synthesis. Besides examining the nature of the bricks and mortar that are the building materials for this synthesis, we also discuss our methodology and how we address the problems that characterize the wide range of single studies (data bricks) on civic service that exist.

Once we understand the nature of the construction materials with which we have to work we begin the actual construction process, examining in greater detail what the data bricks can tell us about the impacts of civic service on those who serve, those who benefit from the service, institutions, and communities. We also begin to construct knowledge about what works and does not work in civic service policy implementation and why. We conclude the construction process by applying the mortar that holds the bricks in place. That mortar is in the form of propositions (generalizations) gleaned from the detailed examination and stacking of the bricks. These generalizations are important not only for what they tell us about civic service but also for what they say about future research in the field. Gaps that become apparent throughout the construction process can guide future researchers interested either in strengthening the current structure of accumulated knowledge or building on that structure.

Finally, in the interests of using this knowledge effectively, we step back and look at the edifice constructed in these pages reflecting on the policy implications of this synthesis for civic service. Research syntheses, write Judith Hall and her colleagues, have several strengths compared to primary research in that they (1) allow for the examination of "information accrued over multiple replications and several operational definitions," (2) bring together alternative explanations of phenomena that have yet to be compared, and (3) "invoke a broader perspective for the understanding of findings from primary research."[3] These strengths improve our ability as researchers, practitioners, and policy makers to reflect seriously about how to best use this knowledge to improve civic service practice and research.

Bricks and Mortar—The Nature of the Evidence

Techniques for analysis of accumulated research have advanced dramatically in the past quarter century. Cooper and Hedges observe, "Two decades ago, the actual mechanics of integrating research usually involved covert, intuitive processes taking place inside the head of the synthesist."[4] Today, literally dozens of techniques are available for estimating effect sizes and producing other, cross-study generalizations. Despite these advances, the techniques that can be applied are highly dependent on the contents of the accumulated research. This dependence is nowhere more evident than in research on civic service.

Understanding the effects of national and community service involves processes operating at numerous levels. The issues involved in these processes range from the psychological (e.g., changes in self-image and self-efficacy) to the interpersonal (e.g., working cooperatively with others, tolerance of diversity in others) to the organizational, institutional, and societal (e.g., community capacity). Accordingly, the kinds of research relevant to assessing the effects of service run the gamut: studies of the relationship between exposure to service and individual development, research on changes in reading and other education outcomes associated with tutoring and similar interventions, cost-benefit analyses, and changes in community networks related to community service initiatives.

Because the issues of interest lie at the interstices of different disciplines and levels of analysis, there is no single type of research evidence to which we can turn. Instead, we are faced with the task of comparing, contrasting, and synthesizing very different kinds of evidence. Each brand of research has its strengths and its limitations, and each implies what kinds of evidence are most relevant and useful. These are the data bricks we have to work with and what make the task of research synthesis in this field so daunting, though not without rewards. As Hall and her colleagues point out, although the value of research syntheses may be limited in terms of making cause-effect statements (which depends entirely on the "inferential strength of the underlying primary data"), nevertheless, syntheses do have merit for "studying the generality of effects," advancing knowledge, and directing future research.[5]

To explore the potential of these merits further, we first examine the sources and quality of existing evidence, especially service-related research since 1990. We then discuss the difficulties implicit in determining criteria for gauging effectiveness of service and developing benchmarks for distinguishing between low- and high-quality research in the field. We conclude this chapter by suggesting ways to address the underlying flaws in the primary data and demonstrating how readers can still learn from the wide variety of studies that currently exist in the field of civic service.

Review of Service-Related Research: Sources and Quality of Existing Evidence

A review of service-related research since 1990 demonstrates that a distinct field of civic service does exist. It is, however, a field characterized by fragmentation and interdisciplinary differences in perspective, terminology, and understandings of the meaning of service.[6] In their article on mapping the field of service, Perry and Imperial summarize results of an analysis of 997 publications on citizen service from an original database of 2,558 records. Their analysis yields the following primary findings. Overall, service-related research is:

- diverse, rich, and considerable in size and scope,
- driven by practice with a high potential for success bias,[7]
- marked by a paucity of research syntheses and interdisciplinary, comprehensive reviews (only 8 of the 997 sources reviewed were meta-analyses),
- characterized by conflicting definitions of service and of service outcomes such that no standardization of outcome measures exists,
- cross-sectional in nature with few longitudinal or panel data available for time-series or comparative research (only 34 of the 997 sources had experimental or quasi-experimental designs; only 12 used panel data),
- dominated by studies that focus on "the psychology of service" by examining individual outcomes (especially attitudinal versus behavioral) at the expense of institutional and community outcomes, and
- marked by significant gaps, especially lack of research on the effects of different types of service on citizenship outcomes.

These findings suggest that the sources and quality of the existing evidence on service lie in the richness of best-practices research but notably lack a well-developed research infrastructure necessary for studies that use longitudinal and panel data, which social scientists consider higher quality research. Because so few research syntheses currently exist, scholars and practitioners face significant barriers to accumulating, interpreting, and effectively using the large body of knowledge on best practices already available. Knowledge for practice involves, at the least, finding a way to assess the effectiveness of service programs. Unfortunately, standardized criteria for gauging effectiveness of service do not currently exist, perhaps for good reason.

Gauging Effectiveness of Service

Practitioners and scholars of civic service agree that one of the purposes of research in the field of service is to inform the practice of service and that to do so requires establishing some criteria for gauging service effectiveness. But the nature of the evidence we currently have on service raises serious questions about the feasibility, or desirability, of developing *universal* effectiveness standards. Increasingly popular support for the virtues of civic service suggests that a growing number and variety of service programs will develop ever more diffuse, often expansive and ambiguous goals and objectives. Service outcomes will necessarily be equally diffuse. It does not help that the intangible nature of some of the purposes of civic service—most recently delineated in the 1993 National and Community Service Trust Act— make measurement of outcomes especially difficult. How, for example, do you measure renewal of civic responsibility and the spirit of community?

The various faces of civic service (expressed through multiple and widely varying goals) may make the research more difficult, and it may force us to look at effectiveness measurements and standards in a new way, but ultimately, a way can be found to gauge effectiveness. In a study of the community-building effects of five civic service programs in one state, for example, we collected a number of universal indicators of community-building based on an ideal vision of what civic service could or should achieve but concluded that such global standards were neither useful nor desirable.[8] More useful standards for successful community building, we argued, will take into account the constraints inherent in any community-building endeavor—constraints imposed by human nature, unique local historical factors, structural inequalities across race and class, economic conditions, and the limitations of local and national institutions.

To measure the effects of these five service programs on local communities, then, we decided to derive community-building standards inductively, through key informant phone surveys, conversations with key community stakeholders, program reports, and success factors identified by program directors from their own experience. We found that, from these various data sources, certain similarities in perspectives on what constitutes successful community building emerged. These included increased community volunteerism, development of new (or strengthening of old) collaborations among community-based organizations, and revitalization of local neighborhoods through civic service signature projects.[9]

This inductive approach, however, is not without its costs. Incorporating unique contextual factors into standards for effectiveness will typically lead to a lack of standardization. This, in turn, significantly limits our capacity to compare outcomes across multiple types of service—a serious barrier to the development of theory in the field of civic service. That we were able to identify similarities in standards for effective community building across these five programs (each quite different from the others), however, suggests that a level of generality does exist that allows some comparability. In situations in which goals (like community building) defy easy definition, are not easily quantifiable, and have outcomes that are time-dependent, inductive case research may prove more useful for building knowledge on civic service than large-scale quantitative research.

Another complicating factor affecting our ability to determine criteria for judging the quality of service outcomes lies in the deliberately devolved nature of today's civic service programs. As the Corporation for National and Community Service knows all too well, "the outcomes [of national service programs] come about through a complex series of partnerships [and] results are achieved through parties [such that] output and outcomes become relative terms depending on one's point of reference."[10] This relativity in perspective characteristic of programs that are, by nature, intersectoral and multiorganizational further limits the capacity of scholars and practitioners to develop universal standards for success that are generalizable beyond similar types of programs. Multiple and different goals, as well as widely varying perceptions of outcomes, create problems for practitioners and scholars who seek to make meaningful statements about relationships between the attributes of service (and/or servers) on outcomes or about the effects of intermediate structures of service delivery on service program effectiveness.

This problem is not new. Organizational researchers cannot, themselves, agree, writes scholar Hal Rainey, that one conclusive model or framework for studying effectiveness exists; rather, many approaches have been tried, each of them found wanting in some respect. That Rainey identifies no less than thirty different dimensions or measures of organizational effectiveness does not bode well for determining criteria for gauging the effectiveness of complex programs like those of civic service.[11]

Multiple understandings (and therefore, standards) for organizational effectiveness make comparison across studies difficult. This has implications for discriminating among high- and low-quality standards for "good" research on civic service. Nevertheless, gauging the effectiveness of service is a challenge worth the effort, paying dividends in stronger and longer-lasting programs, better management of public and private resources, more positive experiences for those serving in various capacities, and a greater number of people being served in a more effective way.

Bricks and Mortar—Addressing Problems in the Evidence

Perhaps a better way of making discriminating choices about the quality of service-related research is the question of purpose—research for what? Knowledge for what? The frequent distinction between knowledge for practice and knowledge for theory building is so commonplace as to be axiomatic. But the debate among scholars and practitioners about the use and control of knowledge—and hence, the methods and types of research—remains as vexing as ever.

Social scientists tend to characterize the debate as that between "traditionalists" (e.g., historians who use ethnographic methods to understand the details of specific phenomena) and "behavioralists" (e.g., political scientists who seek to identify patterns and make explanatory generalizations across a large number of cases); or between those who use qualitative versus quantitative methods. In the more applied field of public management research, the debate is frequently characterized as disagreement between "advocates of knowledge distilled from field experience into generally applicable principles. . . the 'best practice' school. . . [and advocates of] knowledge based on the empirical validation of useful propositions derived from a priori models."[12]

The growing consensus of scholars that service-related research should not just inform the practice of service but also build a body of knowledge useful for making, at the least, contingent generalizations about service outcomes suggests the need to move beyond these disagreements. Methodologist Charles Ragin advocates a research approach that relies on both quantitative and qualitative methodologies—what he calls "a synthetic approach to comparative research" that is both holistic ("so that the cases themselves are not lost in the research") and analytic ("so that more than a few cases can be understood and modest generalization is possible").[13] We believe a synthetic approach to analysis of service-related research is useful when considering what to include or exclude from a research synthesis.

A more inclusive approach to determining research quality suggests that benchmarks for high-quality service-related research should strike a balance between excluding nothing and including only those studies that use experimental or quasi-experimental research designs. The nature of the evidence on service, the complexity of the subject, the newness of the field, the often time-dependent nature of civic service outcomes, and the lack of a research infrastructure necessary to build a body of knowledge about service and its impacts all suggest that this research synthesis should err on the side of inclusiveness—within limits.

Where those limits lie is important. In his book *Public Management as Art, Science, and Profession*, public management scholar Laurence Lynn argues that merely adding to the "already long list of putative principles by canvassing yet another cohort of compliant practitioners for pearls of reflective wisdom" will not suffice as high-quality research. A field of research, he argues, should, at the least, evaluate competing explanations of a phenomenon, attempt to avoid selection bias in building evidence, or avoid "ex post theorizing" in order to develop theory and improve "the analytic skills needed for thoughtful practice."[14]

Lynn's point is well taken. Knowledge for practice suffers when researchers ignore the need for rigor in their research designs. Yet, in a field lacking an adequate research infrastructure and comprehensive, interdisciplinary research syntheses, we may not have the luxury of being too exclusive in discriminating between high-and low-quality research. The current nature of the evidence on service—characterized by a preponderance of cross-sectional studies, self-selection and success biases, and insufficient numbers of longitudinal studies and use of panel data for comparative work—places boundaries on our ability to determine causation. It does not, however, limit our ability to make contingent propositions based on our ability, through research synthesis, to study "the generality of effects" across a wide variety of primary studies; indeed, Hall and her colleagues identify this as one of the major strengths of research synthesis.[15]

Bricks and Mortar—Making Use of What We Have

Even though the quality of the underlying studies limits how much we can take away from this research synthesis, there are still a number of things we can learn. Once again, we turn to Hall and her colleagues, who argue that research synthesis can never be used as a "substitute for primary studies meant to uncover causal relationships," but it can contribute to learning by

> [finding], summarizing, and describing the already existing results of research [and by adding] analyses that shed new light on variations in the phenomenon under study [such that] the synthesist can sometimes make inferences that go well beyond the original results.[16]

We agree. In Parts III and IV of this book, we will begin to stack the data bricks and provide the mortar in the form of generalizations stated as propositions. These will allow the reader to gain a broader perspective on civic service, identify mediating factors that impact the likelihood of positive civic service outcomes, provide insight about what works and does not work in civic service programs, and expose gaps in the current structure of knowledge that need to be filled through further research.

Some readers will look on these generalizations as givens, others will view them as highly speculative, still others will make good use of them in research and practice. Our intent is not to impose any normative standards about what constitutes good or bad outcomes or research; nor do we mean to say about any particular hypothesis, this has or has not been confirmed. Our intent is to offer the civic service community a synthesis of the current knowledge on civic service by carefully examining the nature of the evidence and integrating the research in such a way that practitioners, researchers, and policy makers can make sense of the multiple single studies that currently define the field of civic service.

Conclusion

We began this chapter with an analogy. Research synthesis involves the stacking of data bricks (single empirical studies) according to plan and applying the mortar that holds the bricks together. We extended this analogy further by arguing that before stacking and mortaring, we needed to first scan the landscape upon which we build (the ideal of civic service and its historical manifestation) and then examine closely the quality and nature of the materials we have available for constructing an edifice of accumulated knowledge about civic service.

The primary purpose of this chapter is to describe the bricks, identify problems inherent in assessing their quality, and present our way of addressing those problems. We conclude by asserting that although the nature of evidence on civic service has flaws that limit our capacity to make causal inferences, learning can still occur. The reader can make use of the summary of research findings and gain a clearer picture of what's working in the field of civic service today. To begin to distill this learning, however, we have one more step to complete—a discussion of the methods used in this research synthesis.

4

Methodology

In their discussion of methodology, Harris Cooper and Larry Hedges suggest that research synthesis does not differ from primary research as much as we might think.[1] Both forms of research face similar validity threats, both require careful, systematic consideration of questions to be explored, both require rigor. It is incumbent on the research synthesist to define clearly the boundaries and limitations of the synthesis not only by identifying the quality of the underlying primary research, but also by acknowledging potential threats to validity and limits to causal inferences.

In Chapter 3, The Nature of the Evidence, we focused on the quality and nature of the materials we have for building cumulative knowledge on civic service. In Chapter 4 we consider how to go about working with these materials to assure as credible a structure as possible. First, we consider a key methodological issue: how to define civic service for the purposes of this synthesis. This operational definition is critical for determining the boundaries of the synthesis because the decision about which primary studies to include or exclude will be based on this definition, with subsequent implications for data evaluation, interpretation, and analysis. We conclude Chapter 4 with a discussion of issues affecting our ability to synthesize and draw inferences from such diverse strands of research and a brief overview of the programs included in the synthesis.

Before considering these key methodological issues, however, it is important to return to the basics by restating the research questions driving this synthesis. These are as follows:

- What are the attributes of the research that has been conducted about civic service?
- What are the summative effects of civic service on servers, recipients of service, institutions, and communities?
- What does the research say about civic service implementation?

These questions, supplemented by an operational definition of the principle phenomenon under study—civic service—and a clear understanding of the nature and quality of the primary studies upon which the synthesis rests, set the boundaries for the analysis that follows in Parts III and IV.

Defining Civic Service

When considering the conceptual meaning of civic service, we began with Sherraden and Eberly's 1982 definition that viewed service as a period of time

> given by an individual to the nation or community that embodies two complementary ideas: one, that some service to the larger society is part of individual citizenship responsibility; and two, that society should be structured in ways which provide citizens with opportunities to make meaningful contributions.[2]

This definition is important because it acknowledges the essentially private nature of volunteerism but also emphasizes the public nature of service rooted in institutions that foster civic obligation, social capital formation, and a sense of community.

As we saw in Part I, the historical evolution of civic service in the twentieth century suggests an increasing focus on service as a social institution while still acknowledging the personal and voluntary nature of volunteerism so engrained in the American psyche. Michael Sherraden makes a strong case for institution building in the area of civic service.[3] Building institutions that promote active citizenship, he writes,

> is well underway, but poorly understood. The emergence [of civic service as an institution] has qualities of a social movement, with strong advocates and policy and program innovations [but] theory and research have been limited. Many positive impacts of service are recorded as anecdotal information and widely believed to be genuine, but there is little systematic documentation. We do not know very well how to understand service as an institution. . . [4]

Our conceptual understanding of civic service emphasizes its institutional nature for a number of reasons: (1) we agree with Sherraden's assessment of the need to improve our limited understanding of service as an institution, and (2) we believe that building a research infrastructure relevant for practitioners and scholars demands an institutional focus that moves beyond the study of private individual acts of service. With this understanding, then, we turn to the operational definition of civic service used in this book.

An Operational Definition of Civic Service

How shall civic service be defined for the purposes of this research synthesis? The answer demands thoughtful attention to the pros and cons of alternative approaches that might be taken. One approach would be to define civic service as encompassing research about all service programs with designs similar to the programs administered by the Corporation for National and Community Service (CNCS). This definition would include a heterogeneous array of programs, ranging from full-time residential programs (AmeriCorps*National Civilian Community Corps) to traditional part-time volunteer programs (Retired Senior Volunteer Program) to service-learning programs for elementary school children (Learn and Serve America K–12).

Although it might be desirable to compare programs with widely different characteristics, the number of moderator variables across this heterogeneous research is likely to complicate its analysis and interpretation. A related problem with this approach is the enormous increase in relevant research. Combining the literatures about traditional volunteering with more intensive forms of service would swell the number of studies to unmanageable proportions. Another consideration is that good syntheses already exist for some arenas of service that would be encompassed by defining civic service based on CNCS programs. Service learning research, for example, has been reviewed in several forums.[5] Thus, incorporating service learning into this synthesis would unnecessarily duplicate recent syntheses.

Furthermore, using a federal agency's portfolio of programs to define civic service is convenient, but as the foregoing discussion suggests it is fraught with problems. In addition to the program heterogeneity, research volume, and duplication associated with such an operational definition of civic service, it begs the question of what civic service is conceptually. It also ignores how civic service has differed over time and may serve to screen out relevant studies of earlier programs.

A more productive and defensible way of proceeding is to create a definition of civic service to guide the identification of relevant research. The goal, therefore, is sharpening the conceptual definition of civic service. One source that is useful for thinking about definitions of civic service is Cnaan, Handy, and Wadsworth.[6] The authors discuss different ways that the term *volunteer* is used and identify eleven definitions in the literature. From these eleven definitions, they identify four dimensions of volunteering: free choice, remuneration, structure, and intended beneficiaries. The categories within each of these dimensions are presented in Table 4.1.

The authors argue that the categories within the conceptual dimensions of who is a volunteer represent Guttman scales. Guttman scaling is used when

Table 4.1

Dimensions and Categories of Volunteering

Dimensions	Categories
Free choice	1. Free will (the ability to choose voluntarily)
	2. Relatively uncoerced
	3. Obligation to volunteer
Remuneration	1. None at all
	2. None expected
	3. Expenses reimbursed
	4. Stipend/low pay
Structure	1. Formal
	2. Informal
Intended beneficiaries	1. Benefit/help others/strangers
	2. Benefit/help friends or relatives
	3. Benefit oneself (as well)

Source: Ram A. Cnaan, Femida Handy, and Margaret Wadsworth, "Defining Who Is a Volunteer: Conceptual and Empirical Considerations," *Nonprofit and Voluntary Sector Quarterly* 25, no. 3 (1996): 371.

researchers wish to "establish a one-dimensional continuum for a concept [they] wish to measure."[7] Cnann and his colleagues presented the categories to a sample of respondents to determine whether the participants agreed that the categories defined a volunteer. Those who answered yes at a higher-level category invariably answered yes to a lower-level category. For example, with respect to remuneration, if respondents agreed that stipend/low pay defined a volunteer, then they were highly likely to respond yes to all of the lower-level (1–3) categories. This near perfect hierarchy of responses represents a Guttman scale.

The analysis by Cnaan, Handy, and Wadsworth is helpful for highlighting just how diverse our perception of volunteering is. It also calls attention to qualitative distinctions we often make between "volunteering" and "service." For instance, the character of a volunteer's remuneration—that is, stipend/low pay—is an attribute of many civic service programs. Another attribute of civic service programs is that they are typically formal in structure.

Unfortunately, except for the structure and remuneration dimensions, Cnaan, Handy, and Wadsworth do not provide sufficient criteria for distinguishing studies of civic service from other forms of volunteering. It is possible that civic service programs differ from volunteering along the free choice and intended beneficiary dimensions. But it is unclear whether these two dimensions are programmatic or personal attributes. If they are personal attributes (and they most certainly are, in part, matters of individual determination), information about these dimensions is not available for many studies

Figure 4.1 **Continuum of Service**

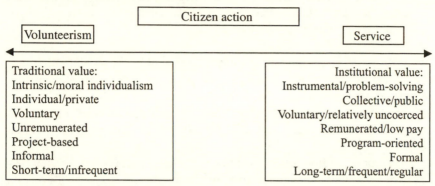

Traditional value:	Institutional value:
Intrinsic/moral individualism	Instrumental/problem-solving
Individual/private	Collective/public
Voluntary	Voluntary/relatively uncoerced
Unremunerated	Remunerated/low pay
Project-based	Program-oriented
Informal	Formal
Short-term/infrequent	Long-term/frequent/regular

Note: Figure 4.1 is our own depiction of the concept of a continuum of service, not Forsyth's.

about civic service. Thus, these dimensions are not very useful for deciding about inclusion or exclusion of particular research.

An attribute not included in this framework, but helpful in deciding which research to include, is the nature of the public problem to which voluntary activity is directed. One feature of many civic service programs, particularly those supported by CNCS, is that they operate in contexts that are not well served by traditional volunteerism. Traditional volunteerism is often project-based and directed toward tractable problems. Civic service programs usually focus on more difficult problems, such as illiteracy, youth violence, homelessness, and welfare dependency. The "tractability of problems" is, to some extent, in the eye of the beholder, but it can be a useful attribute for identifying the domain of studies for the synthesis.

Linda Forsyth, former executive director of the California Commission on Improving Life Through Service, developed a definition of service that implicitly incorporates ideas from Cnaan, Handy, and Wadsworth and other contextual considerations: "Service is differentiated from volunteerism in terms of frequency, duration, training needed to provide the services and criticality of failure to succeed in achieving stated objectives of the service activities."[8] Forsyth and the California Commission refer to the progression from volunteering to service as a continuum of service. Figure 4.1 summarizes in the simplest terms what this continuum of care might look like.

This distinction between volunteerism and service is also evident in Michael Sherraden's definition of civic service as an institution rather than as an individual act. It shares the same logic as that used by Charles Moskos, in his book *A Call to Civic Service.* For Moskos, civic service entails

> the full-time undertaking of public duties by young people—whether as citizen soldiers or civilian servers—who are paid subsistence wages.

[Common] to all such service is the performance of socially needed tasks that the market cannot effectively handle and that would be too expensive for government employees to carry out.[9]

Moskos views service as filling a particular institutional niche that neither the market nor the public sector can fill. As an institution enabling young people to perform their civic duties, service goes well beyond private volunteerism. Its impacts, he argues, must be evaluated in terms of the value of the services performed, not of the good service does to the individual server.[10]

For purposes of this current volume, we take a similarly institutional perspective on service. The perspectives of Cnaan and his colleagues, Forsyth, Sherraden, and Moskos jointly suggest that a synthesis of civic service research look at studies of programs with the following attributes[11]:

- a participant's engagement in service is frequent;
- the commitment to service is long-term, rather than episodic;
- the service is probably remunerated in some way, but at less than market rates;
- the program is formal;
- the program addresses either difficult public problems or needs that have been defined collectively as critical.

These attributes helped us identify a relatively clear-cut set of studies to include in the synthesis. They did not resolve all ambiguities about what to include, however. For example, is participation in four hours of service each day sufficiently frequent to fall on the "service" end of Forsyth's continuum or is twenty hours of service each week "volunteering"? Is a summer of service sufficient to be called "long-term"? Should employment and training programs such as Job Corps, which are similar to civic service youth corps programs, be included? The answers to these and similar questions are important because of their consequences for identifying relevant research.[12]

We made several a priori choices that affected the scope of relevant studies. Because of a tradition of government and nonprofit support for summer service programs, studies of these programs were included.[13] Thus, four hours of service each day for a summer met the intensity thresholds to qualify as civic service. In contrast, studies of the Job Corps were excluded from the synthesis because its members are not engaged in *service*. This decision also excluded a potentially large number of studies of similar programs such as those established by the Job Partnership and Training Act.

Two additional decisions affected the acceptability of studies included in the synthesis.[14] First, we decided to include virtually all studies, regardless of their research designs. The reality is that few studies of civic service meet traditional standards of experimental or quasi-experimental rigor. Rather than impose a quality filter in the selection of studies for the synthesis, quality was taken into account after the fact, when assessing the cumulative weight of findings. Studies of civic service implementation also were included.

Second, a large number of studies that the CNCS calls "accomplishments estimates" were excluded. These estimates are counts of civic service accomplishments categorized by outputs such as houses built, children tutored, and miles of trail restored. They are available for programs such as the Civilian Conservation Corps, the Youth Conservation Corps, and AmeriCorps. Aside from questions about their validity, accomplishment estimates are not calibrated or standardized and therefore it is difficult to judge their significance. This decision disqualified at least twenty studies. Finally, this synthesis covers studies completed and available prior to June 2000.

Drawing Inferences from Diverse Strands of Research

In Chapter 3, we began addressing the first research question driving this study—what are the attributes of the research that has been conducted about civic service? This involved examining the quality and nature of service-related research (the data bricks with which we have to work). The methods used to study civic service are diverse. This is not surprising in light of the long time span from which the studies were drawn, the varied nature of civic service programs, and the varied units of analysis studied in the research, ranging from individuals to organizations to communities. To shed further light on the attributes of civic service research, we continue with an examination of the sampling and data collection methods used in the primary studies and the discussion of research quality begun in Chapter 3.

Sample Size and Sampling Methods

This synthesis included 115 publications but because 15 of them contained more than one study, the total number of studies coded was 139. These studies exhibit a wide range of sample sizes. Small sample sizes are largely a product of research that investigated one or a few programs. Large samples also are well represented across the studies, with seven studies using samples larger than 1,000 and many others greater than 500. Sampling methods represented across the wide variety of studies in this synthesis are summarized in Table 4.2.

Table 4.2

Sampling Methods Used in Civic Service Research

Sampling method	Number of samples	Percent of total
Random	14	10
Judgment or convenience	74	53
Census	43	31
Not reported	8	6

Note: $N = 139$. The number of publications included in this research synthesis is 115; of these 115, 100 contain only 1 study (and therefore 1 sample), 6 include 2 studies (and therefore 2 samples), and 9 publications include 3 studies (and therefore 3 samples). This makes the total number of studies/samples coded 139.

The large majority of samples, 53 percent of the total, are judgment or convenience samples. Although there are no published norms for evaluation or applied research, the predominance of judgment or convenience samples is probably not far from the norm for similar research. The high proportion of judgment or convenience samples is a function of several factors. A number of the civic service studies were exploratory in character, which usually requires judgments about the selection of programs or participants. In addition, the cost of evaluations of civic programs with hundreds of sites would be prohibitive, unless the number of sites studied were reduced to manageable proportions. The percentage of samples selected randomly was 10 percent of the total. Although random sampling is not used extensively in the research, much of the research used censuses of programs, members, or both. Only a small portion of the studies failed to report their sampling methods.

Data Collection Methods

Surveys, interviews, site visits, program records, and several other data collection methods were used individually and together in the research. The data collection method used most frequently was the survey, which was used in 86 of the 139 studies in this synthesis. Two other data collection methods—interviews/focus groups and budget and archival data—follow closely behind the use of surveys (65 studies and 60, respectively). Reliance on a single data collection method was uncommon. Many of the studies used three, four, or even five data collection methods. Using multiple methods is a valuable research strategy because each method has its own strengths and weaknesses; using multiple methods of inquiry decreases the likelihood of research findings reflecting one particular method.[15]

Table 4.3

Research Quality—Study Design

Study design	Frequency
Randomized	2
Nonequivalent comparison group with pretest	10
Nonequivalent comparison group with posttest only	3
Time series	0
One-group pretest and posttest	23
Preexperimental	97
Synthesis	2

Note: N = 137; 2 of the 139 studies could not be coded.

Judging Research Quality

In order to synthesize and draw inferences from such diverse strands of research, we rely on "Judging Research Quality," an essay by Paul Wortman, in the *Handbook of Research Synthesis*. Wortman's review addresses the issue of research quality. We used two indicators suggested by Wortman to measure overall quality of each discrete study reported in a publication—research design and threats to validity.

Research Design

The quality indicator *study design* is an ordinal variable identifying variations in study design. This variable permitted seven options, as shown in Table 4.3. Research designs were arrayed from those with the fewest to those with the most threats to internal validity. The highest quality design is randomization, which allocates subjects to treatment and control groups randomly. The next most trustworthy design is nonequivalent groups with pre- and posttests. On the other end of the spectrum were preexperimental designs. For the most part, these were single-shot case studies or surveys that lacked comparison groups and measurement of effects over time. We also coded two studies as research syntheses because they involved aggregations of a group of studies.

Threats to Validity

The second quality measure is a count measure that has to do with the number of threats to validity present in a particular study. *Validity* refers to how closely an empirical measure actually measures what it is meant to measure, or, put another way, "the extent to which an empirical measure adequately

Table 4.4

Research Quality—Threats to Validity

Threats to validity	Frequency
1	10
2	30
3	47
4	35
5	13
6	1

Note: $N = 136$; 3 of the studies could not be coded.

reflects the *real meaning* of the concept under study."[16] Numerous threats to validity have been identified by research methodologists over the years, each of which has consequences for the types of conclusions we might draw from primary studies and consequently for the research synthesis. Six of the enumerated threats involve internal validity. These threats are history, maturation, testing, instrumentation, selection, and ambiguity about the direction of causal inference.[17] The other four threats address statistical conclusion validity: low statistical power, violated assumptions of statistical tests, fishing and error rate problem, and reliability of measures. Table 4.4 demonstrates the variation in threats to validity (see Appendix B, Table B.1, for definitions) across the 100–plus studies examined in this synthesis.

In general, both indicators of research quality—research design and threats to validity—provide similar perspectives about the distribution of quality across the studies. The design indicator shows that only two studies, less than 2 percent of the research, used randomized designs. A larger but small subset of studies used nonequivalent groups with a pretest. Most of the research falls into the preexperimental category. None of the studies use a time-series design. The threats-to-validity indicator provides a somewhat more favorable picture of research quality. About 7 percent of the research contains only one threat to validity. Another 22 percent is categorized as having only two threats.

For several reasons, we believe that the design indicator is overall a better indicator of quality than the threats-to-validity indicator. The design indicator, for example, made assigning scores to studies easier and more objective. Studies could fairly readily be classified into one of the seven categories. It was more difficult to count threats to validity because of the heterogeneity of the studies and the inadequacy of information about each study. This increased the prospect that threats to validity might be undercounted. Because of our uncertainties about the threats-to-validity quality indicator, we rely

Table 4.5

Civic Service Research Categorized by Type of Publication

Publication	Frequency
Journal	5
Book	3
Thesis or dissertation	8
Government report	72
Nonprofit organization report	16
University report	6
Conference paper	2
Consultant report	3

Note: N = 115.

primarily on the design quality indicator throughout the rest of this analysis.[18]

Bias

Wortman suggests that bias should also be considered as part of the assessment of quality in a research synthesis.[19] Given the research design and heterogeneity of studies on civic service, some types of bias defined by Wortman are difficult to assess. A form of bias that can be assessed, however, is publication bias. This can take different forms. One is systematic oversight of sources used in the synthesis. Although it is impossible to be comprehensive, the systematic search for studies to include in this synthesis was thorough and is not a likely source of bias.

Another related potential for bias lies in the variation across publication forums in terms of standards for quality control, publication of negative findings, and other factors that influence substantive results. Peer-reviewed scholarly journals have reputations for high standards, but this is not true for all journals or all publications appearing in high-quality journals. At the same time, journals also may be biased against null findings, thereby systematically influencing the results reported. Table 4.5 categorizes the studies in this research synthesis by type of publication (*N* = 115). As a percentage of the total, government reports clearly represent the dominant publication forum for these studies (63 percent) in contrast to journals and books (7 percent). This distribution, however, represents only a rough measure of quality and is more descriptive than it is discriminating.

Summary

Overall, judgment of research quality remains difficult. As a group, the studies of civic service rely largely on preexperimental designs. Only a small percentage of the studies, on their face (using research design as a proxy for quality), are high quality. In many instances, the investigators in the studies pay special attention to obtaining multiple sources of data to compensate for their recognition that the designs are not ideal. Collection of data from several sources is one means of developing an accurate picture of the program being studied.

Civic Service Programs in the Synthesis

A final step in setting the boundaries of this synthesis involves identification and description of the civic service programs included in the synthesis. The present study synthesizes research about civic service according to several parameters discussed earlier in this chapter. Hence, civic service programs in the synthesis do not represent the universe of all programs; instead, they represent programs that have been the subject of applied research or evaluation. Table 4.6 provides a brief summary of these programs.

As the table demonstrates, the programs included in the synthesis represent a wide diversity in terms of time periods, programmatic goals, and identities. Only the most knowledgeable observers of civic service are likely to be familiar with all of them. Some of the programs are such distant memories that even people familiar with civic service may have forgotten important details about them. To compensate for differentials in familiarity and memory, we provide brief descriptions of the programs in Appendix C.

Conclusion

In this chapter, we establish the boundaries of this synthesis by discussing issues related to methodology. We first provide an operational definition of civic service to guide our analyses. We then extend the discussion (begun in Chapter 3) regarding the first of the three research questions driving this study—what are the attributes of the research that has been conducted about civic service? We discuss issues of sample size, sampling methods, data collection, and research quality of the primary studies included in the synthesis. We conclude with a brief description of the civic service programs included in the synthesis as background for the findings presented in Part III, Research Synthesis Findings.

This research synthesis is meant to provide a baseline edifice of accumulated knowledge on civic service. In their discussion of the potentials and limitations of research synthesis, Cooper and Hedges conclude that, in the end, "sophisticated literature searching procedures, data quality controls, and

Table 4.6

Civic Service Programs Included in the Synthesis

Program	Year initiated	Current status
Civilian Conservation Corps	1933	Discontinued in 1942.
American Friends Service Committee Work Camp	The Quakers founded the American Friends Service Committee in 1917. The work camps began about 1930.	See www.afsc.org.
Volunteers in Service to America (VISTA)	1964	In 1993, VISTA came under the umbrella of the Corporation for National and Community Service (CNCS) and is now part of the AmeriCorps program within CNCS (AmeriCorps*VISTA)
Foster Grandparent Program (FGP)	1965	In 1993, the FGP came under the umbrella of CNCS and is part of the National Senior Service Corps within CNCS.
Teacher Corps	1964	Discontinued in 1982.
Senior Companion Program (SCP)	Enacted into law in 1972; authorized in 1973; launched in 1974.	In 1993, the SCP came under the umbrella of CNCS and is now part of the National Senior Service Corps within CNCS.
University Year for ACTION (UYA)	1971	Discontinued in 1981.
Youth Community Service (YCS)	1978	Discontinued, but we are unable to determine dates.
Youth Conservation Corps (YCC)	1970	In 1981 budget reductions virtually eliminated YCC. States picked up the idea.
Program for Local Service (PLS)	1973	Discontinued, but we are unable to determine dates.
California Conservation Corps	1976	The oldest and largest conservation corps now in operation.
City Year	1988	In 2003, City Year operated in thirteen sites nationwide.
Georgia Peach Corps	1990	Discontinued in 1994.

(continued)

Table 4.6 *(continued)*

Program	Year initiated	Current status
Public Allies	1991	In 2003, Public Allies operated in ten cities across the country.
AmeriCorps*State and National	Enacted into law in 1993; launched in 1994	Grants over 50,000 service positions per year to community-based organizations.
AmeriCorps*National Civilian Community Corps (NCCC)	Enacted into law in 1993; launched in 1994	In 2003, operates five campuses nationwide to focus on environmental, educational, human needs, and disaster relief projects.
Summer of Safety	Summer 1994	This program was a precursor of ongoing programs supported by CNCS.
Experience Corps	1998	In fiscal 2000, funding for Experience Corps was discontinued.
Seniors for Schools	1997	In fiscal 1999, 428 volunteers served in the program.

Note: There are several reasons for the difficulty in identifying termination dates for some service programs. One is that some initiatives are demonstrations or experiments that may not be formalized in statute. Although these experiments may be documented in formal evaluations, the ultimate disposition of the program has not. Another reason is that much more fanfare accompanies an initiative's startup than its demise. Yet a third reason is that because of reorganizations and other reinventions of programs, the termination of a program is sometimes not sharply demarcated.

statistical techniques can bring a research synthesis only so far."[20] Eventually, judgment of research quality depends on a number of other factors. Techniques are necessary though not sufficient when building sound knowledge through research synthesis. A valuable synthesis of accumulated knowledge, they conclude, should have both

> intellectual quality and practical utility; [it should] clarify and resolve issues [and] result in a paradigm shift [by bringing] to a theory greater explanatory power, [to] a practical program expanded scope of application, and [to] future primary research an increased capacity to pursue unsolved problems.[21]

These are the goals we seek to achieve in this synthesis of civic service research. We seek not only to build theory in the field, but to inform practice by examining linkages between service and outcomes, identifying implementation factors likely to enhance or impede positive outcomes, and by considering implications of current research for civic service policy. We acknowledge that the relative newness of the field of civic service, the methodological issues raised in Chapters 3 and 4, and the relatively rudimentary methods used (compared to standards of other fields and the overall general sophistication of research synthesis methods) place some limitations on this synthesis. The accumulated knowledge presented here, however, represents the most systematic and comprehensive synthesis conducted on national civic service research to date. To this task we now turn in the remaining pages of this book.

III

Research Synthesis Findings

5

Civic Service Outcomes

We observed in the initial chapters of this book that civic service manifests itself in a variety of ways in America—as ideal, as operating programs, and as continually evolving social institutions. In Part III, we look at another manifestation of civic service—as the effects of interventions intended to produce individual and social outcomes. This chapter focuses on the immediate and longer-term outcomes associated with civic service. Chapter 6, Qualities of Successful Programs, looks at variations in program design, leadership, and management to derive a better understanding of how they influence civic service outcomes.

This chapter is organized around the four types of outcomes summarized in Table 5.1. Beginning with a discussion of the effects of civic service on servers, the chapter then goes on to consider the effects on beneficiaries, institutions, and communities. It is important to note that when coding these outcomes, where there was doubt whether it was positive or null, we took a conservative approach and coded the outcome as no effect or null.

Server Outcomes

The cornerstone of many philosophical justifications for civic service is its effect on participants. Among the most prominent of the outcomes predicted to accrue to servers are the following: the development of their job and life skills; a better understanding of, and capacity for, civic involvement; educational opportunities conferred to reciprocate for service rendered; improved self-esteem; greater appreciation of, and tolerance for, diversity; satisfaction from serving; and better health, both physical and mental. The sections that follow provide an overview of these various outcomes, explaining the positive, negative, and null findings associated with each.

Skill Development

The vast majority of skill development outcomes, thirty-three of thirty-eight studies, are positive. A small minority of studies show no effect. These positive

Table 5.1

Outcome Definitions

Outcomes	Definition
Servers	
Skill development	The extent to which the civic service experience leads to improvements in server's job or life skills.
Civic responsibility	The extent to which service enhances the server's understanding of community issues and problems, commitment to civic duty, and/or willingness to participate in advocacy or political processes.
Educational opportunity	The extent to which civic service opens opportunities for further education in the period following service.
Self-esteem	The extent to which the server's sense of personal worth improves as a result of the service experience.
Tolerance for diversity	The extent to which servers' tolerance of people different from them or appreciation of diversity changed as a result of service.
Satisfaction from serving	The server's global effect toward the service experience.
Health	The physical and mental well-being of the server.
Beneficiaries	
Impacts on direct beneficiary	The extent to which service brings about the intended changes in the target of the service.
Impacts on indirect beneficiary	The extent to which service affects relevant third parties who are not the direct targets of the service.
Institutions	
Expansion of service	The extent to which providers are able to increase the number of units of a good or service.
Improvement in quality of services	The extent to which providers are able to improve the quality of existing services.
Creation of new institutions	The extent to which new organizations or organizational units result from the service program.
Communities	
Community strengthening	The extent to which social capital, service networks, or other multiorganizational arrangements are enhanced.
Benefit-cost ratio	The ratio of benefits to costs reported for the program.
Volunteer leveraging	The extent to which civic service participants are able to involve other volunteers.

and no effect studies are assessed in this section to identify which conclusions can be drawn about civic service and skill development.

Positive Findings

Several features of the aggregate of studies finding positive outcomes are noteworthy. One is that the positive outcomes persist across research conducted during a fifty-year period. Riecken's evaluation of the American Friends Service Committee (AFSC) work camps was the first to connect server skill development to service.[1] The most recent is Macro International's evaluations of DC Reads, a collaborative tutoring program for first- through third-grade students in District of Columbia public schools.[2]

A second noteworthy feature of the research is that the positive outcomes are sustained across a range of different types of service programs. They include youth and conservation corps,[3] senior programs,[4] VISTA,[5] University Year for Action,[6] Public Allies,[7] the Teacher Corps,[8] and national service demonstrations.[9]

The single program that leads by far in attracting scrutiny of its skill development outcomes is AmeriCorps. The AmeriCorps research includes preexperimental designs,[10] comparison group designs,[11] one-group pre- and posttest designs,[12] and a separate assessment of AmeriCorps*NCCC,[13] the residential component of AmeriCorps.

What is the precise nature of the skill development outcomes? One type of skill civic service has sought to influence is the skill needed to acquire technical or professional certification in a particular field. The Teacher Corps in the 1970s and Teach for America today are two civic service programs directed at shaping teacher development. The Teacher Corps had some success in broadening teacher-training programs and engaging interns to teach in schools with large enrollments of poor children. Corwin's extensive assessment indicates, however, little consensus about whether the program provided interns with the skills and competencies necessary for teaching in poverty schools.[14]

In addition to specific technical or professional skill development, service learning (integrating service formally into traditional academic curricula) has been used to enhance academic performance. The short-term nature of most service learning excludes it from the definition of civic service used in this synthesis, but one example exists among programs included here. University Year for ACTION (UYA), a 1970s service-learning program, reported success in linking service to academic performance. A survey of thirty volunteers in seven UYA schools showed that 75 percent of the job assignments related to the student's major and grades increased 12 percent over the pre-UYA semester or quarter. Although this is an isolated, small-scale study, it suggests that the claims for service learning's benefits for academic performance may be transferable to intensive service programs.

The nature of the effects of civic service on skill development may be most influential for generalized skills rather than professional skills or academic achievement. One example is provided by Aguirre International's three-year study of the first two cohorts of AmeriCorps*State/National.[15] The study assessed the effects of a member's AmeriCorps experience on life skills, a general set of competencies people need to function effectively in today's workplace and society. The research compared AmeriCorps members and a comparison group on five skills based on the secretary of labor's Commission on Achieving Necessary Skills (SCANS).[16] The five skills are communication, interpersonal relations, analytical problem solving, understanding organizational systems, and technology. Skills levels were measured pre- and postprogram for the AmeriCorps members and at similar intervals for the comparison group. A random sample of 382 AmeriCorps members showed statistically significant gains for all five skills. A comparison group of 732 had no statistically significant changes during the year. In addition, the gains for AmeriCorps members were widespread, with 70 percent reporting significant changes.

Null Findings

Five studies reported that the skills of participants did not change as a result of their service.[17] These studies are generally of high quality. Only one of the five studies, Pence's ethnography of the Wisconsin Conservation Corps' operation in Milwaukee, was preexperimental.[18] Bartlett and Beecroft is one of only two randomized design studies in the synthesis.[19] Grossman and Tierney[20] and Wolf, Leiderman, and Voith[21] used comparison groups with pretest/posttest. In light of the quality of these studies, their findings deserve closer examination.

The five studies share some characteristics that help to account for their variance from the positive findings in the large majority of studies. The four programs—the California Conservation Corps (which was the subject of two of the studies), Youth Conservation Corps, Wisconsin Conservation Corps, and Washington Service Corps summer program—use a youth corps design. They provide work opportunities for youths who are unemployed or who have not worked previously. The programs were designed to give participants exposure to work and the norms of the workplace, but contained few explicit developmental opportunities. The Youth Conservation Corps, the first of the four programs, was mandated by Congress to create opportunities for learning about the environment and natural resource management. The first-year evaluation of the program found very few changes in the low levels of environmental understanding of participants. The results are not surprising, because no resources were explicitly devoted to environmental education during the first year of the program. Adjustments made based on the first year's evaluation resulted in positive effects the second year.[22]

Like the other conservation corps, the California Conservation Corps' emphasis on productive work left little time or resources to devote to formal training or developmental activities. This emphasis means that skill development occurs largely through the work itself. The low skill levels of entering corps members simultaneously magnify the importance and difficulty of skill development. Wolf and her colleagues from Public/Private Ventures conclude: "The CCC has had difficulty developing a workable education program around the heterogeneous needs of the corps members and the demands of the work program."[23] The difficulty of mixing education and job training with conservation work was also experienced in the Civilian Conservation Corps, the precursor of modern youth corps.[24]

Another factor mediating the effects of service on skill development appears to be the intensity of service. The low intensity of service may have been a factor in several of the programs that produced null findings. The Washington Service Corps was a summer variant of the year-round program.[25] Participants spent four days working and one day in educational and developmental activities. The activities focused on job readiness skills, reflection about work and personal experiences, and integration of educational activities. These summer activities had no effect on educational performance in the following academic year as measured by grade point average (GPA), days absent, and whether students failed any classes. Although the program's design and theory of change can be criticized, the short span of service, less than two months on average, may be the reason that no skill development changes occurred.

The length of exposure also may have been a factor in the conservation corps results. Although conservation corps typically call for a year of service, the time served is usually much less. Many conservation corps report high attrition early in the program. In the case of the California Conservation Corps, Wolf and her colleagues found that no significant benefits accrued to members departing in the first four months.[26] Thus, service intensity appears to be an important mediating factor in skill development.

Summary

The breadth of positive findings and their replication across studies using a variety of methods indicate the robustness of the skill development outcomes.

One question that is not entirely answered by the research is which skills are most readily influenced by civic service. The evidence indicates that general life skills are most directly and substantially influenced. This finding reinforces the traditional view that service develops general skills that prepare participants for civic engagement.[27] It is conceivable that service promotes other types of skill development, specifically professional and academic skills, but the evidence does not substantiate this conclusion.

In addition to general conclusions about the impact and nature of service's effects on skill development, the null findings suggest several factors that mediate the service–skill development relationship. Skill development is more likely to occur when it is an explicit goal. Furthermore, longer exposure to service is more likely to produce positive effects.

Civic Responsibility

Civic responsibility involves the extent to which service enhances the server's understanding of community issues and problems, commitment to civic duty, and/or willingness to participate in advocacy or political processes. Civic service is routinely associated with the power to engage people in civic life for the long term.

Positive Findings

Like the skill development research, the studies that found a positive relationship between civic service and civic responsibility are diverse. The earliest study in the sample, Riecken's evaluation of the AFSC work camps,[28] and one of the most recent, a high-quality national study of AmeriCorps*State/ National,[29] found positive relationships between civic service and civic responsibility. Other studies of AmeriCorps produced results consistent with the national study.[30] In addition, research on VISTA,[31] the Youth Volunteer Corps of America,[32] AmeriCorps*NCCC,[33] Public Allies,[34] and civic service demonstrations[35] corroborates the positive relationship between civic service and civic responsibility.

The diversity of programs that discovered positive relationships is noteworthy in two other respects. One is the variation of service intensity across the programs. The AFSC[36] and Youth Volunteer Corps of America[37] were summer programs, at the low end of intensity among the programs in the sample. This suggests that short-term civic service, which may not affect skill development, may produce positive effects for civic education.

Another noteworthy feature of the programs is that civic responsibility was influenced by a diversity of program designs. Traditional conservation and youth corps programs,[38] direct service programs,[39] and capacity building programs[40] produced positive civic responsibility outcomes.

Null Findings

Five studies[41] reported no effects. These programs are less diverse than those for which positive outcomes were found for civic responsibility. With the exception of the Jastrzab et al. study,[42] the other four studies focused on either AmeriCorps*State/National[43] or AmeriCorps*NCCC.[44] Most of these programs were also relatively new, having been founded shortly before the studies were conducted. But if program maturity alone influenced civic responsibility outcomes, it would be difficult to account for positive results in other AmeriCorps programs, which were also new.

The overall quality of the no-effect studies makes it difficult to dismiss their findings as mere aberrations or methods artifacts. On average, the research designs of the no-effect studies are of higher quality than the positive studies. The study by Jastrzab and colleagues, which found no relationship between service and civic responsibility, is one of only two experimental studies of civic service in the synthesis.[45] Most of the other studies that failed to detect an effect used at least a design with pre- and posttests of a treatment group. Most of the studies that found positive effects used only a posttest with the treatment group. The one high-quality exception was the five-year study of AmeriCorps, which used a comparison group with pre- and posttests.[46]

One possible reason for the different results is methods based. The measurement of civic responsibility is not uniform across studies. Variations in operational measures, therefore, could be a factor in explaining differential findings. For the most part, the measures of civic responsibility are self-report survey items rather than behavioral indicators. In addition, the reliability of many of the measures is not known, casting further doubt on what conclusions can be inferred from the research results.

A substantive reason for the variations across studies resides in potential differences among program participants. This prospect is suggested in the study of youth corps by Jastrzab and her colleagues.[47] They found no overall effects on the total sample in a study of participant impacts in four youth corps in 1993–94. Subsample analysis of posttest results revealed, however, that African-American men scored significantly higher than members of the randomly assigned control group on measures of personal and social responsibility and were more likely to have voted in the last election. African-American males in the treatment group averaged nearly 8 percent above controls on the community involvement subscale and over 6 percent above controls on the summary personal and social responsibility scale. The treatment subsample was more than four times as likely to have voted (22 percent of participants versus 4 percent of controls).

What the subsample analysis does not reveal are the reasons underlying the significant changes in the civic commitments of African-American males. It is possible that as a group, they are more alienated than most other groups within American society. The youth corps experience may have been effective in reducing their alienation and increasing their sense of self-efficacy about civic engagement.

Another factor that may account for variations in results across studies is the richness of the civic content[48] or public work[49] in which civic service participants were engaged. A proxy for the civic content of the service is the rating for difficulty of the problems addressed. This rating does not appear to be correlated with the civic responsibility finding, however, because several of the no-effect studies were rated high in problem difficulty. In addition, definitive scores could not be assigned for many of the positive cases because insufficient information was provided about the service rendered. Although this one indicator does not provide conclusive evidence, it appears that the civic content of the service cannot account for variations across civic responsibility findings in the research to date.

Summary

The evidence about the effects of service on civic engagement is less compelling than for skill development. On its face, the number of positive findings exceeds null findings by 3 : 1. Using this ratio alone to judge the effects of service on civic engagement would be misleading. Two subsets of studies with positive findings have common roots, decreasing their independence from one another and, arguably, inflating the count of positive studies.[50] Furthermore, if any form of publication bias suppressed null or negative findings, there is likelihood that the true ratio of positive to no-effect studies is closer than reported here.

A comparison between the positive and no-effect studies reveals possible mediating variables for the differences. Two potential mediating factors are gender and ethnicity. One high-quality study revealed significant improvements for African-American males but no significant changes in the sample as a whole.[51] Another potential mediator is the civic content of service. It is likely that not all service is equal in its potential to influence civic commitments, but the research to date has not identified the service attributes that are critical for producing stronger civic commitments.

Educational Opportunity

Educational opportunity addresses the extent to which civic service opens opportunities for further education in the period following service. Eleven studies showed positive outcomes and one study produced a negative effect.

Positive Findings

Most of the research about educational opportunity is derived from analysis of AmeriCorps or precursor demonstrations after 1990. AmeriCorps*State/ National and AmeriCorps*NCCC provide an education award after completion of a specified number of service hours. Full-time members serve 1,700 hours and part-time members serve 900 hours in a year. The education award is entered in trust for future use toward tuition or qualifying student loans. Thus, the education opportunity issues associated with AmeriCorps are quite similar to those for the GI bill.[52]

Only one study addressed the effects of civic service on educational opportunity prior to the 1990s. The UYA was initiated to allow students to work one year in full-time, voluntary jobs with community agencies and organizations focusing on the solution of specific poverty problems while making normal academic progress toward their degrees. UYA issued grants to universities to select, train, and supervise the volunteers and provide academic credit. Institutions were encouraged to waive or reduce tuition for participants. The volunteer stipends and reduced tuition were factors in attracting participants to UYA, but they did not become the primary motivations.[53]

Negative Finding

In contrast to the studies that found positive relationships, Jastrzab and her colleagues found a negative relationship between service and the likelihood of earning a technical certificate or diploma.[54] The experimental design used in the study gives it substantial credibility. A plausible explanation for the result, however, is the timing of the follow-up and the nature of the outcome. Impact estimates were made at fifteen months after enrollment. The relatively short time between enrollment and follow-up is likely to disadvantage members of the treatment relative to the control group on this outcome because of the likelihood that participants must put their educational plans on hold during their service. Thus, the negative finding probably reflects the choice to defer education rather than a negative dynamic associated with service.

Summary

On the whole, the evidence supports a positive relationship between civic service and educational opportunity. Many individuals who complete a civic service commitment qualify for education benefits according to the terms of the program. Although not all service alumni will avail themselves of the opportunity, most are likely to behave in economically rational ways and draw upon the credits for which they qualify. Because some programs that tie educational opportunity to civic service are relatively new (for example, AmeriCorps), drawing more definitive conclusions about educational opportunity outcomes will need to wait until cohorts of servers mature.

Self-Esteem

Self-esteem refers to a person's sense of personal worth. Service is believed to increase self-esteem. The results of twelve studies support this expectation. Ten studies uncovered positive self-esteem outcomes and two produced null findings.

Positive Findings

The positive findings for self-esteem cut across server demographics and service programs. Youth,[55] seniors,[56] and heterogeneous populations of servers[57] report increases in self-esteem as a product of their service. Self-esteem of servers improved in service programs as varied as Foster Grandparents,[58] youth corps,[59] the California Conservation Corps,[60] Senior Companions,[61] AFSC Work Camps,[62] and VISTA.[63] Self-esteem outcomes are especially compelling for senior programs, where the results have been replicated repeatedly.

Null Findings

The anomaly to these findings is AmeriCorps*State/National. Two studies, encompassing a small sample of programs, found no self-esteem effects. Perry and Thomson, studying five Michigan AmeriCorps programs, detected no change in self-esteem between pre- and posttests.[64] They used Rosenberg's self-esteem scale.[65] In their study of the National School and Community Corps, Fox and Fox[66] report improvements in an eleven-item measure of self-worth. Although they concluded that self-worth increased, they misspecified the model by comparing the self-worth scores of 156 respondents in the pretest with the scores of 78 respondents in the posttest. Any differences in the pre- and posttest scores can be attributed to no more than self-selection bias.

Summary

The predominance of positive findings mixed with a few null findings suggests that civic service has a good probability of producing favorable self-esteem outcomes, but there may be variations across programs. A caution with respect to the self-esteem findings involves operationalization of the self-esteem variable. Most studies used one or a few survey items to measure self-esteem. Item reliabilities typically are not reported so it is difficult to assess how factors such as reliability and social desirability may have influenced the overall pattern of results.

Tolerance for Diversity

Tolerance for diversity is the extent to which people accept those different from them. Service is expected to increase appreciation of diversity. Research about tolerance for diversity is less common than most of the other outcomes discussed here. The overall outcomes are slightly skewed toward findings of no effect rather than positive outcomes.

Positive Findings

The earliest research to show a relationship between civic service and diversity is Riecken's study of the AFSC work camps.[67] Riecken used a scale of ethnocentrism to test the hypothesis that service reduced the amount of prejudice expressed toward racial, religious, and national minority groups. Campers' attitudes were measured prior to service, at the conclusion of the summer, and again ten months after camps had ended. Their ethnocentrism scores declined significantly by the end of the summer and remained significantly lower during the ten-month interval following their service. Thus, their prejudice declined as a result of service.

The other three studies that produced positive results for diversity emanate from single-group, posttest-only studies that relied on self-report, single-item measures of diversity. Participants in VISTA's 1993 Summer Associates Program, a national demonstration, rated dealing with diversity as the area of greatest impact on them.[68] The National Service Demonstration programs, funded under Subtitle D of the National and Community Service Act of 1990, produced results comparable to the 1993 VISTA demonstration.[69] During the second year of operation (1993–94) for the nine programs in the demonstration, participants reported an increased appreciation of diversity and benefits from working with people of backgrounds different from their own.

A study of Northern California civic service programs by Harder+Company Community Research also found positive results for diversity.[70] A survey of 469 participants from fifteen AmeriCorps programs gave learning about people from different backgrounds the highest rating for impacts of their AmeriCorps experience. The rating was 4.42 on a five-point scale. Forty-nine percent of respondents agreed strongly with the statement, "learned about people with different backgrounds." In contrast to the impact rating, only 20 percent of participants rated "being with people from diverse backgrounds" as the best part of their AmeriCorps experience. This placed diversity, fourth in ranking, far behind "working with client" (70 percent), "working with fellow AmeriCorps members" (36 percent), and marginally lower than "working with the community" (26 percent).

Null Findings

Five studies show no effects for diversity.[71] Three of the five studies measured attitudes at pre- and postservice.[72] One of these studies, by Wolf, Leiderman, and Voith, evaluated the California Conservation Corps using a comparison group.[73] The results of this study are revealing about the difficulty of interpreting results about tolerance and diversity outcomes. Both the treatment and comparison groups scored high at baseline. The two groups also exhibited significant changes over time, making it difficult to attribute changes to the program as opposed to other factors, such as maturation. Regression analysis indicated that the treatment group's attitudes toward women in nontraditional jobs may have improved, but this was the only difference detected between the groups on a variety of tolerance indicators.

The results in a Macro International study were difficult to categorize because the survey responses reported and the author's global characterization were shaded in several directions.[74] Twelve AmeriCorps programs participated in the study. Item-by-item results reported in the study range from 75 percent agreeing or strongly agreeing with the statement "The program promotes respect for diversity," to 69 percent agreeing or strongly agreeing with the statement "The atmosphere in the program does not make me feel like I belong." The absence of baseline measures for tolerance and appreciation for diversity and the unknown reliabilities of the measures confound interpretation of the survey responses.

Summary

In some respects, the Macro International study mirrors the mix of outcomes for the diversity construct as a whole. The dynamics underlying the relationship between service and tolerance are complex. Unraveling this complexity is doubly difficult because of the paucity and weaknesses of the research. Weak research designs and measures of unknown reliability and validity call into question attempts to generalize. Frees and colleagues reflect the caution appropriate for this body of research:

> It should be recognized that this analysis is based on self-reports from participants while they were still in the program. Since it was not feasible to collect comparable data for a control or comparison group, we have no way to separate these reported effects from the normal maturation process of youths and young adults, or to compare the experience of program participants with that of non-participants. Moreover, because we have no post-program follow-up data for the participants, we have no way of knowing whether these effects persisted after they left the program.[75]

Beyond the methodological reasons for caution about the research findings, there are probable substantive reasons that account for the variations in results across the studies of tolerance and diversity. The first study of the effects of service on tolerance, Riecken's pathbreaking research on AFSC work camps, provides several insights.[76] Riecken speculated that the changes evident in campers were a function of several mediating factors. One was the reinforcement of individual changes by the groups within which campers worked. Individual attitudinal changes tended to become group norms rather than isolated individual changes.

Riecken also argued that attitudinal changes took hold because of a close connection between the new attitudes and the activities in work camps. Like the reinforcing effects of groups on individuals, campers' opportunities to put their new attitudes into practice reinforced individual changes. Riecken writes:

> Not only did work campers discuss topics like racial prejudice and democratic group action, but they also had opportunities to put these sentiments into action, to participate in nonprejudiced, democratic behavior, while they performed acts of social service for the communities where they worked.[77]

Campers put their new attitudes into action not only with respect to the communities in which they worked, but also in their personal relationships with other campers.

> The culture of the group encouraged campers to be equalitarian, warmly friendly and sympathetic toward each other, and, above all, to respect each other as individuals. Thus, in their day-to-day contacts, in the very nature of their rapport with each other, campers were strengthened in the attitudes in which the greatest favorable changes occurred.[78]

A recent study of diversity in AmeriCorps reiterates and elaborates Riecken's findings of a half-century earlier.[79] Among the mediating factors the study identified were these:

- program design—the program needs to place explicit and implicit importance on diversity in achieving its goals;
- member recruitment—the desired diversity mix needs to be intentionally developed;
- assignments—member assignments in host sites and in teams need to be appropriately structured;
- attention to group conflict—members must have the skills necessary to work through conflicts constructively.

Much like Riecken's conclusions decades earlier, the researchers concluded:

Recruiting a diverse Corps is a necessary but not sufficient step for successfully supporting diversity. The program itself must set the tone and create an environment which values Member diversity throughout the program year. . . . Implementing strategies to support diversity that have not been tailored appropriately to a program's Members may be more divisive than taking no action. A successfully supported diverse Corps of Members can generate more benefits for all parties involved.[80]

Satisfaction from Serving

The server's global affect toward the service experience is the only server outcome for which all studies report positive results.[81] Like the skill development outcome, the positive findings for server satisfaction range across a variety of contexts. These include youth and conservation corps,[82] senior programs,[83] the Teacher Corps,[84] VISTA,[85] and AmeriCorps.[86]

The sources of individual satisfaction appear to be quite diverse. For instance, a 1997–98 study of four AmeriCorps programs in the Pacific Northwest indicates several factors that contributed to member satisfaction.[87] Alumni of the four programs expressed satisfactions associated with the opportunities for personal self-discovery and exploration of career interests, development of interpersonal and technical skills, and contributions to their communities.

The positive findings for server satisfaction should be interpreted with some caution. All the studies in the synthesis involved voluntary participation in civic service—that is, participants in the programs freely chose civic service. None of the programs involved mandatory service. Thus, the self-selection of members into programs may predispose them to express satisfaction with their experiences.

In addition, most measures of satisfaction are single-item survey measures taken after the service is completed, thereby excluding those who leave early, perhaps because they are dissatisfied. Participants who stay are much more likely to express their satisfaction, either because they genuinely valued the experience or because they rationalized the choice in order to reduce cognitive dissonance.

We have no ready benchmarks for satisfaction, thereby making it difficult to specify norms for expected levels of satisfaction. The difficulty of many civic service jobs suggests, a priori, that dissatisfaction with the experience is as likely a prospect as satisfaction. Thus, despite the caution about overinterpreting the findings, the results indicate that server satisfaction is a likely outcome of civic service.

Health

The physical and mental well-being of the server has been addressed solely in the context of senior service programs. This largely results from the early vision of senior service as contributing to productive aging. Service was envisioned as a way to engage seniors so that their physical and mental capacities did not deteriorate from disuse. A by-product of stipended service for low-income seniors was that it gave them financial support to improve their lifestyle and reduce stress.

The volume of research about health has been modest, consisting of only six studies. What is striking about the civic service health outcomes is their persistence over time. Research spanning a twenty-year period beginning in the mid-1960s has consistently shown a positive relationship between health outcomes and service. Another noteworthy attribute of this research is that it is among the most rigorous conducted about civic service.

Positive Findings

Saltz conducted two longitudinal studies of a cohort of foster grandparents at two- and seven-year intervals.[88] The sample consisted of thirty-seven foster grandparents and a comparison group of twenty-two. The foster grandparents demonstrated significantly higher life-satisfaction and adjustment at both the two- and seven-year intervals. Subjective assessments of health and records of absence due to illness compared favorably to the comparison group and to a national housekeeping sample in their age group. A third study of foster grandparents also produced positive results.[89]

Two evaluations of the Senior Companion Program (SCP) found similar positive health outcomes.[90] The more recent and rigorous of the two studies, by SRA Technologies, involved a five-year study initiated in 1979.[91] Active senior companions and persons on the waiting list to become senior companions were compared on mental and physical health in three rounds of interviews conducted over the five years of the study. Entering volunteers showed significant improvement in mental health functioning, while those remaining on the waiting list declined. Volunteers who remained active maintained the level of mental health functioning over the five years of the study, while volunteers who subsequently became inactive declined after they ceased their participation. In addition, active volunteers reported adjusting more positively to the limitations of declining health. In the third and concluding round of interviews, 65 percent of active volunteers, compared to 28 percent of inactive participants, reported that their health troubles did not stand in the way of doing things they wanted to do despite the fact that the groups were similar in illnesses reported.

Null Findings

The one study to find no favorable health effects of senior service focused on the National Long-Term Care Demonstration Research Project, which operated from March 1982 through November 1983.[92] The project sought to determine whether volunteer services, such as those available from the Retired Senior Volunteer Program (RSVP) and SCP, were a viable way of helping elderly persons in need.[93] The project used senior volunteers to provide services to peers needing help. Volunteer services included such things as providing companionship and respite care, preparing meals, and coordinating referral services. Volunteers also helped in communications, home management, chores, and transportation.

Several factors, largely technical in character, may account for why service did not produce health outcome improvements in this study as it had in others. One is that field offices were given significant latitude in selecting the comparison group. This raises questions about the consistency of comparison group selection criteria across sites, their comparability to members of the volunteer (treatment) group, and their comparability to similar groups in previous studies.

Another factor is that the composition of clients under observation was different from normal groups receiving service through typical SCP projects. Half the clients were selected for their high functional capability and half for their low functional capability. It is not immediately obvious how client differences could affect volunteer health outcomes. One possibility is that the clients of low functional capability placed an excessive burden on volunteers, thereby increasing health dysfunctions. The technical report of the research also implies that members of the comparison group may have been used to replace volunteers. If this occurred, the treatment-comparison group distinction would be diluted.

Summary

Research about health outcomes for servers has been confined to seniors. The positive results are consistent with the expressed objectives for senior service programs—that is, improvements in the health of seniors who serve. Although the volume of research is modest, the positive findings have been replicated several times, suggesting that they are robust.

Beneficiary Outcomes

Impacts on beneficiaries involve two subsets of effects: those for direct and indirect beneficiaries. The *direct beneficiaries* are the groups for whom service is targeted—the homeless in the case of Habitat for Humanity, those in need of tutoring in the case of DC Reads, and shut-in seniors in the case of the Senior Companion Program. An *indirect beneficiary* refers to parties who are not direct targets of the service who nonetheless reap benefits from the service.

Direct Beneficiaries

The impacts of civic service on direct beneficiaries involve the extent to which service brought about the intended changes for the target of the service. In the current parlance of the Corporation for National and Community Service (CNCS), this is "getting things done." You will recall from the definitional discussion in Chapter 4 that one of civic service's distinguishing features is that it is often a strategy for tackling difficult problems that requires more intensive effort than can be marshaled by traditional volunteerism. Thus, getting things done is a core expectation of civic service.

All thirty of the studies that investigated direct beneficiary outcomes produced positive findings. Many of the studies are quite recent, assessing results from AmeriCorps,[94] VISTA,[95] or national service demonstrations.[96] Another large subset of studies is focused on senior programs[97] and senior demonstrations. A smaller subset of studies looks at youth and conservation corps programs.

The programmatic context of the research is not a reliable guide to the targets of service. For example, the beneficiaries of senior programs are sometimes seniors, but frequently they are also children in educational or foster care settings. Similarly, AmeriCorps is directed at getting things done in four policy arenas—education, public safety, the environment, and other human needs—but the research involving AmeriCorps is primarily directed at education, with lesser attention to the environment and almost none to public safety.[98]

Education

The intensive evaluation of education-focused service is a relatively recent phenomenon. Eleven studies[99] have appeared since 1997. Prior to the mid-1990s, only one study[100] was conducted about the role of civic service in education, and it focused on higher education.

The education-focused research follows several different strategies for identifying impacts on direct beneficiaries. Some research[101] investigates specific learning tasks, such as reading, and gauges the progress of the target group using standardized tests. Other studies address the impacts of service on the school as a social organization, assessing how the service intervention affects a variety of factors known to improve education outcomes.[102] Yet other research involves the synthesis and secondary analysis of local outcome studies.[103]

An example of research on specific learning tasks is Macro International's evaluation of DC Reads.[104] The DC Reads program was initiated in 1997. By the 1998–99 school year, it brought together a partnership of the District of Columbia public schools; Communities in Schools (CIS), a nonprofit organization; eight local universities, led by Georgetown University; and the CNCS. In its second year, DC Reads operated in sixteen schools. About 500 students, mostly second graders, were tutored by a total of 340 tutors. By the fourth semester of operation, the tutoring curriculum was a blend of Book Partners and Reading One-to-One, which served a wide range of students, including those with very low reading skills.

Four schools served as primary sites for the evaluation of DC Reads. The core instrument for measuring outcomes was the Reading Performance Battery, which contains eight components. Most tests were administered three times, at the beginning, midpoint, and end of the school year. Students improved most dramatically in phonemic awareness, the matching of sounds to their symbols, and in four of the other seven components of the test battery.[105] In addition, tutored students made greater gains on the Stanford Achievement reading tests than did nontutored students. Tutored students gained nearly twice as much as nontutored students during the course of the school year.

Achatz and Siler's study, which was exploratory in character, took a broader look at education outcomes created by a civic service program in a study of what foster grandparents do in Head Start programs.[106] The authors conducted intensive observations of foster grandparents in six classrooms. In effective classrooms, they observed that foster grandparents engaged in a range of positive interactions with children over the course of the day, including listening attentively and acknowledging their progress and accomplishments. The foster grandparents developed and reinforced prosocial behaviors through modeling, encouraging children to try new activities, and acknowledging individual contributions to group activities. Foster grandparents also helped children make productive choices and redirect misbehavior by providing children with constructive guidance and feedback. Achatz and Siler concluded that these caregiver behaviors contributed to positive developmental outcomes for children in four areas: (1) emotional well-being, (2) social and behavioral skills development, (3) language development, and (4) cognitive development.

A third strategy for identifying outcomes in the education arena is synthesis of local program evaluations.[107] Seniors for Schools is an initiative of the CNCS as part of the America Reads Challenge. It sought to recruit adults over age fifty-five to help children read independently by the end of the third grade. Sites in nine states participated in the first two years of the program. Each of the nine sites conducted local evaluations using standardized and nonstandardized reading skills tests. Project Star synthesized results from the nine studies.[108] It found that 88 percent of the students improved their reading skills during the 1998–99 project year. Sixty-nine percent of the tutored students whose grade-level change was measured achieved increases of one full grade or more.

Senior and Long-Term Care

Elder and long-term care is a close second to the education focus, but the research about seniors has a far longer history than research on most other civic service programs. Research about the effects of civic service on the senior population is dispersed across each of the last four decades of the twentieth century, dating to 1968.[109] Most of the research has concentrated on two programs—Foster Grandparents and Senior Companions[110]—but a few studies have other foci. [111]

The senior-related research about direct beneficiaries is unique in that there are typically two beneficiaries: the caregiver and the recipient of care. Among the reasons for the dual emphasis is the character of civic service programs targeted to seniors. Both the Foster Grandparents and Senior

Companions programs require an income test to determine eligibility because they are intended to benefit low-income seniors. In addition, the programs are conceived as means to support productive aging. Thus, while the Senior Companion Program seeks explicitly to provide service to aging Americans, it also addresses needs of senior caregivers.

The research indicates that civic service has been successful in meeting needs of both senior caregivers and recipients. Caregivers benefit on several dimensions—economic, physical and mental health, and social. An early evaluation of Senior Companions found that caregivers placed high value on three benefits from the program: the opportunity to help others, the stipend, and the chance to be active.[112] Research has consistently demonstrated that low-income seniors benefit from service stipends.[113] Saltz's longitudinal study of foster grandparents identified social and health benefits for senior participants.[114] Foster grandparents showed positive effects on life satisfaction and adjustment after one and two years of participation and again after seven years. Although the indicators of effects on health of participants were mixed, Saltz concluded that foster grandparenting had positive effects on the perceived health and vigor of many participants.

Although many senior programs originated for the benefit of participants, they also have been shown to produce significant benefits for seniors who are serving others. Repeated evaluations of senior civic service programs have shown client improvements in areas such as social resources, adjustments to health limitations, and functional independence.[115]

Other Positive Findings About Direct Beneficiaries

Few of the other studies that produced positive findings for direct beneficiaries zero in on a particular service or type of activity. Several of the studies addressed corps programs—conservation corps, youth corps, and urban corps—but they did not provide fine-grain analysis of the services provided and how the direct beneficiary effects were produced.[116]

Summary

The volume of evidence for civic service as a strategy for ameliorating public problems is compelling. The number of positive findings and the absence of null or negative findings is important evidence for the efficacy of civic service as a problem-solving strategy. The limitations of the extant research are that its service-arena coverage is relatively narrow, and it does not provide much information about the difficulty of the public problems addressed. Research about education dominates the sample of studies. Studies of effects on seniors and environment and conservation work are prominent, but less common than education. These limitations of the research notwithstanding, however, the strategy to use civic service to get things done appears to be paying off.

Indirect Beneficiaries

Service programs may be targeted at a variety of beneficiaries—among them homebound seniors, teens in crisis, and youth struggling to read at grade level. In the course of serving the intended target population, service programs may produce benefits for third parties who are not the direct targets of the service. Although research about indirect beneficiaries is sparse, it is useful to review what we know about this facet of the outcomes from civic service.

Positive Findings

Six studies identify positive outcomes for indirect beneficiaries of service.[117] Schools provide several examples in which indirect beneficiaries gain from service.[118] Seniors for Schools (SFS) is one example. Its primary emphasis is student outcomes, especially reading and literacy. But in the course of trying to achieve these outcomes, seniors also worked with parents and families. Each of the four SFS sites sought to involve parents in the schools. Sites also developed activities to promote literacy enrichment in the home. The reported result was that parents took a more active role in the schools and were better prepared to support their child's development.[119]

Programs for seniors also are productive contexts for providing benefits to individuals who are not direct targets of the service. Frail and disabled older adults are the primary target of SCP. Because so much assistance for older adults is provided in the home by relatives, senior companions often provide significant relief for family members. [120] Respite for caregivers is an indirect and, in some circumstances, a primary benefit of the service program.

Null Findings

A study of the Teacher Corps is the one exception to the positive findings among the studies of indirect beneficiaries.[121] As part of their in-service responsibilities, Teacher Corps interns studied toward a college degree, served in low-income area schools, and performed community service for the low-income families and their children. Service to teachers and students in the classroom was an intern's primary role; community service was secondary.

The result was that the service in the community was slighted. The time pressures on interns were heightened by the supervising teachers' perceptions that the time interns spent in the community reduced their value as assistants to the teachers. The interns themselves felt that they did not spend enough time in the classroom. The result was that the community derived few benefits from the community service requirement of the in-service program.

Summary

Despite limited evidence, civic service appears to generate benefits for indirect beneficiaries. It is difficult to identify how widespread or predictable these benefits are, given the limited evidence. Research in service contexts such as education and long-term care suggest that such benefits could accrue consistently.

Why is there so little research about indirect beneficiaries? One reason, as the distribution of research between direct and indirect beneficiaries implies, is that it is less consequential to improve the situation for third parties than it is to ameliorate the needs of the direct targets of service. Another reason that there is so little research is the problem of attribution. Even with some direct beneficiaries, it can be challenging to attribute effects with confidence. With indirect beneficiaries, the number of variables in play can quickly become overwhelming. Yet a third reason is that it is sometimes difficult to distinguish between direct and indirect beneficiaries. This seems to be particularly true for programs like Senior Companions, where the needs of the server, the served, and third parties may be integral to the design of the program. Thus, despite the lesser importance of indirect beneficiaries, it is important to capture the outcomes of civic service for third parties in order to produce an accurate picture of the full benefit of civic service programs.

Institution Outcomes

Institution outcomes encompass the effects of civic service on service-delivery organizations. They may involve temporary changes in either the quantity or quality of goods or services produced or longer-lasting changes in service-delivery organizations. In general, changes in the quantity or quality of output are relatively low threshold outcomes; that is, they should be expected in most circumstances. In fact, productivity—that is, quantity and quality of services—should correlate with impacts on beneficiaries. If this is the case, the positive results discussed in the preceding section are precursors to positive effects of civic service on quantity and quality.

The creation of new or the transformation of existing institutions is, a priori, far more difficult to achieve. Unlike changes in service quantity or quality, which can usually be achieved using existing operating structures, changing institutions requires participants to accept the need for change and to design and implement new structures.

Service Expansion

Service expansion is the extent to which providers are able to increase the units of a good or service produced as a result of a civic service intervention. Twenty-three studies investigated this outcome and all reported a positive increase in services. The results cut across the range of civic service programs. Among continuing programs investigated in the research are AmeriCorps*State/National,[122] AmeriCorps*VISTA,[123] the Senior Companion Program,[124] and various youth conservation and service corps.[125] Three of the programs, UYA,[126] Youth Conservation Corps,[127] and the Teacher Corps,[128] have been discontinued. Several studies also looked at service expansion in the context of civic service demonstrations.[129]

The way in which civic service programs expand is illustrated in the evaluation of the civic service demonstration programs funded under Subtitle D of the National and Community Service Act of 1990. The demonstrations were intended to test models for a civic service program. Nine demonstration programs provided more than 1.1 million hours of service in 1993–94. Frees and colleagues found that 85 percent of project sponsors indicated that only some of the work completed by program participants, or none at all, would have been done in their absence. Among the new activities initiated were these:

- For a community-based education center, a corps member planned and taught algebra and geometry lessons for a summer math camp and conducted or assisted at math study or tutoring sessions, averaging thirty-three sessions per week, during the school year;
- For a community-based human services organization, a corps member developed, organized, and ran a children's recreation program at a public park, with activities scheduled after school and four to six hours each Saturday;
- For a local branch of a national affordable housing organization, a corps member supervised and worked with 460 volunteers in the completion of eight homes and the startup of five more.[130]

The Lower Yakima Valley Summer Reading Tutoring Project illustrates how AmeriCorps has been deployed to expand reading programs.[131] In late spring 1997, Washington State's Office of the Superintendent of Public Instruction (OSPI) initiated a summer school program for kindergarten and elementary school students. The nineteen schools selected for the program exhibited the lowest, nationally normed test scores in Washington over a four-year period. Ninety percent of the children in the two districts in the lower Yakima Valley from which schools were selected qualified for free or reduced lunches and about half their parents had only a sixth-grade education. Twenty-four AmeriCorps members helped the two schools implement a concentrated reading improvement program. The deployment of the AmeriCorps members permitted the schools to carry out their plans quickly and efficiently. The results of the program were daily one-on-one reading with the children and an increase in their enthusiasm for reading and reading skills.

Service Quality

Service quality refers to the extent to which providers are able to improve the quality of existing services. The results of the research for service quality are quite similar to those for service expansion. All twenty-four studies that involved service quality outcomes produced positive findings.[132] These studies overlapped significantly with those discussed in conjunction with service expansion.

An important question to be asked about this outcome is: Do improvements in service quality permit service providers to increase quality to a threshold that produces benefits disproportionate to investments? Although the question has not been investigated explicitly, there is some evidence from the descriptions of programs that this may be the case.

The Experience Corps illustrates how a civic service program can enhance quality along several dimensions, thereby increasing prospects for successful impacts on service recipients. The program was designed to engage the talent and skills of older Americans to assist low-income children in inner-city elementary schools. The Experience Corps intervention enhanced service quality in concrete ways. It increased the level of personal attention given to students. Volunteers spent fifteen hours or more each week working one-on-one with small groups of students. The presence of the volunteers reduced the ratios of adults to students. Reducing the ratios was important in light of circumstances in many of the schools—large class sizes, growing enrollments, low parental involvement, students working below grade level, and tight constraints on new funding. Beyond reducing the ratios, the volunteers provided much needed academic support. Students were able to spend more time on task. Interactions between volunteers and students permitted the volunteer to assess comprehension, bolster study habits, and monitor students' adjustment to the classroom. A by-product of the process of providing academic support was that the volunteers became mentors to the children. Thus, the Experience Corps intervention affected service quality by increasing personal attention, reducing adult-student ratios, increasing academic support, and providing mentoring.

The D.C. Reads program is another example of how an intervention can affect service quality.[133] The nonprofit running the program, CIS, introduced several effective practices that had not been applied widely in D.C. schools prior to the initiative. They included: using research-based curricula; planning regular, frequent, and well-structured tutoring sessions; and engendering positive, caring relationships among students, staff, and tutors.

Institution Creation

Institution creation involves the extent to which a civic service initiative produces new organizational forms or organizational units. Civic service initiatives often include institutional change goals such as reforming existing institutions or filling voids in service delivery networks. Achieving these goals may require some form of institution creation, ranging from new service units in existing organizations to entirely new organizations.

Several generalizations about the institution creation research are worth noting by way of introduction. The volume of research related to this outcome is small relative to most other outcomes. Only ten studies are categorized as addressing institution creation.[134] Half of the research predates 1990. The findings of the research are mixed. Six of the ten studies produced positive findings and four found no effect.

Positive Findings

The role of civic service on institutional development is concretely documented in Aguirre International's study of a sample of sixty AmeriCorps programs.[135] In interviews with the administrators of these programs, 17 percent indicated that new organizations providing new services resulted from participation in AmeriCorps. This often entailed creating new stand-alone organizations that met AmeriCorps goals and received its funds. The final report provides several examples of these new stand-alone organizations:

> An unusual alliance of three different water authorities—local, state, and federal—was formed to perform environmental services. All three entities had existed before AmeriCorps, but the alliance and the resulting institution and services they provided were new. In another case, a new national

direct organization provided services through individual placements in three states. In a final example, one new program forged links between five Indian tribes with a history of animosity toward each other to work on improving a common ecosystem.[136]

In the sixty-program AmeriCorps study, 40 percent of the administrators responded that they added new services in an existing organization. In some cases, the new services sought to build on existing competencies. For example, one agency

> that provided job training and support services to farm workers began providing pesticide safety training in Spanish. The agency was already familiar to many farm workers and forged new alliances with farm employers who were relieved to be able to direct workers to safety classes in their native language.[137]

Some organizations incorporated direct service into missions that had not previously included such responsibilities. Checkoway's description of the effects of AmeriCorps at the University of Michigan is one example of such an organizational transformation.[138]

Another perspective about institution creation is provided in studies of forty-five VISTA projects.[139] In interviews conducted during site visits to the projects, the investigators inquired about project self-sufficiency as a proxy for institutionalization. They found that after the first year of VISTA involvement, 13 percent of the projects were completely self-sufficient and 4 percent were partly self-sufficient. After two years, 18 percent were fully institutionalized and 13 percent were partially institutionalized. Staff expected 90 percent of the projects to continue in some form after the VISTA volunteers left. Overall, the results indicate a high probability of long-term survival for the new VISTA-sponsored projects.[140]

An earlier study of twenty-seven affiliates of UYA[141] produced similar results. Institutionalization of university service-learning programs was measured by the extent to which universities adopted a menu of ten new practices, such as funding an office of experiential education or establishing credit for off-campus volunteer service-learning activities. In addition to inquiring about the extent to which practices consistent with acceptance of service learning were adopted, project directors were asked about their perceptions of institutionalization. Seventy-eight percent of the project directors reported moderate to complete institutionalization. These results are comparable to those of Beecroft and Gallant,[142] suggesting good survival rates for institutions created by civic service projects.

Null Findings

Three of the four studies that produced null findings investigate the Teacher Corps, a 1970s program.[143] As Corwin notes, the Teacher Corps was a multifaceted program whose results are not easily summarized.[144] The inference from the three studies, however, is that the Teacher Corps was not successful in reforming the profession and organizations that were its target. Corwin concluded:

> Ironically, whereas the program was intended to effect change, the same principles and processes that had shaped the organizations it was trying to alter modified it. The organizational character of this change agent—and the change-agent character of the Teacher Corps organizations—produced status dilemmas, conflicts in goals and roles, political constraints, local resistance, co-optation strategies, and the other problems noted.[145]

In a study of five AmeriCorps programs in the state of Michigan, Perry and Thomson concluded that most of the programs did not design themselves to be sustainable but tended to see AmeriCorps funds primarily as a means to provide community-based organizations with money for the duration of the grant.[146] When asked whether the expansion of programs resulting from AmeriCorps member activities would continue without AmeriCorps, nearly all partner organization directors indicated that it would be difficult to keep programs going without AmeriCorps help.

The findings in the context of Michigan's AmeriCorps are consistent with a descriptive study intended to guide outcome and impact measurement in VISTA. The authors observe that impacts of VISTA on sponsoring organizations appear to be a

> concern of the larger program, not of the specific sponsors. This meant that sponsors did not normally think in terms of questions about impacts on their own organizations. . . . Sponsors were somewhat more likely to think in terms of sustaining VISTA project activities. For the most part, the concern was not how to sustain the project after the VISTAs, but rather how to ensure continued assignments of VISTAs.[147]

The experience of the Youth Community Service (YCS) provides a good illustration of the difficulties of one strategy of building organizational capacity.[148] Grassroots organizations can be an excellent source for innovation and commitment to local objectives. At the same time, it can be very difficult to get them involved in such initiatives.

Summary

The evidence as a whole about the effects of civic service on institution creation fails to show any clear patterns. The volume of research is small and the findings are mixed. Rather than drawing a conclusion about this outcome, it is more productive to speculate about potential reasons for the mixed results.

One impediment to achieving a better understanding about the relationships between civic service and institution creation is definition and measurement of the concept. Most of the research failed to give this outcome any clear conceptual or operational definitions. Several of the studies settled for self-reports from project or program directors. In the long run, this research strategy is not likely to produce reliable and readily interpretable results. The study of UYA, where a concrete set of organization policies and practices was used to define operationally the degree of institutionalization, is an exception.[149] More attention to definition and measurement of the institution creation outcome is needed.

Given that institution creation is a probable result of civic service, not a certainty, research about this outcome should be attentive to mediating variables. Which variables are likely to affect the success of institution creation? The studies reviewed here are not very helpful in this regard, but they suggest some possibilities. For instance, it is plausible that institution creation success varies across types of programs. Direct service programs, such as AmeriCorps for example, may have a better institution creation success rate because they are more discrete and tangible than reform-oriented programs such as the Teacher Corps.

Community Impacts

The fourth and final set of impacts reviewed in this chapter involve communities. Community outcomes are distinct from institutional outcomes in that they are inter- or multiorganizational rather than organizational in character. The word *community* is used in ordinary discourse in several ways, which are compatible with how it is used here. One definition refers to a contiguous and identifiable geographic unit. This is certainly one way in which *community* is used here—that is, to refer to a neighborhood or local political jurisdiction. Another way *community* is sometimes used is to refer to the good of society, to interests beyond oneself. The logic underlying benefit-cost ratios is compatible with this sense of community, which relates to the wider society and not just a neighborhood or political jurisdiction. A final sense of *community* is found in reference to relationships that connect elements of a jurisdiction together. This meaning of *community* is closely associated with *community* strengthening.

Community Strengthening

Community strengthening refers to the extent to which service networks or other multiorganizational arrangements are improved by civic service. One illustration is the work of Habitat for Humanity in communities in the United States and abroad. Habitat helps individuals builds homes using a self-help model. Its role in communities is often more far-reaching, however. Habitat staff and volunteers bring community members, governments, corporations, and other private partners together around local housing needs, ranging from increasing the stock of affordable housing to reducing homelessness. It is these focused networks that we have in mind when we refer to community strengthening.

Positive Findings

Eleven studies found positive results for community strengthening.[150] The studies are well distributed both temporally and programmatically. One of the common means by which civic service programs strengthen communities is by developing consortia or alliances of existing organizations, typically consisting of a coalition of community organizations.[151] In the context of AmeriCorps, the coalitions permitted organizations that were too small to sponsor the minimum number of AmeriCorps members to collaborate to address community needs.[152] In some instances the coalition worked, and in other instances it did not.

Often these coalitions had little in common other than geography and thus were not able to field strong service models. In other cases, however, strong consortia developed and the individually placed AmeriCorps members focused on an overall service goal. For example, a coalition of schools and local nonprofits provided an enrichment program to the children at participating schools. In another case, AmeriCorps members in different social service agencies coordinated the services of their sponsor and its partner organization to improve neighborhood services to community residents. Many of the other studies of community strengthening consist of self-reports from participants about whether they perceived improved partnerships across organizations.[153]

Null Findings

Five studies were coded as finding no community strengthening as a result of civic service. Two of them looked at the Teacher Corps, which was created in 1964 and discontinued in the early 1980s, after major evaluations by the U.S. General Accounting Office and a consortium of organizations funded by the Ford Foundation and headed by the National Education Association.[154]

The other three studies that produced null findings focused on AmeriCorps.[155] The AmeriCorps Watershed Project consisted of 201 restoration and 353 monitoring projects completed in 133 watersheds.[156] Only 45 percent of the ninth- to twelfth-grade participating students responding to a postprogram survey agreed with statements that their community needed them or that they felt they were important to their community. Responses did not differ significantly from preprogram levels. Among the study's limitations were low response rates and survey questions that had questionable validity and reliability.

Perry and Thomson found some evidence for increased levels of cooperation across community-based organizations, such as jointly writing grant proposals and sharing expertise and corps members.[157] They found few operational examples of collaboration that extended beyond the individual missions of each partner organization. They concluded that the contribution of AmeriCorps was essentially additive, the sum of individual actions through individual organizations, rather than multiplicative—that is, the creation of new and sustained linkages between organizations whose capacities grew as a result of the blending of individual missions.

The National School and Community Corps provides services and after-school activities for students and parents in Philadelphia and New York City. Fox and Fox's evaluation used community observers to assess community outreach.[158] The observers were asked to rate the impact of sites as "enormous," "major," "good," "balanced," and "limited." None of the observers rated the impact as enormous at any of fifteen sites. The impact was rated as major at only three of the sites. Of the remaining sites, six were rated as good, one as balanced, and five as limited. These ratings showed a decline from 1996–97, when six sites were rated as having enormous or major impact.

Summary

Overall, the findings for community strengthening are positive. Despite the positive findings, the civic service community-strengthening relationship merits further scrutiny. Among the reasons is the nonnegligible percentage of null findings, limitations in the conceptualization and measurement of the community-strengthening concept, and the absence of clear and compelling models of change underlying the relationship.

Benefit-Cost Ratios

The benefit-cost ratio is a measure of the effects of a program on the entire economy, the net social benefits and costs.[159] The ratio was used historically to evaluate the utility of public works projects, but more recently it has been applied more widely to assess the social utility of human investment programs, intergovernmental grants, and government regulatory activities.[160] The broad scope of the ratio makes it an appropriate indicator of community impact.

Fourteen benefit-cost analyses are reported in the civic service literature and summarized in Table 5.2. Six of the studies focus on AmeriCorps*State/National programs.[161] Four assess benefit-cost ratios for conservation or youth corps programs.[162] The other four studies assess AmeriCorps*VISTA,[163] Foster Grandparents,[164] and several civic service demonstrations.[165] Because the models tested in the demonstrations are, in fact, quite similar to or overlap with youth corps and AmeriCorps programs, the majority of the benefit-cost analyses focus on a similar subset of programs.

The benefit-cost analysis that has received the most attention is Neumann, et al.'s assessment of three dissimilar AmeriCorps programs: AmeriCorps for Math and Literacy in Austin, Texas, and Columbus, Ohio; Project First, a multisite project operating in Atlanta, Charlotte, and New York; and East Bay Conservation Corps (EBCC). Benefits were stated in terms of individual benefits to corps members—corps members receive a small stipend for their service, averaging about $7,500 a year, and a $4,725 education award to pay back past college loans or fund future education expenses[166]—and in terms of societal benefits, such as reduced crime, less welfare expense, and enhanced earnings due to educational attainment. Across the three programs, the study found a benefit range of $1.60 to $2.60 per dollar of federal outlays. Benefit ranges were slightly lower ($1.50 to $2.20), but remained positive, when federal outlays were aggregated with the matching funds of the grantees. In 1995, the U.S. General Accounting Office (GAO) reviewed the work of Neumann and his colleagues at the request of Senators Bond and Grassley. GAO found the methodology reasonable and consistent with the normal standards for such studies.[167]

A similar benefit-cost analysis of two Washington State AmeriCorps projects found the benefits of the two projects exceeded costs by a ratio of 2.4 to 1 using a 2 percent discount rate and 1.8 to 1 using a more conservative 5 percent discount rate.[168] In one project, fifteen members (five full-time and ten part-time) spent about four hundred hours per week working for a school district in a variety of capacities, such as reading and ESL tutors, library staff during lunch hours, after-school enrichment coordinators, and recruiters for adult volunteers. In the second project, fourteen members (twelve full-time, two part-time) worked with a city government on renovating a stadium, constructing a children's playground, and creating a farmers' market.

Three cost-benefit analyses were conducted in conjunction with evaluations of Minnesota's AmeriCorps programs.[169] Analysts calculated cost-benefit ratios for three different types of programs—educational enhancement, judicial system initiatives, and property/housing rehabilitation—for 1994–95, 1995–96 and 1996–97. They found benefits exceeding costs for the three-

Table 5.2

Summary of Benefit-Cost Studies of Civic Service

Study	Program	Years	Benefit-cost ratio
Aguirre International, *Making a Difference*	Sample of forty-four AmeriCorps* state/national programs	1994–95 and 1995–96	1.66
Booz, Allen, Public Administration Services, *Cost-Benefit Study of the Foster Grandparent Program*	Foster Grandparent Program	Between 1965 and 1971, but the precise years are not specified.	1.14
California Conservation Corps, *California Conservation Corps, 1976–1979*	California Conservation Corps	1976–79	1.2
Carlson and Strang, *Volunteers in Service to America*	AmeriCorps*VISTA	1994	1.4
Control Systems Research, *Program for Local Service*	Program for Local Service (PLS)	1972	1.9
Frees, et al., *Final Report: National Service Demonstration Programs (Subtitle D)*	National service demonstration projects	1993–94	1.3
Jastrzab, et al. *Impacts of Service*	Eight conservation and youth corps	1993–94	1.04
Neumann, et al., *Benefits and Costs of National Service*	• AmeriCorps for Math and Literacy	1994–95	2.51 (lower range) to 2.58 (upper range)
	• Project First		2.02 (lower range) to 2.15 (upper range)
	• East Bay Conservation Corps (EBCC)		1.59 (lower range) to 1.68 (upper range)

Study	Program	Year	Benefit-cost ratio
Public Interest Economics—West, Economic Impact of California Conservation Corps Projects	California Conservation Corps	1979	1.2
Shumer, *YouthWorks AmeriCorps Evaluation: A Cost-Benefit Analysis*	• Education enhancement	1994–95	Range from 1.23 to 1.65
	• Juvenile crime		2.94
	• Construction training of at-risk youth		3.90
Shumer and Cady, *YouthWorks AmeriCorps Evaluation: Second Year Report 1995–1996*	• Education enhancement	1995–96	Range from 1.34 to 1.93
	• Juvenile crime		2.15
	• Construction training of at-risk youth		1.94
Shumer and Rentel, *YouthWorks AmeriCorps Evaluation Project: Third Year Report 1996–1997*	• Juvenile crime	1996–97	2.26
	• Project Pride for Living		1.65
	• Habitat for Humanity		2.45
Wang, Owens, and Kim, *Cost-and-Benefit Study of Two AmeriCorps Projects in the State of Washington*	Two Washington State AmeriCorps programs	1994–95	2.4 (2% discount rate) 1.8 (5% discount rate)
Wolf, Leiderman, and Voith, *California Conservation Corps*	California Conservation Corps	1984–85	.96

year period by ratios ranging from 1.5 for educational enhancement to 2.7 for judicial system and housing rehabilitation programs.

The most extensive benefit-cost analysis of AmeriCorps was conducted by Aguirre International as part of its impact evaluation of AmeriCorps*State/ National.[170] Forty-four programs were sampled. The benefit-cost ratio for the sample was $1.66, which reflected benefits valued at $53 million and costs of $36.7 million.

The four benefit-cost studies of conservation corps, three of which look at the California Conservation Corps, yield more modest ratios than the AmeriCorps analyses. The ratios range from .96[171] to 1.2.[172] The eight youth corps included in the study of Jastrzab and her colleagues returned $1.04 in benefits for each dollar spent, which is within the range established by the other studies conducted in the 1970s and 1980s.[173] Thus, the benefit-cost ratio for conservation and youth corps appears to be stable over time.

The ratios for the other benefit-cost studies are comparable to those for the conservation corps. AmeriCorps*VISTA's was calculated at 1.4,[174] Foster Grandparents at 1.14,[175] and national service demonstrations at 1.3.[176] The ratio for Foster Grandparents, which was calculated almost thirty years ago, may not be a good indicator of the ratio today. Costs, program benefits, and other factors could have changed. The Program for Local Service (PLS) produces a ratio of 1.9, which is relatively high.[177] PLS was designed and structured more like AmeriCorps than the other programs. If AmeriCorps is used as its benchmark, the 1.9 ratio is not out of line.

Although the sample of studies is small and, therefore, generalizations should be drawn with caution, the benefit-cost ratios are higher for AmeriCorps than the other programs. The average of the lower range of the ratio across the six studies of AmeriCorps is 2.07. For the other six programs, it is 1.35. The AmeriCorps average is elevated by relatively high ratios for two of Minnesota's programs (each 2.7). The ratio of 1.66 from Aguirre International's representative sample of AmeriCorps programs is much closer to the average for non-AmeriCorps programs.[178]

Summary

Do the generally positive benefit-cost ratios indicate that civic service is satisfying unmet social needs by producing a favorable ratio of social benefits to costs? The evidence suggests strongly that civic service, to borrow from the AmeriCorps motto, is "making a difference."

Volunteer Leveraging

Volunteer leveraging refers to the extent to which civic service participants are able to involve other volunteers. One of the best ways for civic service participants to enhance a civic ethic lies in their potential to engage other citizens in voluntary activity. The synthesis database identified sixteen studies that investigated volunteer leveraging. The findings for all sixteen studies were positive. The findings cut across most types of civic service program (for example, direct service, capacity building programs, and senior programs) over a period of almost thirty years. One type of program that is not represented is conservation corps. Because they typically emphasize member development and environmental projects, conservation corps give relatively little attention to using service participants to recruit or coordinate additional volunteers. This probably accounts for the absence of conservation corps from this subset of studies.

The research provides many examples of how civic service participants leverage other volunteers. A study by Development Associates, Inc. reports that former VISTA supervisors and VISTA volunteers attribute the recruitment of thirty-five additional community volunteers per sponsoring organization to VISTA volunteers.[179] Using a sample survey of nearly 10 percent of corps members in the 1995–96 class, Aguirre International found that, on average, each corps member recruited, trained, and supervised sixteen non-AmeriCorps volunteers, generating 246 hours of non-AmeriCorps volunteer service per corps member.[180] Calculations based on quarterly reports of five AmeriCorps programs over a two-year period indicate that, together, corps members at five AmeriCorps programs generated nearly 6,000 non-AmeriCorps volunteers.[181] Similar findings are reported for University Year in Action,[182] senior programs,[183] and DC Reads.[184]

Although civic service participants may help to increase the overall level of voluntary activity in a community, an infusion of volunteers may or may not expand longer-term community capacity. Moret concluded from her analysis of Connecticut's AmeriCorps programs that the responses of stakeholder's (parents, community leaders, and children) showed that volunteer networks are established and take hold, thereby increasing long-term capacity.[185] In contrast, Perry and Thomson's field research indicates that few AmeriCorps programs strategically sought to build their long-term base of volunteers.[186] Of the five programs studied, only one had a deliberate strategy for generating volunteers. The remaining programs tended to be more concerned with generating volunteers around discrete service projects. One key informant interviewee referred to this kind of volunteering as "project volunteerism" or "white bread volunteerism" where "volunteers from churches, colleges, and other organizations (though well-meaning) come and go without really being in tune with the local neighborhoods in which they volunteer."[187]

If AmeriCorps' goal (and that of civic service generally) is to institutionalize a service ethic through generations of volunteers in local communities, strategies to link short- and long-term volunteer leveraging may be necessary. A recent study by Research Triangle Institute of the value added from civic service acknowledges the simultaneous importance of the operational and strategic sides of volunteer leveraging implied in Perry and Thomson's study of AmeriCorps programs in Michigan.[188] Based on field research and systematic textual analysis of interviews, the Research Triangle study concludes that successful civic service programs (specifically AmeriCorps*State/ National) simultaneously mobilize resources and develop collaborative relationships as a means to build capacity.

Conclusion

The synthesis of research about civic service outcomes shows a broad range of effects, which are summarized in Table 5.3. These effects impact servers, beneficiaries, institutions, and communities. Positive outcomes exceed null or negative effects by better than a 7:1 ratio. One fact about the range of potential outcomes that may go unnoticed is worth highlighting—almost none of the studies found any significant negative results.

The impact of civic service as it has been designed and implemented in the United States affects some outcomes more strongly and consistently than others. Civic service appears to have particularly salutary effects on server skill development and satisfaction, direct beneficiaries, service quantity and quality, and volunteer leveraging.

The synthesis also indicates that civic service generates positive effects in other areas. These include civic responsibility, educational opportunity, self-esteem, physical and mental health, indirect beneficiaries, and community strengthening. The magnitude of evidence for these positive outcomes is substantial, but not as compelling as for the other outcomes. One of these outcomes, civic responsibility, appears to be mediated by several factors, among them gender and ethnicity and the civic content of the service.

The evidence for tolerance for diversity and institution creation did not show clear effects associated with civic service. The reason for this conclusion varies across the two outcomes. Tolerance for diversity appears to be sensitive to several mediating factors that affect whether outcomes are positive, null, or negative. In the case of institution creation, the volume and quality of the research prevents concluding other than that the findings are equivocal.

A relatively large number of benefit-cost studies complement the inference from the synthesis of other outcomes that civic service is an efficient and effective problem-solving approach. In all but one of fourteen studies, benefits exceed costs. Conservation corps, which typically tackle a difficult

Table 5.3

Summary of Civic Service Outcomes

Outcome	Positive	No effect	Negative
Servers			
Skill development	33	5	—
Civic responsibility	14	5	—
Educational opportunity	11	—	1
Self-esteem	10	2	—
Tolerance for diversity	4	5	—
Satisfaction from serving	33	—	—
Health	5	1	—
Beneficiaries			
Impacts on direct beneficiary	30	—	—
Impacts on indirect beneficiary	6	1	—
Institutions			
Expansion of service	23	—	—
Improvment in quality of services	24	—	—
Creation of new institutions	6	4	—
Communities			
Community strengthening	11	5	—
Benefit-cost ratio[1]	13	—	1
Volunteer leveraging	16	—	—

[1]Benefit-cost ratios greater than 1 are reported in the positive column; ratios less than 1 in the negative column.

two-pronged task of conservation work and youth development, yield ratios slightly above 1. Ratios for AmeriCorps*State/National average about 1.7 : 1, and for other types of programs, around 1.3 : 1.

Extracting generalizations about civic service outcomes is challenging, but we have nevertheless succeeded in synthesizing important details about the effects of civic service in this chapter. The next chapter takes on what is conceivably a more difficult challenge. It seeks to identify qualities of successful programs—ways in which program design, leadership, and management contribute to producing the types of positive outcomes we discussed above.

6

Qualities of Successful Programs

Positive outcomes from civic service are important for validating large public and private investments. It may be even more important to know how such outcomes are produced so that they can be replicated. This chapter synthesizes findings about program qualities that enhance prospects for successful civic service. These findings provide program leaders with important benchmarks for assessing the performance of their programs and for managing processes that are consequential for producing positive results.

The discussion in this chapter is organized around eight themes from the synthesis for which counts[1] are presented in Table 6.1: program management; training; member recruitment and retention; cost and funding; sponsoring agency; effective leadership; program visibility; and administrative burdens.

Program Management

Program management subsumes matters of program design and operation. The breadth of this category helps to explain the frequency with which program management appears as an issue in the research. Thirty-seven studies refer to some facet of program management.[2]

Program Design

The design of service programs has received little explicit attention in the research. Many studies, however, provide insights about design features that are consequential for program results.

Clear Focus, Manageable Scope, and Structural Simplicity

There are many reasons why civic service programs that are focused and relatively simple have a good chance of succeeding. A clear focus is likely to reduce the number of target populations, make it easier to communicate the goals of the program to key stakeholders, and simplify the management of the program.[3] A

Table 6.1

Implementation Issues Cited in Civic Service Research

Issue	Frequency
Program management	37
Training	42
Attrition/retention/recruitment	36
Fiscal management	23
Sponsoring agency	20
Effective leadership	13
Program visibility/awareness	8
Administrative burdens	6

program that is difficult to communicate to outsiders or too complicated for them to understand is not likely to garner broad community support.[4]

Congruence Between Program Duration and Goal

Because individual and community changes take varying periods to effect, a program's duration must suit its goals. For example, a 1993 summer service program designed to have positive effects on educational performance during the following academic year failed to achieve results.[5] We speculated that the null finding might have been a product of the short duration of the program. Similar concerns were raised about a more recent summer reading program.[6] This caution should not be construed as a criticism of programs of short duration, but rather as the need to assess the appropriateness of a program's duration in the context of its goals.

Geographic Dispersion of Members

The geographic dispersion of members is problematic.[7] It definitely needs to be considered in the context of whether a program is viable. If a choice is made to create a dispersed program, its consequences must be managed. With regard to Volunteers in Service to America (VISTA), changes in program structure were recommended so that there were more medium-sized, multicounty projects rather than statewide or local projects.[8]

Applying an Effective Change Theory

An equally important insight about implementation is that programs need to apply a sound change theory. By this we mean that the outcomes envisioned by a service program are predicated on a causal theory that is at least plausible if not already proven. This generalization is intuitively reasonable and consistent with long-standing dictums from program implementation research,[9] but it is frequently overlooked. One exception is a study of AmeriCorps literacy programs that explicitly assessed whether the practices used were consistent with effective tutoring practices.[10] The research surveyed 360 AmeriCorps*State/National programs providing literacy tutoring. They found that most tutoring programs had some structural and instructional features (for example, coordination of tutoring activities with the classroom curriculum and adequate intensity of tutoring activities) that researchers considered important for positive reading outcomes. Almost half the tutoring programs used well-known, widely used models. They concluded that the use of effective tutoring practices was fairly widespread. The important lesson is that many programs adopted an effective model for changing reading abilities as a precondition for mounting a successful change effort.

Project Selection

Several studies provide insights about operational details that also have a bearing on program design. One theme is that the selection and planning of projects has a significant impact on achieving program goals.[11] An obvious problem associated with poor project selection and planning is inefficient use of resources. Another liability of poor selection and planning of projects is dissatisfied civic service participants.

Goal Setting and Outcome Measurement

An extension of the idea of better selection and preparation for projects is goal setting and measurement of project results.[12] The character of the goals makes a difference. Successful programs tend to set goals that are realistic, tangible, and measurable.[13]

Team or Crew Leaders

A consistent research finding is that team or crew leaders are highly consequential for the effectiveness of civic service initiatives. This finding is particularly prominent in research about youth corps,[14] but is referred to in other programs as well.[15]

The reasons that team leaders are so consequential for service effectiveness are manifold. In some circumstances, the team leader is an important trainer. The Marin Conservation Corps, for example, did much of its skills training in specialty crews.[16] Specialties ranged from carpentry to landscaping to tree surgery. The specialty crews needed supervision by experienced professionals to assure that appropriate skills were transmitted to crew members and contract work was done correctly.

Team leaders are also important agents in implementing program goals, particularly when teams work in highly decentralized locations.[17] Team leaders facilitate team productivity and member development. Team leaders may be responsible for managing crews at work sites, counseling members, and enforcing rules. This front-line supervisory activity affects productivity and member identification.

Team leaders also serve as role models and mentors who can play important roles in youth development.[18] Their selection and training should therefore be a significant program management concern. The quality of support and supervision that team leaders receive also should be a continuing concern.

Relations Between Staff and Corps Members

Relations with specific team leaders are important to program success, but the more general psychological feel of the program, what organizational psychologists refer to as *organizational climate*, also is consequential. An early study of the Youth Conservation Corps found a strong relationship, for instance, between camp scores on participation and interpersonal relations and corps member satisfaction.[19] The participation index measured the extent to which corps members were involved in camp governance. The interpersonal relations index tapped how corps members related to camp staff.

A recent study of the California Conservation Corps returned to the climate theme first raised twenty-five years earlier. The author found that corps members perceived a lack of positive reinforcement for their contributions. They felt slighted when educational, physical training, and other services were not delivered effectively. The study concluded that "The CCC is a climate where corps members' work is emphasized but is not rewarded or praised. Perceptions of exploitation can arise."[20]

An early national study of VISTA found that effectiveness of supervision was an important variable related to project outcomes.[21] The investigators used a broad definition of *supervision*. Volunteer respondents were asked to consider all aspects and sources of supervision, not just their supervisor. The study obtained information about the frequency with which volunteers received supervisory assistance and support through group meetings, one-on-one meetings, phone calls, and site visits. The positive relationship between effectiveness of supervision, broadly defined, and project outcomes reinforces the view that relations between staff and corps members are a significant determinant of outcomes.

These relationships are also an important element in developing a program that supports diversity.[22] Managerial attention to group conflict and relationships at sites hosting members is key to creating a climate that produces constructive outcomes with respect to tolerance for diversity.

Staff Motivation

One factor in staff motivation is likely to be the ability of programs to offer adequate salaries. Although program directors and staff are highly committed to what they do, there is a question about their ability to sustain their commitment. For example, in AmeriCorps programs in the Pacific Northwest, researchers concluded that programs may face staff turnover due to their inability to offer competitive salaries and adequate staff support.[23]

Salary is not the only factor affecting staff turnover. A program's ability to meet staff expectations is very important. Providing realistic job expectations and on-the-job support can go a long way to reduce staff turnover.[24]

Uncertainties about funding can make it very difficult to do the advanced planning, staff recruitment, and support development necessary for a successful program. Thus, timely funding of program grants can be critical.[25] Despite the Summer Reads Initiative's success as part of the America Reads program, one of the reported limitations was that funding decisions as late as June 1 prevented some programs from planning and staffing as effectively as they might have with earlier notification of funding.

Communications

Another implementation lesson synthesized from the research is to communicate expectations clearly. Failure to clearly communicate expectations resulted in misunderstandings about the role of Summer Reads tutors: "As one tutor said, 'The teachers didn't know what to do with us.'"[26] One way of diminishing miscommunication is to increase the participation among program stakeholders. In the context of Summer Reads, this meant greater involvement for teachers. "Members/tutors working in school-based programs believed that teachers should participate in student selection, program planning, and tutor training, so that all parties have a common understanding about roles and responsibilities."[27] A national study of VISTA found that something as simple as sharing the project narrative with the volunteer was an important way of communicating expectations to improve project outcomes.[28]

Decentralization of program delivery simultaneously magnifies the need for effective communication and increases the difficulty. In an early study of AmeriCorps, for example, Shumer and Cady[29] reported difficulties in communication and working relationships between site directors and site personnel. They reported inconsistencies between what programs expected of members working at community sites and what community personnel understood to be the purpose of member placements. The evaluators anticipated that these communication problems would be resolved, but they would require active management and attention.

Summary

The research that addresses program management issues shows that civic service is much like other contexts—good management is necessary for producing results. Effective communications, supervision, team leadership, and motivation all play a role in generating favorable results. The design of the service program also is a determinant of success. Programs that have a clear focus, apply an effective change theory, set goals, and evaluate outcomes have a higher probability of succeeding.

Training

Training is a programmatic consideration about which there are differing perceptions of need. An image of traditional volunteers is that they can drop into a given situation, be given a minimum of direction, and contribute effectively to a particular task or initiative. The image of the traditional volunteer is at odds with reality, as reflected consistently in the volunteer literature.[30] There is every reason to expect, therefore, that training is even more critical for success when service is deployed to solve significant social problems. This inference is born out by the frequency with which training surfaces as an important component of civic service programs. Forty-two studies in the synthesis acknowledge the importance of training.[31]

Civic service has evolved so that today training is viewed as a critical ingredient of success. Training is often a prerequisite for ensuring that the work volunteers do can be meaningful.[32] The evolution of the role of training in the voluntary sector generally and in civic service in particular is reflected in senior programs, which at one time were ambivalent about the need for training and now recognize its importance to their effectiveness.[33]

As a means of human capital development, training can serve a variety of functions. One obvious function of training is cognitive and skill development. Training is essential, for instance, in developing the understanding and skills of service participants so they can effectively deliver specific services, such as tutoring.[34]

Training sometimes is necessary to support specialized roles (such as team or crew leader),[35] specialized goals (such as tolerance of diversity), and special populations (such as learning-disabled students or teen tutors who have little workplace experience).[36] Some civic service programs have learned from experience that training needed to be enhanced to meet the needs of the populations served and required augmentation to be effective.[37] The Experience Corps, for example, sought to improve reading levels directly by tutoring children and to increase parental involvement to support long-term improvements in learning.[38] But the abilities of service deliverers to achieve these goals depended on both their competence and confidence in these arenas. The evaluation of Experience Corps concluded that service participants would have benefited from familiarity with well-tested reading curricula, such as Reading Coaches, Reading Recovery, and Book Buddies, to improve the abilities of low-performing students. The volunteers' sense of efficacy in the area of parent involvement also merited further training.

Training members at the lower end of the education and income spectrum has proven to be difficult. Training in youth and conservation corps where employability is an objective has also been problematic.[39] These difficulties may simply reflect that success is lower when the level of challenge is higher. They also reflect inherent tensions between goals. Among the reasons conservation corps encounter difficulty in delivering educational programming is the tension between service and job training expectations. Shumer and Cady identified a similar tension in the context of AmeriCorps programs.[40] The experimental Youth Community Service (YCS) of the late 1970s encountered similar problems. Joint sponsorship of the program by the Department of Labor and ACTION created some goal tensions between community service and employment goals.[41]

The developmental opportunities that come with training can be an important resource for member recruitment and a means to sell participation in a program.[42] Having clear goals for member development is one of the important ingredients for success.[43]

Even when training is accepted as an integral part of a civic service program, its effectiveness may be diminished by suboptimal choices about how training needs are assessed and how training is delivered. Training should not be too costly or delivered in ways that do not improve results. Training must be efficient and effective—these are two essential requirements for training intended to support civic service initiatives. Among the documented problems encountered in civic service is the formality of training and associated costs and learning transfer. An early analysis of the California Conservation Corps recommended that relatively costly formal academy training be converted to on-the-job training as a means to decrease costs and improve effectiveness.[44] More recently, Summer Reads encountered similar problems with training transfer. National Civilian Community Corps (NCCC) and VISTA coordinators recommended changing the predominant training mode to a more interactive format.[45]

To summarize, training has become an essential feature of effective civic service programs. It improves the prospects that services are delivered effectively and members develop appropriately. The challenge for service programs is to deliver the necessary training effectively and efficiently.

Member Recruitment and Retention

Attracting and retaining a quality cadre of civic service participants is a pivotal issue in civic service, just as it is in military service. Fully thirty-six of the studies refer to member recruitment and retention.[46]

Member recruitment and retention are vital for the effectiveness of many civic service programs. Recruiting members with appropriate aptitudes, skills, and motivations directly affects whether substantive outcomes are achieved. Recruitment is also vital for achieving process goals such as member diversity.[47] Program success also is heavily dependent on member retention. High rates of attrition in programs such as the California Conservation Corps (where only 20 percent of the members stay a full year) is important in light of findings that show no effects from service for those who stay less than four months.[48] High attrition was also reported to detract from the effectiveness of the Milwaukee Service Corps and various youth and service corps.[49]

Attracting Members

In studies of community health workers and Michigan AmeriCorps programs,[50] the investigators concluded that there were clear advantages in recruiting local members. Local members knew the community, were more likely to stay, and were less costly to maintain. Coupled with the research finding that nonresidential programs can be as effective as residential programs,[51] recruiting local members should be strongly preferred to alternatives. Programs are not precluded from using nonlocal recruits, but the choice to nonlocal recruits should be purposive, growing out of distinctive program goals. For example, Zuvekas, Nolan, and Tumaylle argue that nonlocal recruits would be useful in some contexts, such as rural areas, where local talent is hard to find.[52]

The ability to recruit sufficient numbers of servers may depend on how the relevant pool is defined. For example, AmeriCorps is generally perceived as youth oriented. Tschirhart's study of older volunteers in AmeriCorps suggests that more aggressive recruitment of seniors could pay significant dividends for AmeriCorps.[53] An earlier program, YCS, was designed to have adult volunteers support counseling and programming services for youth volunteers in local nonprofit organizations.[59] The demonstration site in Syracuse, New York, abandoned the design when it failed to recruit adults to provide services to youth in the program. Although the report suggests several reasons for the failure of this component of the program, the prospect that expectations about ability to recruit adult volunteers were overly optimistic cannot be dismissed.

For many who serve, the availability of a stipend is an important enabler. Some stipend recipients report that they would serve even if they did not receive a stipend. But most are barely able to sustain themselves on the typical remuneration and many others discontinue their service because of the economic hardships.[55] The evidence about the experiences and sacrifices of those who serve in stipended civic service programs—which means the vast majority of those engaged in intensive service programs—calls into question criticisms of "paid volunteers."

Despite its importance, the stipend is not the most important factor in attracting most people to service.[56] Participants probably weigh most strongly opportunities to meet community needs, followed by career-related experiences. This suggests that neither altruistic nor egoistic motives dominate participants' calculus to join—motives are decidedly mixed.

The availability of variable service commitments also affects recruitment of civic service participants. This implementation lesson was first learned in University Year for ACTION (UYA).[57] When it was created in 1973, UYA allowed students to work for one year in full-time, voluntary jobs with community agencies and organizations focusing on the solution of specific poverty problems while making normal academic progress toward their degree. After three years of operation, program directors were asked what changes would need to occur for the program to sustain itself after federal funding had ended. A large majority of the program directors answered that more flexible terms of service were key to sustaining the program. The variety of models they proposed included full-time, part-time, and semester programs.

AmeriCorps*State/National has undergone an evolution similar to that of UYA. The preferred model is full-time service, but options have been created to build in more flexibility for people to serve part-time. The most recent example of using variable service commitments to influence recruitment is the AmeriCorps Education Awards program. The Corporation for National and Community Service (CNCS) developed the education awards program as an alternative structure intended to increase AmeriCorps opportunities while lowering the per-member cost. In its first year, the education awards program enrolled 9,475 members. Adding the education award option to the AmeriCorps program appeared, at least initially, to meet the goals for which it was designed—that is, "to increase the number of AmeriCorps programs, members, and sponsors at a limited cost to the federal government."[58]

As noted in conjunction with the discussion of training, member development is an integral part of attracting and retaining people to civic service. Griffiths' study of math and literacy tutors found that the opportunity to acquire skills during civic service was an important means for attracting participants.[59]

Factors such as the predictability of program startup and timeliness of funding also influence recruitment. Freedman and Fried noted that the slow startup of the Experience Corps delayed the recruitment of volunteers.[60]

Retaining Members

Motivating people to commit to service is essential for effective programs, but the promises of successful recruitment can be squandered if members are not retained. Member retention is affected by several factors, including the expectations that members bring to their service, the quality of their experience, and program rules and climate.

A common problem in the retention of civic service participants is managing expectations.[61] The high hopes that often are placed on civic service programs bring with them a host of risks. One of these risks is that prospective participants bring unrealistically high expectations with them to the service experience.[62] If these high expectations cannot be met, which is often the case in the messy and challenging situations that civic service programs regularly tackle, then participant satisfaction is bound to suffer. The result can be disaffected participants and dropouts.

Differences in server motivations need to be considered in the management process. Individuals bring a variety of motivations to service. The ability to retain servers demands that managers respond to these individual motivational differences. Tschirhart's study of age-related differences among AmeriCorps members illustrates the importance of responding to individual motivational differences.[63] She notes that AmeriCorps is not aggressively pursuing older individuals despite the potential benefits—mentoring, informal training, and modeling—of increasing age diversity. Any plan to increase age diversity is complicated by differences across age groups. Tschirhart notes: "AmeriCorps members aged 50 and over appear to mirror 'pure' volunteers more than their younger colleagues." The implication is that service opportunities must permit servers to fulfill their different needs. Despite the importance of addressing these differences from a recruitment and retention perspective, satisfying heterogeneous motivations is challenging. As Tschirhart observes, "This may be a challenge when [older individuals] are asked to work side by side with individuals with significantly less work experience and different interests."[64]

Another issue that arises with regard to retention, particularly in the context of corps programs, involves the application of disciplinary rules.[65] Corps programs such as the California Conservation Corps and NCCC use quasi-military rules to maintain discipline. Although these rules were valued and effective as part of the Depression-era Civilian Conservation Corps, their efficacy has been questioned repeatedly in the context of more recent corps programs. When surveyed in 1996, participants who were leaving the NCCC responded that they wanted to see the "petty aspects of the military" eliminated.[66] Evaluators of the San Francisco and Milwaukee Conservation Corps concluded that too much emphasis on strict disciplinary rules was counterproductive. Rosenblum and Leiderman, commenting on the San Francisco Conservation Corps' experience, concluded:

> Although strict rules are necessary to facilitate learning and high productivity, enforcement has created a rate of turnover that has strained the staff, caused difficulty in meeting production and funding goals, and interfered with the corps' ability to deliver formal educational programs.[67]

The discussion about program management emphasized the importance of staff-member relations for the quality of member experiences. This importance is reinforced in the research on member attrition. Bartlett and Gallant found that program management accounted for a large share of the attrition among VISTA members.[68]

Summary

To summarize, many of the general parameters of successful civic service recruitment and retention are well known. Successful recruitment hinges on defining appropriate pools of prospective servers, enabling servers by offering a variety of formats or stipends that eliminate barriers to participation, and organizing programs of service that appeal to prospective members. The appeal of civic service to prospective servers depends on factors such as its perceived social good, its relevance to servers' career goals, and server developmental opportunities.

The retention of civic service participants overlaps, in part, with considerations relevant to recruitment. The appeal of civic service must withstand an individual's passage from nonparticipant to participant. This requires that service programs manage the expectations of prospective participants so that they are realistic and so that unmet expectations are minimized. Program managers must also work to meet the needs of participants to increase their satisfactions and motivation. Generally, the quality of supervision and minimization of arbitrary rules are likely to positively influence retention.

Fiscal Management

Although the costs and financing of civic service are referred to less frequently than the most prominent implementation issues, they appear often in the literature.[69] What is more, they are the object of intense debate. The themes in the literature can be organized around three issues: costs per member, funding strategies, and financial sustainability.

The centrality of costs and financing for civic service is borne out by the rise and decline of civic service programs over the years. The history of program life cycles presented in Chapter 2, Policy Evolution, is evidence of the volatility. Funding for civic service programs has been so unpredictable from year to year that some advocates of civic service take the cycle of a funding rise, decline, and rise again for granted. In his study of the institutional impacts of AmeriCorps on the University of Michigan, Barry Checkoway indicates that, from the outset, he "viewed AmeriCorps as an episode in the history of American social programs which do not have a record of steady advance, but rather follow a cycle whose legacy is measured by what is left behind after the cycle concludes."[70]

Alternate funding sources are critical for sustaining civic service programs. A small number of civic service slots are sustained solely by private funds. This is true of faith-based service programs such as the Jesuit Service Corps. But most civic service programs, such as City Year and conservation corps, even when they receive private monies, rely to some extent on public funds. The reality is that public funds are typically allocated for a fixed period after which alternate sources of funding must be acquired. The results of a 1993 study of VISTA are revealing. Alternate funding was selected overwhelmingly as the steepest barrier to continuing VISTA-related services after VISTA support ended. Over 80 percent of the program supervisors pointed to the unavailability of alternate funding as a significant barrier to continuation.[71]

Cost per Member

Cost per member and administrative cost per member are important benchmarks, referred to repeatedly in congressional reports,[72] agency evaluations,[73] independent assessments,[74] and policy monographs.[75] Cost per member is not a new issue. In fact, it was salient even during the era of the Civilian Conservation Corps (CCC), the earliest civic service program included in our synthesis. In his dissertation about the CCC, Sherraden notes that the cost per member of the CCC was higher than other contemporary youth employment programs such as the Works Progress Administration and National Youth Administration.[76] The CCC's bipartisan popularity in Congress and broad public support permitted it to thrive, but it could not be sustained by the combination of labor shortages and costs that arose with the onset of World War II. One of the rationales for the Program for Local Service was that its "organized volunteers" could be recruited, trained, and supported effectively at two-thirds the cost of VISTA and previous similar programs. Thus, cost per member is a durable issue in civic service.

Congressional attention was most recently directed to costs per member in two U.S. General Accounting Office (GAO) reports about AmeriCorps*State and National.[77] For program year 1994–95, GAO estimated CNCS resources at $17,600 and total resources per participant at $26,654. In program year 1998–99, per participant resources from the CNCS were $14,857 and overall resources were $23,574.

Although the research gives attention to costs, relatively little scrutiny is focused on sorting out the cost differentials between, for example, stipended volunteers and paid staff. One reason for the absence of such a focus is concern about volunteers displacing paid staff. Comparing volunteer costs to paid staff would symbolize tacit acceptance of substituting volunteers for paid staff. In some contexts, such displacement may be acceptable, but it is generally not when the federal government subsidizes costs.

Despite this potential source of reluctance to compare the costs of stipended volunteers and paid staff, the differential between the costs for volunteers and paid staff is one benchmark for assessing the value added by volunteers. Some research suggests significant cost differentials between stipended volunteers and paid staff. The evidence from a 1998 study of community health workers reveals that costs (salary, benefits, supervision, administration, and overhead) ranged from $9,104 to $64, 866 per year.[78] Costs for AmeriCorps members, who were a subset of the larger population of community health workers, ranged from $19,130 to $20,775, including the education award. This compared favorably to the costs for non-AmeriCorps community health workers, which ranged from a low of $9,104 in Northwest Michigan to a high of $64,866 in Alameda County, California. The high costs in Alameda County are the product of mandated civil service salary provisions. In Syracuse, New York, the one community where AmeriCorps and non-AmeriCorps community health workers served side by side, the costs were $20,775 for AmeriCorps members and $24,313 for non-AmeriCorps staff.

Funding Strategies

The concerns of Congress and others about cost per member, together with the collaborative character of most civic service programs, magnifies the importance of how civic service programs are funded. Although the federal government has historically funded large portions of civic service, other governments, nonprofit organizations, corporations, foundations, and philanthropists are alternative funding sources.

Civic service programs have demonstrated capacity to garner support. From October 1990 through September 1993, the Senior Companion Program (SCP) and the Administration on Aging implemented the Joint Initiative for the Vulnerable Elderly.[79] The program encouraged states to expand services for frail elderly citizens, particularly those eighty and older. From the outset, participating sites were expected to develop nonfederal support to continue the services after the third year. By the year after the demonstration ended, ten of thirteen sites had found alternative funding sources and only three had not. Six sites had one or two new sources of financial support, but four sites had developed diverse funding portfolios, getting support from at least four and as many as eight sources. Among the best sources of support were state governments, special events, foundations, and Medicaid waivers. The median support was $15,400, enough to fund 4.3 of the projected five staff members at each site.[80]

A successful funding strategy used by some civic service programs, including those sponsoring the Joint Initiative for the Vulnerable Elderly, is fee-for-service or cost-reimbursable contracts. The Marin Conservation Corps is an example of a program that has been highly successful using cost-reimbursable contracts.[81] Despite the success of cost-reimbursable funding, some analysts dispute the desirability of "reimbursement dollars" because of their potential for displacing the idealistic heritage of conservation and corps member development.[82]

Funding was a factor in the demise of the Teacher Corps, but it turned on the timing of grants and their adequacy to induce change. Although the Teacher Corps was authorized $100 million per year, only a portion of the funds, ranging from $10 to $37.5 million, was appropriated in any year. Costs per intern were significant. In ten programs studied by Corwin, average costs ranged from $4,369 to $10,375 per intern.[83] Funding was split between school systems and universities, with one-sixth to one-third going to the universities. This distribution of funds may have marginalized the program in some universities, but congressional delays in funding seriously exacerbated the problem.

The Teacher Corps strategy for leveraging limited investments in local institutions also diffused program impact. The strategy was to rotate funds among programs as a means to influence institutions with marginal funds.[84] It sought to provide short-term funding with the expectation that universities and local schools would cover increasing shares of the outlays. In the words of the former director of the program, "The Teacher Corps was never supposed to be a sustaining program. It was to provoke change, then move on."[85] The strategy failed. Too few resources were allocated for too short a period to sustain the innovations envisioned by the multi-goal program.[86]

Financial Sustainability

The strategies grantors choose to support civic service programs are closely tied to long-term financial viability and independence. The ability to take civic service to scale depends on increasing the financial viability and independence of civic service programs.[87]

The research on civic service consistently refers to barriers to financial sustainability. Indicative are the findings of a recent report about AmeriCorps in four western states:

> An AmeriCorps goal is for programs to eventually become self-sustaining with 100 percent of program funds from local sources. After four years of operation, most programs are not approaching that goal. Several programs have made strides toward generating local support (up to 40 percent locally).[88]

An important consideration in sustaining programs financially is the capacity of community-based programs to raise funds. One of the conclusions of an analysis of the Foster Grandparent Program is that such capacities are usually underdeveloped. Thus, training and dissemination of information about fund-raising techniques that will help sponsors to sustain programs is a vital step in the direction of sustainability.[89]

Summary

Based upon synthesis of research findings, it is reasonable to conclude that we know a great deal more about costs per participant, and concerns related to these costs, than about funding strategies and financial sustainability. The research indicates that, over the years, federal funding has been highly sensitive to costs per participant. Thus, holding down average costs per member is likely to be critical for future funding growth. Cost minimization must simultaneously be coupled with strategies to diversify and increase the portfolio of funding resources for civic service programs. One step in increasing funding is to improve service leaders' competence in fund development.

Sponsoring Agency

Sponsoring agency manifests itself in two ways in the literature. One, at a macrolevel, entails how responsibility for civic service is shared between political entities, such as federal and state governments. The other manifestation is microlevel, involving the configuration of agencies that is most effective in supporting civic service efforts locally. The attention to these issues is substantial, being mentioned with about the same frequency as cost and funding.[90]

The issue of how responsibility for civic service is distributed within our federal system is, of course, an extension of a debate that occurs across public programs. Many observers recognize the need for balancing the federal and state roles.[91] This balance is visible, for example, in AmeriCorps, where financing and management are shared between the federal government and state commissions. As Smith and Jucovy argue, the issue becomes divisive when the generally accepted principle of federal-state balance is perceived to be in disequilibrium.[92] They suggest that this was the case during the early years of AmeriCorps' implementation. The imbalance was driven by greater federal readiness at the outset of AmeriCorps, the unevenness of state capacity, and the desire of federal officials to assure high quality in civic service programs.

The problem of maintaining a balance between federal and nonfederal interests arose much earlier in the YCS, which was established in the late 1970s. Gittel and her colleagues describe the relationship between ACTION and the local agency in Syracuse, New York, responsible for implementing the initiative as "a continuing trial and error process."[93] A local board of directors who would develop relationships with local government, social service delivery systems, and grassroots organizations was envisioned as the leadership for YCS. In addition, designers intended the program to be a partnership between a federal agency and the local community. Disagreements between ACTION and the local board arose, however, over questions of policy, program definitions, and implementation practices. ACTION's attempt to promote local operation of the program (while simultaneously maintaining control of important policy and implementation determinations) was not sustainable.

With regard to local sponsors, the research carries several generalizations. One lesson extracted from a case study of the San Francisco Conservations Corps is the advantage of having an independent nonprofit agency run the program. The reasoning is that nonprofits, unlike governments, are better able to develop broad sources of funding. Rosenblum and Leiderman conclude:

Its status as an independent non-profit agency has enabled the corps, unlike a government department or agency, to obtain a mix of funding and to develop a broad political constituency. These make possible flexibility in program design and suggest the likelihood of long-term financial security.[94]

Although many civic service programs rely on nonprofit grantees, Rosenblum and Leiderman's generalization implies something more expansive than current arrangements. For many nonprofit host sites, civic service is not their primary mission. Rosenblum and Leiderman are suggesting that dedicated nonprofits, in the long run, are more sustainable than alternative arrangements. In a subsequent report that was part of the larger Youth Corps Assessment Project, Wolf and Branch suggest that federal funding of the Young Adult Conservation Corps had the advantage of minimizing fund-raising efforts, but simultaneously subjected the corps to uncertainties and restrictions that seriously affected operations.[95]

Because many civic service programs are delivered by organizational collaborations, the issue of what makes good participants in these collaboratives is directly relevant to the issue of sponsoring agencies. The role and performance of the collaborative are segmented in the literature between "lead agencies" and "partners." One study suggests, however, that the distinction can be taken too far. The overall relationship among members of the collaborative should be framed as a service partnership rather than a lead or host agency hierarchy.[96]

With respect to the lead agency role, Perry and Thomson note that it must have credibility and legitimacy in the local community.[97] They ascribe to the lead agency a catalytic role in promoting connections and cohesion among partners. The lead agency is charged with monitoring and involving partner sites, disseminating information and maintaining open lines of communication among partners, and developing relationships with media. In a study of Senior Companions, Griffith comes to similar conclusions.[98] She also suggests that project leaders need to establish information systems that ensure timely availability of information across the network of partners. Responsibility for fund-raising to sustain programs is also likely to fall disproportionately to project leaders and the sponsoring agency.

Among partner organizations, attributes such as a compatible mission, high priority for the development of participants, clear expectations for supervisors of participants, and adequate support structure are important for constructive program involvement.[99] Jucovy and Furano conclude that nonprofits that are too bottom-line-oriented are less successful placements.[100] Such placements often prove mutually unsatisfactory because participant development is a minor concern and supervisors' production expectations cannot be met.

Griffith, based on research that found that partnerships between agencies can have a significant impact on program effectiveness, advises that programs make connections with experienced partners and use the network of local, experienced organizations.[101] In these partnerships, it is important to keep the lines of communication open between all key players. Among the attributes of effective partnerships are that they are mutually beneficial for a variety of reasons, including credibility, technical support, publicity, and service expansion, and they involve established organizations with a solid reputation in the community.

The research provides important insights about the details of establishing a network of capable and effective sponsoring agencies. A lesson learned from demonstrations supported by the 1990 National and Community Service Act is that sponsoring organizations should be screened through a competitive site recruitment process akin to the process organizations use for employee recruitment.[102] Following the screening and selection process, the agencies selected should receive thorough orientation and training sessions. These steps are likely to improve results by assuring that the service partners have similar understandings about what is expected of them and common interests in civic service. Coordination and priority differences among service partners in programs such as the Youth Conservation Corps reflect the need to employ these operating principles.[103]

The experiences of the Youth Volunteer Corps (YVC) add further depth to the understanding of sponsoring agencies.[104] The YVC is an intensive four- to eight-week summer program for youth ages eleven to eighteen. Teams of eight to ten youngsters do community service projects and enrichment and reflection activities. Each YVC affiliate is housed in local sponsoring agencies such as the YMCA or Boys and Girls Club. The types of sponsors chosen were crucial to the success of the programs. Sponsors whose missions focused on direct service and youth programming produced the most successful YVC programs. The match between YVC goals and sponsor mission increased the prospect that sponsors were experienced in youth leadership, fund-raising, and community organizing and were able to perform the tasks to establish, operate, and maintain a YVC. This conclusion is consistent with studies of civic service in other arenas.[105]

Another finding of the YVC study is that when sponsors are independent of the national organization, their loyalties invariably reside with their employer. Ford describes the situation in YVC:

> Since Project Directors are employees of the sponsor and not YVCA, there can be conflicts over program features, use of the YVC name and logo, and percentage of time spent on YVC. Funding for the position almost

always comes from the sponsoring agency and thus virtually guarantees where loyalties reside in a conflict.[106]

This conflict of interests has consequences for both program design and incentives as well as expectations for coherence across levels in national programs. The divided loyalty phenomenon is as much an issue for government-sponsored programs as it is for programs like YVC.

An early study of Foster Grandparents assessed two alternatives for organizing projects.[107] In one variant, the grantee/delegate model, a grantee agency assumes overall responsibility for a project, but delegates operating responsibility to another agency. The grantee generally retains responsibility for meeting federal fiscal requirements, but does not participate in day-to-day operational matters. In a second variation, the grantee model, the delegate agency is eliminated and the grantee assumes the delegate's operational functions. A large majority of the grantees, delegates, and project directors preferred the grantee model. Interviewees perceived that the grantee/delegate framework added to administrative costs, introduced an unnecessary middleman, and produced an unwieldy bureaucratic structure.

Leadership

Executives and top managers responsible for leading civic service initiatives have several responsibilities, among them establishing strategic direction, supporting a culture conducive to service, and acquiring financial and human resources. This implementation issue is more narrowly drawn than the others, but it surfaces in more than a dozen studies.[108]

The importance of leadership for effective civic service was recognized early in its evolution. Sherraden's analysis of the CCC acknowledged how pivotal leadership choices were in its record of success.[109] Even before publication of Sherraden's historical review of the CCC, Riecken's evaluation of the American Friends Service Committee work camps gave leadership a prominent role in the effectiveness of service. In reflecting about the camp director's leadership role, Riecken observed:

> He is faced with the large task of not only establishing the camp physically, but of seeing to it that work, educational, and recreational patterns are established, that contact with members of the local community is secured and maintained, that a plurality of previously unacquainted and diverse individuals are transformed into an effective working and learning group.[110]

The lessons learned about leadership from early civic service programs have currency today. Moret's evaluation of AmeriCorps programs in Connecticut found that leadership styles were important to success but they were also uneven and potentially ineffective.[111] She uncovered inconsistencies between the vision and mission of AmeriCorps and styles of leadership. AmeriCorps members expected leaders and staff to model behaviors and to project an image of AmeriCorps throughout the community. The evaluation found inadequacies in the shared vision of principles of leadership, how they were operationalized, and how to communicate based on the principles.

Connecticut's experience is a microcosm of the national level. Strong leadership surfaced as a critical success factor in Aguirre International's national study of AmeriCorps.[112] The quality of management and leadership varied tremendously across programs. The evaluators found that organizations with leaders who had a clear vision of how to use AmeriCorps members were more successful than leaders whose ideas were unclear or nebulous.

Effective leadership appears to be especially critical for summer service programs.[113] Summer programs often involve young members whose developmental needs simultaneously require more structure and nurturing. In addition, summer programs are brief, seldom extending more than eight weeks in duration. Thus, the attributes that effective leaders bring to programs—clear vision and goals, management skills, and priorities for member development—become critical.

Leadership can refer not only to personal responsibilities and attributes, but also to institutional attributes. Driebe investigated how participants in civic service presently define leadership in civic service.[114] She found no single source of leadership, but widely dispersed leaders at all organizational levels, ranging from the CNCS to the states to nonprofits.

The theme of leadership within the civic service system underlies the implementation of AmeriCorps. Which roles will accrue to the state and federal governments and how will leadership be divided? According to Smith and Jucovy, the National and Community Service Trust Act of 1993 envisioned a strong role for state community service commissions.[115] However, commissioners had limited capacity and inclination to assume active roles. The early years following AmeriCorps' implementation, therefore, were characterized by typical staff-driven organizations rather than active, citizen-led enterprises. Strong executive directors, high quality, energetic staff, and a preexisting service infrastructure characterized states that provided strong leadership.

Program Visibility

The visibility of a service program—that is, the extent to which it is publicly recognized—is a relatively recent issue that has received limited attention in the research.[116] The issue surfaced in the 1990s and, with only one exception, has been confined to AmeriCorps.

The findings of a formative evaluation of the AmeriCorps Pinellas program—a public safety initiative in Tampa, Florida—are representative of some reports that touch on public visibility.[117] The evaluation surveyed three categories of stakeholders: (1) AmeriCorps Pinellas members in the program, (2) law enforcement and corrections agencies to which members were assigned, and (3) the service recipients and organizations within the community that the program served. The three groups of stakeholders gave summary scores on "awareness of concept" ranging from 3.99 (members) to 4.28 (agencies) to 4.44 (service recipients) on a five-point scale where five meant high awareness. The author concluded, however, based on open-ended responses by law enforcement and corrections agency personnel and service recipients, that improvements were needed in publicizing the program within the community. He recommended increasing efforts to publicize program activities on radio, television, and newspapers.

What is perhaps most interesting about the AmeriCorps Pinellas report is that it did not reveal its unstated assumptions about *why* improvements were needed in publicizing the program. By what standards did the author judge public awareness to be inadequate? What difference would more visibility make? There are, of course, reasonable answers to these questions, but they do not surface in the report.

Among the reasons for concern about public visibility is whether AmeriCorps receives appropriate credit for what it does in communities. People's level of recognition of a service program indirectly affects their perception of its value and their political support. Thus, if members of a community are unaware of voluntary service that is rendered below prevailing rates, they are unable to confer proper credit. The conclusions from a study of four Pacific Northwest AmeriCorps programs reflect this reasoning:

> AmeriCorps often provides service through existing organizations and service delivery mechanisms. . . . This design minimizes redundancy and has helped AmeriCorps maintain a lean structure. It also means that AmeriCorps members blend into communities and organizations and may not seem different from other agency staff. Community members don't always take notice as to how these volunteers are funded, even if they do appreciate their contribution.[118]

Another potential consequence of visibility is the ability to attract resources. Driebe's national study of AmeriCorps found this was a concern across levels within the federal-state-nonprofit system that delivered AmeriCorps.[119] Her respondents felt that the public was confused or unaware of AmeriCorps' national identity. Driebe concluded that "the public's confusion led to difficulty in recruiting members, educating the state legislature, and securing funding from sources beyond the Corporation. These problems, in turn, affected the sustainability of the program."[120] Thus, there is a perceived link between program identity and the ability to attract human and financial resources.

Program visibility may also influence community strengthening. To the extent that AmeriCorps members are recognized within their communities and the populations from which they are drawn, their example of service may help to energize communities.[121] The national evaluation of AmeriCorps' first two years of operation articulates the logic of the connection between visibility and community strengthening:

> An important part of galvanizing communities is visibility. AmeriCorps members are important role models for their community. This is particularly true for members drawn from the communities served. Both disadvantaged members who are turned around by AmeriCorps and members who are successful on their own play important roles. It is important for communities to see members giving back to their communities.[122]

The lesson that the report draws from this reasoning is that AmeriCorps programs should maintain a high community profile through visible service projects and by using AmeriCorps logos, t-shirts, and other materials.

The visibility–community strengthening logic is reinforced by a study of community building in Michigan's AmeriCorps.[123] The study of five programs from 1995 and 1997 found little media attention. In general, awareness was limited to the small circle of organizations within which corps members worked. A key informant survey of influential community members conducted early in 1996 and again in 1997 found that awareness of local AmeriCorps programs did not change significantly. Most community members interviewed had little understanding of what AmeriCorps participants had done (or do) in their communities. One longtime resident and community leader responded when asked about familiarity with the local AmeriCorps program:

> I know so little about the program that I am not sure I can comment. But that's the point. I am on all these boards and have been active in the community for many years, yet I know very little about this program locally or what its goals and achievements have been.[124]

There is some evidence that establishing an identity for programs like AmeriCorps may be more complex than simply increasing marketing of the program. In 1997, the CNCS initiated the Education Awards program, which gives education awards in return for specified terms of service. During the first year of the program, eighty-nine operating programs were allocated 12,254 education awards. The first-year evaluation found that members typically identified more strongly with their sponsoring organizations than with AmeriCorps.[125] Members had little knowledge about the AmeriCorps program. The results of the evaluation are sensitive to the education award program's design, which puts members at some distance from the core concept, but they also reflect divided loyalties inherent in the structure of a program that is the product of collaboration among several organizational entities. The phenomenon of divided loyalty is probably exacerbated by members' proximity to local sponsors and distance from the national funder.

Administrative Burdens

Because many civic service programs involve grants-in-aid from federal to local governments or nonprofit organizations, the grants typically come with strings attached and administrative requirements. These requirements are invariably mentioned in the research disapprovingly, for example, when they overburden administrative staffs or appear to add little value to administrative processes. This issue does not arise frequently and is of relatively recent origin, appearing in the research only since the expansion of civic service programs with passage of the National and Community Service Trust Act of 1993.[126]

Red tape—too much unproductive paperwork—is the most frequent administrative-burden theme. Like program visibility, many of the references to administrative burdens occur in the context of studies about AmeriCorps* State/National.[127] Member frustration with the amount of paperwork was a recurring theme in surveys of AmeriCorps members in Montana, Oregon, and Washington during program years 1995–96 and 1996–97.[128] Concerns about paperwork, however, do not appear to be confined to one geographic area. The issue of paperwork arose consistently in a national study of AmeriCorps and devolution of federal programs. Based upon interviews and concept mapping, Driebe concluded, "The paper trail surrounding the administration of an AmeriCorps program was documented as endless, confusing, redundant, and overwhelming."[129] Similar concerns about paperwork and administrative requirements were documented in Michigan's AmeriCorps.[130]

AmeriCorps*State/National is not the only program singled out in relation to paperwork burdens. Summer Reads, an initiative mounted by AmeriCorps*VISTA and AmeriCorps*NCCC, also drew complaints about paperwork burdens from participants.[131] Coordinators and partner representatives requested that the paperwork be streamlined so that more resources could be expended delivering services. Similar feedback was received from sites participating in Seniors for Schools.[132]

Some administrative difficulties involve integrating new programs into existing administrative systems. For example, the special status of AmeriCorps members presented challenges to organizations attempting to integrate them into their administrative systems. For example, Fear and colleagues recounted the challenge of incorporating AmeriCorps members into the Michigan State University payroll system:

> Were AmeriCorps members University employees? It was clear in one sense they were: they were to be paid through a University payroll account. Or, were AmeriCorps members "compensated" volunteers, with the University serving a financial pass-through function? It took months, many meetings, and periods of intense negotiating to enable us to appoint members within the framework of the existing MSU employee union contracts. It was finally agreed that they were employees, and the University selected an appropriate employee designation. But to get from start to finish, University attorneys were involved, the Federal and State governments were consulted, and systems in place in other states and at other Michigan universities were investigated.[133]

Conclusion

This chapter has synthesized qualities of successful programs from the myriad factors identified in civic service research. Three qualities are most frequently associated with success: program design and management, member training, and recruitment and retention. Program designs that are clearly focused, purposeful, and grounded in sound theory are likely to succeed. Effective communication, supervision, team leadership, and motivation are qualities critical for program management.

Member training is an essential feature of quality programs because it simultaneously increases the likelihood that service will be delivered effectively and enhances member development. Successful recruitment and retention depend on defining appropriate pools of prospective servers, enabling individuals to serve by offering a variety of formats and rewards that reduce barriers to participation, creating programs that appeal to servers, and minimizing arbitrary rules and other factors that reduce the satisfactions of serving.

Five other factors get less attention in the literature, but they are also consequential for the success of many civic service initiatives. These factors are fiscal management, characteristics of the sponsoring agency, leadership, program visibility, and administrative burdens.

Part III has looked in detail at what we know about civic service. The next chapter takes stock of our collective understanding, drawing upon our knowledge of the history, outcomes, and implementation of civic service.

IV

Summing Up
and Taking Stock

7

Drawing Conclusions About Civic Service

The preceding chapters presented a fine-grained look at the results of civic service research in a series of outcome and implementation categories. The purpose of this chapter is to step back and look at these results with a wider lens. If you will recall the analogy used in Part II, this chapter represents the point at which we apply the mortar that holds the edifice of accumulated knowledge on civic service together. This mortar is the "stuff" that allows us to learn; it comes in the form of propositions or generalizations gleaned from the integration of the wide range of primary studies here examined. As Cooper and Hedges assert,

> [r]esearch syntheses attempt to integrate empirical research for the purpose of creating generalizations. Implicit in this definition is the notion that seeking generalizations also involves seeking the limits and modifiers of [those] generalizations.[1]

In this chapter, we seek to achieve both—to create generalizations and to identify the limits and modifiers of those generalizations—by addressing the following two questions: (1) What light does the synthesis shed on cause-effect relations involving service, its design, implementation, and effects? (2) What are the implications for future research? On the limits of making cause-effect statements from research syntheses, it is important to remember our discussion in Part II. We cannot, in the words of Judith Hall and her colleagues,

> with any confidence ascribe causality to a relationship based on review evidence alone. The boundaries to how much we can learn about causation with research synthesis are defined by the underlying primary studies. Research integrations cannot be used as a substitute for primary studies meant to uncover causal relationships. They may, however, provide guidance for the directions for new primary research.[2]

Given the nature and quality of civic research discussed in Part II, we need to make clear that the propositions in this chapter are not cause-effect statements. They are general statements about relationships between variables that provide a foundation for future empirical analysis. Later on in the chapter, we identify the limits and modifiers to these generalizations under the heading, Research Needs. Both the propositions and the research needs identified in this chapter are ultimately meant to provide guidance for new primary research that will only strengthen the edifice of knowledge about civic service built in these pages. Although the answers to the two questions driving this chapter are grounded in the research synthesis, it is necessary to draw on other sources for interpretive and contextual information.

Generalizations About Civic Service and Its Outcomes

In the following discussion, we offer five propositions about service based on the research synthesis. Figure 7.1 presents a composite of all five propositions in terms of the relationships among service, implementation, and outcomes. For simplicity, the schematic uses four blocks of variables: service attributes, server attributes, implementation, and outcomes (individual, institution, and community outcomes). We break this larger schematic into its component parts, discussing each proposition separately. We conclude the discussion by returning to the composite figure and summarizing what we have learned through the research synthesis. Together, the propositions present a richer, more complete model of service than we previously had.

Civic Service and Its Outcomes

> **Proposition One**: The documented outcomes of civic service are positive over time and across units of analysis.

Many Americans refer nostalgically to the Civilian Conservation Corps (CCC). The foundation for this nostalgia is clear. The CCC was a cornerstone of Franklin Roosevelt's New Deal initiatives that helped to pull America out of the Great Depression. Nostalgia for the CCC should not be misinterpreted to mean that it achieved better results than recent civic service initiatives, however. The outcomes of civic service are consistent over time. Research on domestic civic service, all of it produced in the last half of the twentieth century, shows consistently positive results during each of the last five decades.[3]

The positive results were produced even as the level of scrutiny paid to civic service increased in the last decade of the twentieth century. More

Figure 7.1 **Relationship Among Service, Implementation, and Outcomes**

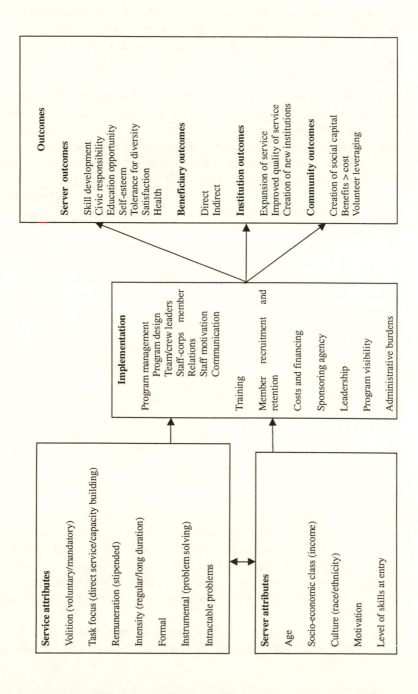

research is available for the 1990s than for any previous decade. Much of this research is the result of two developments: the creation of the Corporation for National and Community Service (CNCS) and the intense spotlight given President Bill Clinton's signature program, AmeriCorps.

From the outset, the CNCS was intended to be a model for government reinvention.[4] It placed the issue of civic service program results front and center. Eli Segal, the first chief executive officer of the CNCS, chose to emphasize accomplishments above member development, thus magnifying the importance of measuring and monitoring results. In addition, because the CNCS launched new programs like AmeriCorps and introduced new provisions such as an education award for civic service, evaluation became more prominent as a means of understanding and measuring the consequences of new initiatives.[5]

Congressional criticism and the 1995 shift in control of Congress from the Democratic to the Republican Party assured further attention to civic service programs in the 1990s. Controversy over a 1995 General Accounting Office report documenting the cost of AmeriCorps to the American taxpayer and political fallout from the granting of AmeriCorps monies to the advocacy group Association for Community Organizations for Reform Now (which allegedly used AmeriCorps members to lobby for legislation and participate in political demonstrations) fueled the flames of partisanship in Congress over civic service. The CNCS's decision to contract with national evaluators, like Aguirre International, to produce annual accomplishment reports[6] served to defuse some of the conflict because the CNCS was able to document concrete results of corps member activities.[7]

The patterns of results across units of analysis—servers, beneficiaries, institutions, organizations, and communities—also show consistently positive results. The largest volume of research by far has been done on the effects of service on servers. This is consistent with a recent report about service-related research as a whole, which concluded that the individual level of analysis was more accessible and therefore more frequently studied than other units of analysis.[8]

Regardless of how much research has been conducted on a unit of analysis, the results are consistently positive. Eight-five percent of the results for servers are positive. The ratios rise to 97 percent in the case of beneficiaries and 93 percent for institutions. Research findings on community outcomes approach 90 percent positive. Figure 7.2 summarizes the relationships between service and outcomes for which our synthesis found consistently positive outcomes.

In the interests of service scholarship, it is important to interpret these positive outcomes with caution. The body of research on civic service is

Figure 7.2 **Relationships Between Service and Outcomes**

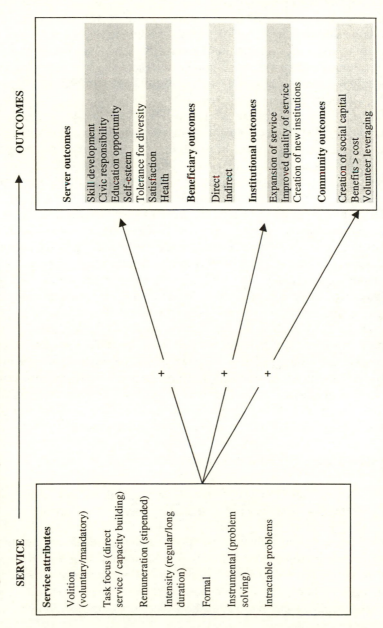

Note: Areas in gray demonstrate overall positive results; areas not in gray—tolerance for diversity and creation of new institutions—demonstrate equivocal results.

marked by a number of flaws making the data bricks that we discussed in Chapters 3 and 4 potentially unstable. Nevertheless, the propositions based on these findings can be used as guideposts for new primary research.

Although the research findings are largely positive, they are not definitive for all outcomes. In the case of two outcomes, tolerance for diversity and institution building, the mix of research findings produces ambiguous results. As the discussion suggests in Chapter 4, Methodology, the difficulty in clearly defining and measuring complex constructs like tolerance, diversity, and institution creation compromises the ability of researchers to document clear cause-effect relationships.

Figures 7.3 and 7.4 summarize what the research seems to suggest about the relationship between service, tolerance for diversity, and institution creation. The mediating factors of program design and program management play a key role in determining the nature of these outcomes. It is unlikely, for example, that tolerance for diversity will occur without deliberate implementation tactics such as an organizational culture that values diversity or the design of a program that explicitly incorporates diversity into civic service activities. As you will recall from our discussion of Riecken's study on the American Friends Service Committee (AFSC) work camps in Chapter 5, Civic Service Outcomes, merely recruiting a diverse group of corps members, though important, was not sufficient to support tolerance for diversity.

Mediating factors also play a role in successful institution creation. Although the studies reviewed do not shed a great deal of light regarding mediating factors likely to affect the success of institution creation, there is some evidence to suggest that the tangible and more immediate impacts of programs specifically designed to provide direct service may lead to more institution creation than reform-oriented programs designed with more ambiguous, long-term goals focused on institutional change. Clearly, the findings suggest that for each of these two outcomes, tolerance for diversity and new institution creation, high-quality primary studies are needed.

Individual Mediating Characteristics and Outcomes

> **Proposition Two:** The effects of service (high and low intensity) on individual outcomes are mediated by server characteristics.

Although many factors influence the service-outcome relationship depicted in the preceding proposition, differences in server attributes are one of the most likely and prominent factors. Individuals bring different motivations, experiences, abilities, and other attributes to their service. Variations in these individual attributes can reasonably be expected to influence how service affects key outcomes.

Figure 7.3   Relationship Between Service and Tolerance for Diversity Mediated by Program Design and Management

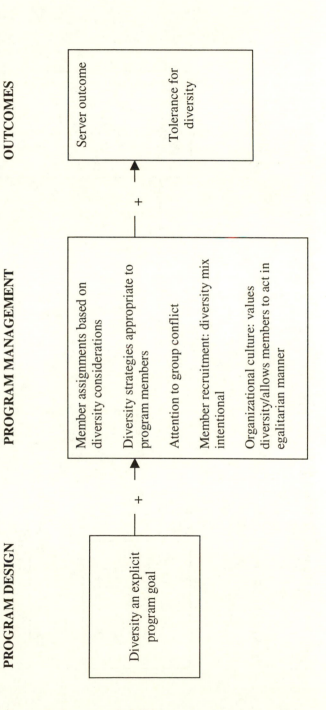

124

Figure 7.4 **Relationship Between Service and Institution Creation Mediated by Program Design**

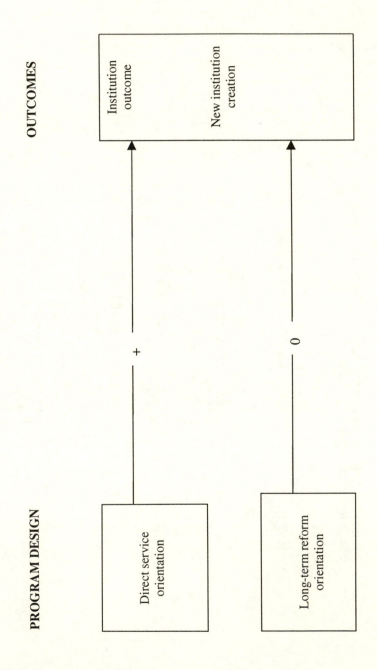

PROGRAM DESIGN

OUTCOMES

Several findings from the synthesis illustrate the general point of the proposition. The lower the member skills at entry, the less likely service will succeed in changing participants' skills. Even if, in the long run, service has transformational effects on some individuals, there is a question of what it can achieve in the short run, particularly when members are seriously deficient on a range of skills. Service may not be the best or right intervention for individuals who lack basic job skills, social skills, and other developmental benchmarks that are critical for labor market competency.

The synthesis suggests that the relationship between service and skill development is more nuanced than the preceding discussion reflects. One of the nuances involves the type of skills civic service programs seek to develop through service. Service is more influential on generalized life skills than on technical or certification skills. The differential effects seem plausible in that general life skills must be practiced and acquired in social settings. Technical skills involve more esoteric knowledge that may not be readily acquired in a service context alone. Furthermore, the synthesis seems to suggest that the greater the intensity of service (long-term/frequent), the greater the likelihood of positive generalized life skill development.

In contrast to the service intensity–skill development relationship, the service intensity–civic responsibility relationship is equivocal. Service intensity does not appear to be a requisite for instilling civic responsibility. Low-intensity service is as effective as high-intensity service for producing improvements in civic responsibility. The dynamics underlying this generalization are not entirely clear, but several are defensible given the research. One dynamic is that less intense service opportunities are associated with programs whose primary goal is development of civic responsibility. This is certainly true of many summer programs for youth, such as the Youth Volunteer Corps of America,[9] that are reported in the research. More intense service experiences, like the Civilian Conservation Corps or AmeriCorps, are likely to have other primary goals.

Another interesting finding suggested by the synthesis is the mediating effects of another server attribute—gender and ethnicity—on the development of civic responsibility. As discussed in Chapter 5, one high-quality study in the synthesis did demonstrate a significant increase in civic responsibility among African-American males with no significant changes for the sample as a whole. Overall, however, the research to date does not provide sufficient information about the mediating factors likely to enhance the development of stronger civic commitments. The relationships summarized in Figure 7.5 are meant to identify hypotheses suggested in the synthesis that need further research.

126

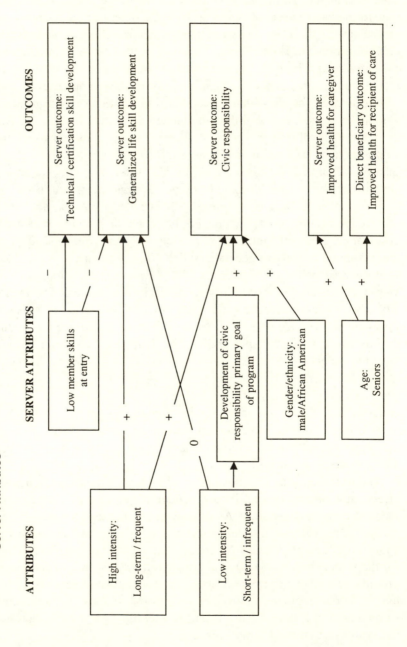

Figure 7.5 **Relationship Between Service and Individual Outcomes Mediated by Service Intensity and Server Attributes**

Besides service intensity and server attributes, the synthesis also identi-fied another individual mediator affecting service and individual outcomes: age. Research on seniors suggests at least two ways in which the age of the server mediates the outcomes of service. Civic service has successfully met the needs of both senior caregivers and the recipients of that care by improving the quality of life of both groups, including but not limited to increased social resources, functional independence, and adjustments in life-satisfaction.

Service Goals and Outcomes

> **Proposition Three:** The type and number of service goals are con-sequential for service outcomes.

A long-term debate in civic service revolves around the question, "Who ben-efits?"[10] Some civic service advocates suggest that the server is the primary beneficiary; others claim that society should be the beneficiary. The synthe-sis suggests that the two goals can comfortably coexist, but that society should receive the higher priority.[11] In addition to placing public-benefit ahead of personal benefit, the evolution from service as a server benefit to service as a public problem-solving strategy has been effective in improving the sustainability of service, resulting in greater legitimacy and, not surprisingly, an increase in service opportunities.

The inference that member skills at entry mediate service-outcome rela-tionships is confounded by the fact that service programs addressing the most needy youth in American society typically pursue multiple goals. For example, many conservation corps seek to train unskilled youth, preserve the environment, and instill participants with a service ethic. This is not sur-prising given that the preamble to the 1993 National and Community Ser-vice Trust Act identifies no less than eight expansive goals for civic service programs, equally demanding and often conflicting.[12]

In his book *The Bill*, Steven Waldman describes the AmeriCorps program as the "public policy equivalent of a Swiss Army knife [in] one affordable package."[13] This Swiss Army knife characteristic necessarily creates adminis-trative complexity that poses a significant threat to the likelihood of successful civic service outcomes. The research synthesis suggests that civic service can achieve many goals, but few are achieved by serendipity. The Civilian Conser-vation Corps is an example of a complex program that worked because re-sponsibilities were clearly allocated among cooperating departments.[14]

Clear roles and responsibilities fall within one of the key implementation issues identified in the research synthesis: program management (which in-cludes program design and operation). As the discussion in Chapter 6,

Qualities of Successful Programs, suggests, a number of mediating factors identified in the research can enhance the likelihood of positive service-outcome relationships in programs with multiple, often conflicting goals. Programs, for example, designed with a clear focus (such as direct service rather than societal reform), manageable scope, and structural simplicity are more likely to achieve their goals than are complex, geographically dispersed programs (especially those that also demonstrate incongruence between service intensity and time required to reach goals). Furthermore, effective management strategies (as the implementation literature asserts) may help to mitigate the effects of multiple goals.[15] Figure 7.6 summarizes these mediating effects.

Individual Mediating Characteristics and Implementation

> **Proposition Four:** Implementation tactics can mitigate the mediating influences of server characteristics.

Besides the mitigating effects of management and design on programs with multiple goals, the research synthesis suggests additional variables that intervene and may mitigate the adverse effects of server attributes on service-outcome relationships.[16] Figure 7.7 summarizes these additional variables, not least of which is the importance of volunteer training.

As the discussion in Chapter 6 suggests, the volunteer literature strongly underscores the critical role training plays in successful service outcomes. But training, though necessary, is not sufficient to assure successful achievement of service goals. The training must be both effective and efficient. Our research synthesis and the volunteer literature suggest that on-the-job training may be more effective and less costly than formal academic training for service. Capacity of program staff to accurately identify training needs is equally important for successful service outcomes.

This capacity is closely linked with leadership that demonstrates a clear vision for how to best use corps member resources to achieve service goals. Supplemented by this vision, clear goals for member development, and experienced team and crew leaders, effective and efficient training can greatly mitigate low member skills at entry and the adverse effects of low income and educational attainment among participants in civic service programs.

Devolution, Collaborations, and Service Outcomes

> **Proposition Five:** Interorganizational and intersectoral relationships are consequential for service outcomes.

Figure 7.6 **Mediating Factors Affecting Relationships Between Service Goals and Outcomes**

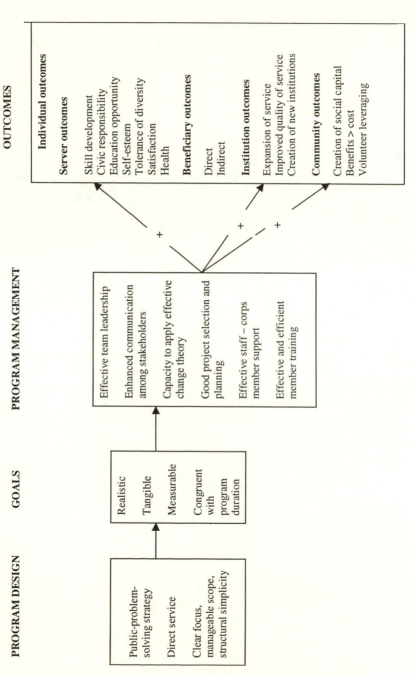

Figure 7.7 **Implementation Tactics Mitigating the Influence of Server Attributes on the Relationships Between Service and Outcomes**

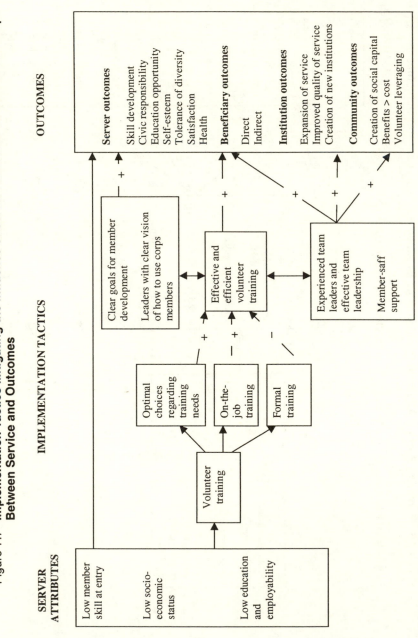

From its inception in 1993, the AmeriCorps program was deliberately designed as a federal-state-local public-private partnership. As the discussion of sponsoring agency in Chapter 6 illustrates, determining the right balance of responsibility among the three different sectors *and* among local sponsoring agencies and host sites is critical to successful achievement of service outcomes. The research synthesis suggests that certain factors may prove particularly important for enhancing the likelihood of positive service-outcome relationships, especially between service and positive community outcomes such as community strengthening or creation of social capital. Mediating factors range from operational issues, like open lines of communication and clarity of expectations, to external factors, like organizational credibility, legitimacy, and solid reputations in local communities.

Insights gained from the research synthesis suggest that the collective action problems of these interorganizational, intersectoral partnerships pose significant threats to the achievement of successful community outcomes. Divided loyalties, miscommunication, unclear expectations, and lack of careful screening and selection of sponsoring and participating agencies are only some of the many factors that constantly threaten to derail the achievement of civic service goals.[17]

Research Needs

We began this chapter with two questions: (1) What light does the synthesis shed on cause-effect relations involving service, its design, implementation, and effects? (2) What are the implications for future research? We turn now to the second of these questions. The synthesis identified explicit and implicit research needs. As Cooper and Hedges caution, it is incumbent on the research synthesist not only to create generalizations but to seek the limits and modifiers of those generalizations.[18] The research needs discussed in this section represent what we believe are the limits and modifiers of the five propositions presented earlier in this chapter. Null findings related to the service-outcome relationship across many of the studies suggest the need for further refinement in research methods and design to better understand the factors that mediate this relationship.

Mediating Variables

As the preceding discussion of potential causal relationships reflects, one surprise finding is the mediating relationships that were identified. Attendant to the mediators identified in the synthesis is the need for research about them; we do not readily understand these mediators within the context of the relationship between service and outcome. Individual attributes such as member skill at entry, age, gender, ethnicity, educational attainment, and socioeconomic status emerge from the synthesis as important mediating factors. The synthesis was less successful in finding mediators that explain variations across programs, such as specific service attributes critical for producing stronger civic commitments; the mediating effects of quality of service program and individual service experience on the development of self-esteem; or the factors that influence the creation of new service institutions, especially mediators that affect participants' willingness to accept and implement reform. This gap merits attention in future research.

Underdeveloped Research About Implementation, Outcomes, and Programs

The synthesis also exposed many areas where research is underdeveloped. At the individual level of analysis, underdeveloped areas of research on the impacts of service on servers and beneficiaries (direct and indirect) range from ignorance about which skills are most substantially affected by service to lack of reliable and consistent measures for satisfaction from service. We also have a relatively narrow and limited view of service as a problem-solving strategy.

At the institutional level of analysis, the primary gap in research lies with the institution creation outcome. Clearly, the complexity of this outcome makes it difficult for researchers to define this construct conceptually and operationally. This, in turn, makes it even more difficult to identify valid measures. The key areas ripe for research lie in identifying and examining mediating variables that enhance or decrease the likelihood of this outcome occurring. Which service attributes, for example, affect the likelihood of institutionalization of service in local communities? How do service programs that take a direct service orientation differ from those that make institutional reform a primary goal? How do programs with different orientations compare across variables such as institution creation, community strengthening, or benefit-cost ratios? Research at this institutional level will generate hypotheses and help to inform research on community outcomes.

Like institutional outcomes, community outcomes are equally amorphous and difficult to define conceptually and operationally. Clear logic models underlying the relationship between service and community strengthening need to be developed to improve our conceptual understanding of how service changes communities. Despite the value of cost-benefit studies for improving our knowledge of the impacts of service on communities, struggling with the more difficult issues implicit in research on community building cannot be avoided if we want to gain a deeper understanding of service and its impacts.

Given that attitudinal outcomes are more easily conceptualized and measured than institutional and community outcomes, it is not surprising that most of the service-related research has been done at the individual level of analysis, especially examining what Perry and Katula call "the psychology of service."[19] This gap in the current body of research needs to be filled. Examining implementation tactics as mediating factors in the service-outcome relationship provides one way to fill that gap. Each of the eight implementation themes discussed in Chapter 6—program management, training, member recruitment and retention, fiscal management, sponsoring agency, leadership, program visibility, and administrative burdens—represents areas ripe for research, and the policy implementation literature provides a rich field from which to draw insights and hypotheses concerning mediating effects.

Each of these themes needs to be examined individually and in various combinations using logic models like those presented earlier in this chapter. Which implementation tactics work synergistically to enhance certain outcomes more than others? Why? What are the implications of these synergies for the design of civic service programs? Do funding strategies differ in civic service contexts compared to other policy settings? How is financial sustainability realized given the unique political and programmatic barriers characteristic of civic service programs? How does leadership change when practiced in a shared-power setting across sectors and within local communities?

Overall, the field of civic service represents a relatively new area for research when compared to older fields and literatures like interorganizational relations, implementation, public management, and organizational behavior. Harris Wofford, former CEO of CNCS, once characterized the field as a "kind of R&D experiment."[20] From this perspective, the field has benefited from having developed a large best-practices literature. The focus now needs to shift to the underdeveloped area of behavioral research. Greater emphasis needs to be placed on rigorous research designs and longitudinal studies examining the service-outcome relationship through the mediating factors identified in this synthesis.

Concept Definition and Measurement

Aside from less than optimal research designs that characterize many civic service studies, another vexing weakness in the research is the validity and reliability of measures. This limitation of the research is multipronged. Part of it stems from the lack of clarity about core constructs in service research.

Concepts like service, community building, public work, and civic responsibility often are either poorly defined or not defined at all.

Even when key constructs are adequately defined, they may not be adequately or consistently measured. The reliabilities of measures are frequently unknown. As noted earlier, this was the case for self-esteem, which has often been measured by a single survey item. Compounding these problems is lack of standardization of concepts and measures. The concept of civic responsibility, for example, may be defined in widely different ways by different researchers despite carrying the same concept name across studies.

An example of a construct that begs for clearer definition and measurement is what Charles Moskos calls the "civic content" of service. With regard to civic content, he writes, "It is upon some such norm of fulfillment of civic obligation, upon some concept of serving societal needs outside the marketplace, upon some sense of participation in a public life with other citizens that the idea of national service builds."[21] Although Moskos is relatively precise about what he associates with civic content, his definition is complex, referring simultaneously to social norms, beneficiaries, and collective action. The complexity of his definition has not been matched by equally sophisticated measurement.

Echoing Moskos, Harry Boyte argues that "from the perspective of civic education, the weakness of community service lies in a conceptual limitation [namely that service] lacks a vocabulary that draws attention to the public world that extends beyond personal lives and local communities." Boyte is concerned that most service programs focus on the private nature of service by emphasizing personal growth at the expense of learning political skills such as public judgment, negotiation, and public accountability. He believes the personal language of many service programs seldom signals the reality of effective citizen action. Community service, from Boyte's perspective, needs a "conceptual framework that distinguishes between personal life and the public world," one that places service explicitly in the public realm by bringing diverse groups of people to "work together effectively to address public problems," what Boyte calls "problem-solving politics."[22]

A rare effort to conceptualize how service activates responses is provided by Yates and Youniss. They contend that three dimensions of the service experience trigger the development of civic responsibility: agency, social relatedness, and moral-political awareness.[23] Perry and Katula adapt these dimensions in creating a theory of change about how service affects citizenship. They suggest that the three primary mechanisms are intellectual stimulation, socialization, and practice. By placing these mechanisms within a theory of change, Perry and Katula not only better conceptualize the constructs themselves, but also clarify where these mechanisms fit within the larger research context, determining whether and how service affects citizenship.[24]

We need more theories of change (or logic models) when conceptualizing service-outcome relationships that allow us to think more systematically and analytically about the complex relationships that define both the practice and study of civic service. In order to better understand civic service's impacts on people, institutions, and communities, specifying theories of change can provide a means of identifying hypotheses to be tested and gaps that need to be filled by high-quality primary research.

Other Research Needs

Besides conceptual clarity, our synthesis identifies yet other research needs, not the least of which concern the nature of the questions being asked about the relationship between service and outcome. Much of the research investigates issues with low probabilities of "disconfirmation." Did service increase? Did quality improve? We need to ask more substantively challenging questions, some of which have already been identified in the previous discussion.

Outcome questions should also involve consideration of benefit-cost ratios, outcome benefits in relation to investment increments. For example, the ability of civic service programs (particularly those supported by public dollars and stipended participants) to solve public problems should be compared to the effects of individual voluntarism (expressed through the nonprofit sector). A sample of social initiatives (of the type showcased in recent analyses of social entrepreneurship)[25] could be compared to a sample of civic service programs. Comparisons could be made on a number of dimensions, among them impacts on beneficiaries, costs, and efficiency. In addition to comparing discrete indicators of inputs, outputs, intermediate outcomes, and impacts, an examination of the environment of conduct would be important. We suspect that successful public and private initiatives share a great deal in common.

Conclusion

William James's idealistic vision of a civic service that retains the "martial virtues" without resorting to militaristic tendencies has not necessarily panned out.[26] But perhaps James should not be held to too high a standard. After all, his vision was utopian. As we discussed in Chapters 1 and 2, in a liberal democracy such as the United States, civic service can best be understood as filling a niche that military service cannot fill (as opposed to replacing military service, as James envisioned).

In this chapter, we have taken a less ambitious approach to civic service and its potential to influence positively individuals, institutions, and communities. Our research synthesis provides a broad picture of the service-outcome relationship that allows us to reflect upon potential cause-effect relationships. More important, it offers insight into the mediating factors that influence this relationship and underscore its complexity. Many challenging questions that emerge from this review of civic service research need to be addressed—questions that demand greater attention to conceptual and operational definitions, identification of logic models that include mediating factors, and rigorous research designs, preferably longitudinal and comparative in nature. Following this research agenda will not only increase the legitimacy of the field of civic service in academic circles; it will also positively influence the practice of citizen service by enlarging and improving our understanding of service as a foundational concept of democracy.

Cooper and Hedges conclude their *Handbook on Research Synthesis* with this important point. "A research synthesis," they write,

> should never be considered a replacement for new primary research. Primary research and its synthesis are complementary parts of a common process; they are not competing alternatives. [A] synthesis that concludes a problem is solved, that no future research is needed, should be deemed a failure. Even the best architects can see how the structures they have built can be improved.[27]

We see the identification of gaps in the edifice of accumulated research on civic service constructed in this book as one of its most important contributions to the field. Scholars can examine these gaps, now that they have been identified, and design new primary research capable of testing hypothesized causal relationships identified in these pages.

"In a liberal democracy," write Perry and his colleagues, "government intervention in an otherwise private domain must be adequately justified."[28] Research on civic service plays a critical role in that endeavor. The civic service policy cycle in which we currently find ourselves suggests that a change may have occurred in the national ethos regarding service. Bipartisan congressional support and sustained popular support for civic service underscore the importance of developing a carefully designed research agenda that can inform future civic service policy and improve the likelihood of achieving positive service-outcome relationships. It is to policy that we now turn.

8

Policy Implications

The synthesis of civic service research has been fruitful for identifying both potential cause-effect relationships and gaps in the research. Now that we have explored what the research has to say about civic service, we can consider the ways in which the findings can be used on a larger scale. This chapter examines the policy implications of the research synthesis for civic service. What are the implications for public policy? Although the answer to this question begins with the results of the research synthesis, it also is necessary to draw on other sources for interpretive and contextual information.

We begin by discussing three policy issues that we believe are brought into perspective by the research synthesis. These issues involve the objectives for civic service, tradeoffs between results and innovation, and the scale of civic service. We then turn to the superordinate issue of what we envision as the future for civic service.

The Evolution of Civic Service's Objectives

As the history of civic service demonstrates, many objectives have been pursued in the context of civic service programs. The objective functions of civic service are not uniform across programs, but highly varied.[1] Some programs emphasize primarily member development, some community building, others public works, and still others mixes of these objectives.

The objective functions of civic service have evolved in ways that permit some generalizations about optimal objective structures. The optimal mix of objectives is a mix of public and member benefits. Concrete public benefit may be the more important of the two objectives. Programs that attain concrete public benefits appear to be more successful than programs seeking to achieve generalized or diffuse objectives. When programs achieving concrete public benefit can simultaneously transform members in significant ways, then the objectives of civic service are optimized. A corollary is that missteps with regard to either public or member benefit can be devastating for a service program.

Several examples illustrate these generalizations. The Teacher Corps, created in 1965, pursued an ambitious set of goals that sought to reform teacher development and engage schools in their communities. Its goal was, quite simply, institutional reform. It failed, however, both in articulating concrete alternatives to the status quo and in developing a case for sustainability. The Teacher Corps ended in 1982.

Teach for America, founded in 1989, shares much in common with the Teacher Corps, including a similar name and the goal of creating a national teacher corps that will reform education in America. But with the name and overarching goal the similarities end. Teach for America which is partly funded by the Corporation for National and Community Service (CNCS) seeks to reform education in two novel ways—by producing results and by bringing in fresh blood to teach in low-income districts. Wendy Kopp, Teach for America's founder, describes the initial reactions to her teacher-corps model:

> I learned that the dominant belief held that teachers, just like doctors and lawyers, needed to be trained in campus-based graduate programs before entering the classroom. From this vantage point, the only acceptable way to improve teaching was to ensure that schools of education raise their selection standards and make their programs more rigorous. Proponents of this view were reluctant to invest in Teach for America, whose recruits would go through only a short pre-service training program before entering the classroom.[2]

Despite the limited investments in formal corps member training, Teach for America has succeeded where the much better funded Teacher Corps failed. More than 90 percent of principals who hired Teach for America members rated them as good or excellent on twenty-three indicators of successful teaching.[3] The majority of principals reported that corps members were "strongly advantageous" for their schools.

The evolution from member benefit to public problem-solving strategy has been effective in gaining greater legitimacy for service and growing service opportunities. At the same time, the meaningful service and training needed to fulfill the service strategy have paid enormous benefits for participants. Although the benefits of some early service programs were weighted toward member benefits while others attempted to address growing social needs, the evolution of the civic service movement in the past decade has been toward successfully accomplishing both sets of goals simultaneously.

As the experience of the Civilian Conservation Corps (CCC) attests, no specific mix of objectives assures a program's survival. Despite its successes and popularity, the CCC was short-lived, closing its camp doors less than a decade after its creation. But the demise of the CCC was associated with both the resolution of the problem for which it was created—substantial unemployment triggered by the onset of the Great Depression—and a larger public concern—World War II. Furthermore, the glow of the embers left by the CCC experience helped to ignite new service programs in later years, among them youth conservation corps and AmeriCorps.

Tradeoffs Between Accomplishment and Innovation

A recurring issue in studying and ultimately developing civic service programs and movements is the tension between accomplishment and innovation. Corwin asserts that choices must often be made to achieve gain, even if the choices reduce the chances for true innovation in civic service programs.[4] To understand Corwin's argument is to face the realization that the number and types of organizations with the capacity to administer civic service programs effectively may be limited. Inclusion of certain organizations under the civic service umbrella, whether for political expediency to increase program diversity or for more general purposes, may do more harm than good for the overall effectiveness of the program itself.

Furthermore, Corwin would argue, the administrative complexity involved in increasing the number or types of organizations involved in civic service may simply create internal program confusion and red tape that actually can undermine the efforts for program success.[5] In the case of Teacher Corps, for example, attempts to create an innovative program for increasing the supply and proficiency of teachers in poverty-stricken areas led to an enormously complex network of participating organizations. Elementary, secondary, and postsecondary schools became key participants along with local communities, program staff, and legislative members. The implementation structure became a mirror image of struggles among the same parties who contested the enabling legislation for the Teacher Corps. The communication and administrative demands became so great that despite the innovative structure of participating organizations within the program, Teacher Corps was handcuffed in its ability to accomplish the goals for which it was established.

AmeriCorps, on the other hand, has demonstrated more, albeit limited, success in pairing innovation in program design and structure with accomplishment of desired benefits. Several questions need to be addressed on this front. The first question concerns the development of the right mix or balance of innovation and accomplishment within programmatic lines. Is the goal to establish previously untried techniques or should the emphasis be placed on the levels of outcomes of particular service programs? As we noted in the preceding section, producing results is a critical part of the objective function for civic service, but producing social innovation should merit some risk taking. But how much is appropriate and how should it be built into program oversight and accountability?

The new millennium and the transition in political leadership in Washington have done little to resolve the debate over accomplishment-innovation tradeoffs. In fact, the early initiative of the Bush administration to expand social service provision to "faith-based" organizations may fuel the tradeoff debate. The White House essentially is attempting to reverse bureaucratic obstacles to the participation of faith-based organizations, the inclusion of which is itself quite innovative for national service. The intended payoff of this innovation lies in increased provision of needed services through existing organizations, thereby reducing the overall cost to the American people of providing those services. But, as Lenkowsky points out, the issue is still far from straightforward.[6] Constitutional issues as well as questions of accountability and the effectiveness of faith-based organizations to provide services are clear evidence that the accomplishment-innovation debate is alive.

Taking Civic Service to Scale

In two influential books about civic service published in the late 1980s and early 1990s, Charles Moskos and William F. Buckley Jr. proposed programs for civic service. Moskos's proposal calls for comprehensive voluntary civic service, a "full-time undertaking of public duties by young people—whether as citizen soldiers or civilian soldiers—who are paid subsistence wages."[7] The comprehensive program would be administered by a Corporation for National Youth Service (CYNS), functioning as a public corporation like the Corporation for Public Broadcasting and similar to CNCS, which was subsequently authorized in 1993. VISTA and Peace Corps were slated to retain their administrative homes and reside outside CYNS. Housed within CYNS would be mission-based signature programs geared to specific needs such as Alzheimer's and AIDS. The large majority of servers would be in state and local, not federal, programs. Moskos proposed funding these programs with block grants to the states from CYNS. Moskos's 1988 proposal for voluntary civic service departs from his earlier insistence on compulsory service as the only means for avoiding a societal division between the "haves" and "have-nots."

William F. Buckley Jr. criticizes Moskos's proposal and offers his own vision for universal civic service in his book *Gratitude,* published just two years later. In his ideal, Buckley sets forth the essentials of a service franchise model of civic service:

- a "conscious mobilization of social, philanthropic, and civic enthusiasm for the idea of national service,"
- establishment of a National Service Franchise Administration, whose primary function would be to provide information to states and individuals about appropriate service opportunities,
- the provision of federal financial educational aid only to those who have completed civic service or are scheduled to do so in the near future,
- sufficient uniformity across states so the service program is truly national,
- the imposition of sanctions by Congress on states deviating from the national intentions for service, and
- provisions that permit students who go on to college before completing national service to serve during or after college.[8]

What is striking about both the Moskos and Buckley proposals is their similarity, despite the authors' criticism and countercriticism. Beyond the programmatic qualities of existing or proposed service programs, both authors envision the purpose of civic service less as a way to provide economic, educational, or material benefits to participants and beneficiaries and more as the means through which to return a national ethos to America's younger generations, an ethos not widely seen in America since World War II. The essence of their envisioned ethos is that each individual citizen owes a debt to society, a debt to those who have gone before and have sacrificed for the greater good of the country. In Buckley's terms, all Americans, particularly younger generations, owe a "debt of gratitude" to their country. Civic service provides an outlet for youth to repay this debt.

In at least one respect, the visions articulated by Charles Moskos and William F. Buckley Jr. are realities today. Options for civic service are more extensive today than perhaps at any other time in American history. Opportunities for civic service may be found in AmeriCorps; youth, conservation, and faith-based corps; and a variety of grassroots organizations. The past several decades have witnessed an explosion in the range of civic service projects and programs.

Regardless of the individual supplemental benefits of each program, civic service has grown increasingly diverse in terms of the types of programs offered. From the CCC of the 1930s to senior citizen programs such as the Senior Companion and Foster Grandparents programs to AmeriCorps in the 1990s, different programs have been designed to target different segments of the American population. Individuals today can choose to participate in service programs tailored to their particular interests, be that military, environmental, educational, or another interest.

Scale is the primary difference between today's circumstances and the Moskos and Buckley visions. The number of civic service slots referred to by Moskos and Buckley ranged from 600,000 to 1.6 million.[9] In comparison, although no official counts are available, the total number of participants in all current civic service programs is probably no more than 100,000.

How to enlarge the number of civic service slots has been thoughtfully addressed in several quarters.[10] In essence, the issue is one of supply and demand. Not only must demand for civic service be increased among the public in general, but the supply of quality service opportunities must be enlarged as well.

Several potential strategies have been suggested to accomplish this increase in supply and demand, including increasing the flow of funds to service organizations and enterprises that have shown themselves successful in recruiting qualified participants and raising matching funds. The downside to such a strategy is, of course, that it perpetuates only existing programs instead of enlarging the mix of available service opportunities. The need to develop new programs capable of attracting new pools of participants is in keeping with the Moskos and Buckley proposals. For those individuals not interested in traditional civic service opportunities, including present-day AmeriCorps programs, expansion of civic service into other social arenas might prove attractive.

The number of civic service slots is an issue closely associated as well with the shift away from singularly public service programs to jointly administered and funded efforts. Expansion of public-private cooperation is precisely what Eli Segal and Shirley Sagawa, top executives at the founding of the CNCS, address in *Common Interest, Common Good*.[11] No longer are joint public-private ventures simply one possibility in the development and implementation of civic philanthropic enterprises. The growing difficulty in obtaining funds from traditional public and nonprofit sources necessitates a shift in the sources and purposes for service programs. Such a shift, however, comes at a price. Private corporate or fraternal enterprises must be persuaded of the benefit (not primarily to society in general, but to their own financial well-being) of supporting expanded civic service forays. Doing so would further the transparency of government's role in civic service.

Arthur Brooks also examines the effect of governmental funding on private donations to nonprofit organizations.[12] Brooks's conclusion that, within the realm of social and human service provision, private donations are inversely related to the level of governmental funding—the assumption being that private organizations and individuals consider government-funded nonprofits as quasi-governmental and therefore less attractive—lends credence to the necessary, growing role of private involvement in civic service.

The necessity of the "invisible hand"—in a role reversal for government, its most effective role is best not seen—is vital for building a network of civic service providers.

Concluding Observations

In considering the optimal objective function for civic service, the tradeoffs between program accomplishments and innovation, and ideas for increasing the scale of civic service, we have come full circle to broad themes addressed in the initial chapters of this book. We began with William James's search for an alternative to war's disciplinary function, a moral equivalent of war, as he looked forward to the twentieth century. As we look forward at the beginning of the twenty-first century, what is our long-range vision for civic service? In what ways is our vision influenced by the findings of the research synthesis?

Although America's political landscape is likely always to be characterized by the competing political ideologies of classic liberalism and classic republicanism, we believe that civic service has begun to develop a more harmonious relationship with both political ideologies. Many of the attributes of our current civic service—its voluntarism, pluralism of opportunities, and reliance on private nonprofits for setting the action agenda—originate in the ideals of classical liberalism. At the same time, our growing acceptance of a redefined and broadened volunteerism, which includes stipended service and government's role as a partner and catalyst for civic service, attest to the harmony developing between classic republicanism and civic service.

One symbolic manifestation of the developing harmony between our civic service institutions and competing political ideologies is the remarkable continuity between the Clinton and Bush administrations with regard to important structures for civic service. CNCS, created during the Clinton administration, has become a key feature of the Bush administration's vision for partnerships with the voluntary sector. President Bush and congressional supporters like Senators John McCain (R-AZ) and Evan Bayh (D-IN) have proposed expansion of AmeriCorps, one of President's Clinton's most prominent domestic initiatives. This proposed expansion comes in the face of budget deficits and spending pressures that are even more constraining than those faced during the Clinton administration.

The debate about the nature of civic service and American political philosophies does not do justice to one reality of our commitment to civic service. Regardless of the competing values associated with civic service, our research synthesis suggests that it is deeply rooted in American pragmatism. America turned to civic service during the Depression to put men back to work, during the Great Society to ameliorate poverty, and, most recently, to improve the education performance of those most at risk of being left behind.

It is this picture of pragmatism that we draw from our synthesis of civic service that most sharply distinguishes our vision of civic service from the ideal of William James and the more recent visions of Charles Moskos and William F. Buckley Jr. We have turned to civic service in extraordinary times to produce extraordinary results. By the same token, as a country, we have been unable to leverage our regard for civic service as a means for restoring civic obligation on a large scale. An irony of our conclusion that civic service is a manifestation of American pragmatism is William James's intellectual leadership of the highly influential, early twentieth-century philosophical movement known as pragmatism, which asserted that the meaning of any idea was a function of its practical outcome.

As much as we are persuaded of the morality of Buckley's view that our culture should be characterized by a deep sense of gratitude, we do not believe that gratitude can be imposed or easily manipulated. To the extent that gratitude is a cultural phenomenon, it must flow from the sentiments of the people and cannot be imposed upon them. Our synthesis suggests that culture-related outcomes—for example, civic skills—are less predictably tied to civic service than other outcomes. Restoring what Bellah and his colleagues refer to as "habits of the heart," the spirit of community demands more than the creation of new civic service institutions.[13] It is likely to require reinforcement by changes in many of our institutions, including our political institutions. We will not restore an ethos of civic obligation by creating new civic service institutions without simultaneously reinvigorating our political institutions and restoring their integrity.

Our review of the evolution of civic service and synthesis of its outcomes leads us to conclude, in contrast to Moskos and Buckley, that civic service is first a way to provide economic, educational, or material benefits to beneficiaries and participants and only secondarily the means through which to restore a national ethos to America's younger generations. Like William James's earlier view that national service could be turned from military to pacifist pursuits to benefit civil society, we believe that Moskos and Buckley place too much faith in using civic service to restore an ethos not widely seen in America since World War II. As Robert Putnam's generational analysis in *Bowling Alone* suggests, we may be incapable of restoring the ethos of the World War II generation without a similar national crisis.[14] September 11, 2001, was indeed a crisis, but, as wrenching as it was for American society, it had neither the intensity nor the duration to trigger the civic transformation we associate with the World War II generation. Putnam's analysis of

September 11's aftermath suggests that it is likely to have modest and perhaps temporary effects for civic engagement.[15]

We believe that public officials and society's leaders should go beyond mere lip service to the value of civic service and institute inducements and rules in public policy that elevate its economic and social recognition, much like Buckley's proposals.[16] But unlike James, Moskos, and Buckley, we envision a future civic service that is pluralistic, voluntary, and funded by subsidies from a variety of governments together with infusions of private support. This civic service is much closer in character to de Tocqueville's ideal than James's.

For de Tocqueville, a fundamental reality of democracy is that its citizens, as free and equal participants in the demos, are, in the end, "powerless if they do not learn voluntarily to help one another." The capacity for joint action, what he calls "the science of association," is what represents the hope for "civilization itself."[17] In a postindustrial world, characterized by increasingly complex social problems and concerns, we view civic service as one valuable means for developing *pragmatic* joint action that involves individual citizens and the social, economic, and political institutions they create, to more adequately meet the demands of the twenty-first century. The cumulative structure of knowledge of civic service built in these pages offers scholars and practitioners of civic service an opportunity to stand back, reflect upon, and test the link between pragmatic joint action and civic service.

V

Appendices

═══ Appendix A ═══

Searching the Literature

The rapid growth of research about service is quite recent,[1] but the techniques of research synthesis are mature, fairly well developed, and assume a critical mass of research.[2] The objective for the synthesis was that its coverage be exhaustive of all research meeting the defined inclusion criteria. A variety of channels were used for finding relevant studies. Some of them were formal (for example, print and electronic journals) and many of them were informal (for example, personal contacts and solicitations).

Two circumstances strongly influenced the search process. One was the development by the senior author of a research bibliography about civic service in 1998–99. The other was his sabbatical year at the Corporation for National and Community Service (CNCS) in the academic year 1999–2000. The bibliography and the senior author's presence at CNCS were enormously useful for tracking down many relevant sources.

Early in the search process, we discovered that the parameters (such as intensity) used to define and bound the civic service literature were not good terms for searching for research. Few research studies appear, for instance, under the terms *stipended* or *intensive service*. We started, therefore, with an alternative tactic, which was to search for research about identifiable service programs. The Civilian Conservation Corps (CCC) and AmeriCorps are familiar names to those in the civic service community and to the public. But there are many more service programs—some of them obscure and dating back decades—with which we were not familiar. We were aided in identifying the names of service programs by a very thorough CNCS Web page that recounts the history of national service. The Web site names ten past and current civic service programs.[3]

Searches of Electronic Databases

The formal names of twelve civic service programs, listed in Table A.1, were used to search three electronic databases. The databases used were the Library of Congress Online Catalog, Dissertation Abstracts, and the Grantmaker Forum Service-Related Research database.

Library of Congress

The Library of Congress Online Catalog is a database of approximately 12 million records representing books, serials, computer files, manuscripts, cartographic materials, music, sound recordings, and visual materials in the Library's collections.[4] The online catalog also provides references, notes, circulation status, and information about materials still in the acquisitions stage.

Dissertation Abstracts

The Dissertation Abstracts database is an index of over 1.3 million dissertations and master's theses from 1861 until the present. More than 40,000 titles are added each year, covering all fields of research, including education, business, sociology, political science, religion, and psychology. Each record contains all bibliographic information and a detailed abstract. The database is updated quarterly.

Grantmaker Forum

The Grantmaker Forum database contains 2,558 bibliographic records and abstracts of service-related research published between 1990 and 1999. The database was constructed by searching nine databases using a variety of search terms related to service-related activities. The databases used were Academic Search Elite; Book Where; Dissertation Abstracts International; ERIC (education); Government Documents; PAIS (public affairs); International Political Science Abstracts (IPSA); SocioFile (sociology); and PsycINFO (psychology). The search for the synthesis was confined to 997 records in the database that used some form of scientific method that increased the prospect that the retrieved item would contain research.[5]

Literature Reviews

The search for sources also benefited from prior literature reviews. The two most comprehensive were prepared by CNCS staff.[6] Book-length studies by Richard Danzig and Peter Szanton[7] and by Charles Moskos[8] were also useful for identifying research.

Table A.1

National Service Programs Subject to Electronic Search

Program
Civilian Conservation Corps (CCC)
Volunteers-in-Service to America (VISTA)
National Teacher Corps
University Year for ACTION
Youth Conservation Corps
California Conservation Corps
Young Adult Conservation Corps
Jesuit Service Corps
City Year
Teach for America
Public Allies
AmeriCorps

CNCS Archives

In addition to electronic searches and literature reviews, the CNCS archives were searched for unpublished reports and other studies that might have been overlooked in previous reviews and syntheses. This process uncovered a few additional reports that were not cited elsewhere.

═══ Appendix B ═══

Civic Service Synthesis
Coding Protocol

A central question informs the coding of the literature: "Which retrieved evidence should be included in the review?"[1] In theory, this question implies a vast array of choices involving complex methodological and substantive issues. As a practical matter, however, the underdeveloped status of civic service research and the larger goals of the synthesis simplified the options enormously.

The coding instrument was divided into eight major divisions. In brief, the divisions contained the following types of information:

- *study information*—basic identifying information for the study, including author, title, publisher, year published, and who supported the research;
- *service attributes*—descriptive information about the service performed, such as the name of the service program, the program's focus, service intensity, and remuneration;
- *server attributes*—demographic characteristics of servers, including income, age, and race;
- *sample characteristics*—the type of sample and its size;
- *methods information*—methods of data collection used in the research and ratings of quality;
- *outcome variables*—the outcomes addressed by the study, classified by server, served, institutions, and community;
- *findings*—whether the finding for a particular outcome was positive, negative, or no effect;
- *implementation*—issues associated with the implementation of the program, divided into eight categories including program management, program visibility, and funding.

Coding Protocol

Study ID (three-digit identifier):

Study Information

Author(s):

Title/Publisher:

Source:
   1—journal
   2—book
   3—thesis or dissertation
   4—government report
   5—nonprofit organization report
   6—university report
   7—conference paper
   9—consultant report

Year Published:
   (9999—not reported)

Study Auspices:
   1—funded by program
   2—independently funded
   3—not specified/cannot be inferred

Notes:

Service Attributes

Name of the Service Program:
   1—AmeriCorps*State/National
   2—AmeriCorps*NCCC
   3—VISTA or AmeriCorps*VISTA
   4—Foster Grandparent Program
   5—Senior Companion Program

6—Civilian Conservation Corps
7—California Conservation Corps
8—Youth Conservation Corps
9—Teach for America
10—Teachers Corps
11—National School and Community Corps
12—Public Allies
13—Youth Volunteer Corps of America
14—Georgia Peach Corps
15—Experience Corps
16—Various Youth Conservation and Service Corps
17—Wisconsin Conservation Corps
18—National Service Demonstrations
19—New York City Volunteer Corps
20—Marin Conservation Corps
21—San Francisco Conservation Corps
22—Seniors for Schools
23—American Friends Service Committee Work Camp Program
24—University Year for ACTION
25—Youth Community Service
26—Washington Service Corps
27—Hawaii Youth Service Corps
28—AmeriCorps*State/National, AmeriCorps*VISTA
29—AmeriCorps*NCCC, AmeriCorps*VISTA
30—AmeriCorps*All
31—AmeriCorps*State/National, AmeriCorps*NCCC
32—Program for Local Service
33—Summer of Safety
34—Pennsylvania Conservation Corps
35—City Year

Service Focus:
1—education
2—public safety
3—environment
4—health
5—other (specify):
6—mix of services
7—not specified

Acknowledged Difficulty of Problem(s):
   1—problem(s) widely viewed as very difficult
   2—problem(s) viewed as moderately difficult
   3—uncertain problem difficulty
   4—problem(s) viewed as moderately solvable
   5—problem(s) viewed as easily solvable
   6—not able to ascertain

Remuneration:
   1—none at all
   2—expenses reimbursed
   3—stipend/low pay
   4—not able to ascertain

Free Choice:
   1—free will (the ability to voluntarily choose)
   2—relatively uncoerced
   3—obligation to volunteer (i.e., mandatory service)
   4—not able to ascertain

Service Intensity—number of hours per week:

Service Intensity—number of weeks continuous service:

Service-learning component:
   1—yes
   2—no
   3—not specified

Team versus individual orientation:
   1—service is performed in teams
   2—service is performed both individually and in teams
   3—service is performed individually
   4—not able to ascertain

Notes:

Server Attributes

Income:
1—Under $5,000
2—$5,000–less than $10,000
3—$10,000–less than $15,000
4—$15,000–less than $20,000
5—$20,000–less than $25,000
6—$25,000–less than $30,000
7—$30,000–less than $40,000
8—$40,000–less than $50,000
9—$50,000–less than $60,000
10—$60,000–less than $70,000
11—$70,000–less than $80,000
12—$80,000–less than $90,000
13—$90,000–less than $100,000
14—$100,000 or more
15—mix of income levels
16—not specified

Race/Ethnicity:
1—diverse, heterogeneous sample
Homogeneous sample composed of (specify):
2—White, non-Hispanic
3—Black/African American
4—Hispanic/Spanish origin/Latino
5—American Indian or Alaska Native
6—Asian American or Pacific Islander
7—not specified/unable to ascertain

Age:
1—less than 18
2—18–23
3—24–35
4—36–49
5—50–59
6—60 +
7—heterogeneous
8—not specified

Gender:
    1—female
    2—male
    3—mixed
    4—not specified

Notes:

Sample Characteristics

Sampling Study I:
    1—random
    2—judgment or convenience
    3—not reported
    4—census, no sampling

Sampling Study II:
    1—random
    2—judgment or convenience
    3—not reported
    4—census, no sampling
    8—not applicable

Sampling Study III:
    1—random
    2—judgment or convenience
    3—not reported
    4—census, no sampling
    8—not applicable

The total sample size, Study I:
    9999—not reported

The total sample size, Study II:
    888—not applicable
    9999—not reported

The total sample size, Study III:
    888—not applicable

Notes:

Methods Information

Data collection methods, Study I (circle all that apply):
    1—survey
    2—interviews/focus group
    3—case study
    4—observations
    5—site visit
    6—records/archival information/budget data
    7—test results/health assessments
    0—documents/literature review/review of evaluations

Data collection methods, Study II (circle all that apply):
    1—survey
    2—interviews/focus group
    3—case study
    4—observations
    5—site visit
    6—records/archival information/budget data
    7—test results/health assessments
    0—documents/literature review/review of evaluations

Data collection methods, Study III (circle all that apply):
    1—survey
    2—interviews/focus group
    3—case study
    4—observations
    5—site visit
    6—records/archival information/budget data
    7—test results/health assessments
    0—documents/literature review/review of evaluations

Study I: Quality of study ratings (design):
    1—randomized
    2—nonequivalent with pretest
    3—nonequivalent with posttest only

4—time series
5—one-group pretest/posttest
6—preexperimental
7—synthesis

Study II: Quality of study ratings (design):
    1—randomized
    2—nonequivalent with pretest
    3—nonequivalent with posttest only
    4—time series
    5—one-group pretest/posttest
    6—preexperimental
    7—synthesis
    8—not applicable

Study III: Quality of study ratings (design):
    1—randomized
    2—nonequivalent with pretest
    3—nonequivalent with posttest only
    4—time series
    5—one-group pretest/posttest
    6—preexperimental
    7—synthesis
    8—not applicable

Study I: Quality of study ratings (count of threats to validity):
    88—not applicable

Study II: Quality of study ratings (count of threats to validity):
    8—not applicable

Study III: Quality of study ratings (count of threats to validity):
    8—not applicable

Notes:

Outcome Variables

Outcomes:
    Server Outcome 1: Skill development
        1—yes
        2—no

Server Outcome 2: Civic responsibility (including knowledge of civic affairs)
    1—yes
    2—no

Server Outcome 3: Educational opportunity
    1—yes
    2—no

Server Outcome 4: Self-esteem
    1—yes
    2—no

Server Outcome 5: Tolerance for diversity
    1—yes
    2—no

Server Outcome 6: Satisfaction from serving
    1—yes
    2—no

Server Outcome 7: Health
    1—yes
    2—no

Served Outcome 1: Impacts on direct beneficiaries
    1—yes
    2—no

Served Outcome 2: Impact on indirect beneficiaries
    1—yes
    2—no

Served Outcome 3: Specify
    1—yes
    2—no

Institution Outcome 1: Expand service
    1—yes
    2—no

Institution Outcome 2: Improve quality of services
    1—yes
    2—no

Institution Outcome 3: Create new institutions
    1—yes
    2—no

Community Outcome 1: Community strengthening
    1—yes
    2—no

Community Outcome 2: Benefit-cost analysis
    1—yes
    2—no

Community Outcome 3: Volunteer network/leveraging
    1—yes
    2—no

Notes:

Findings

Server Finding 1: Skill development
    1—no effect
    2—positive
    3—negative
    8—not applicable

Server Finding 2: Civic responsibility
    1—no effect
    2—positive
    3—negative
    8—not applicable

Server Finding 3: Educational opportunity
    1—no effect
    2—positive
    3—negative
    8—not applicable

Server Finding 4: Self-esteem
    1—no effect
    2—positive
    3—negative
    8—not applicable

Server Finding 5: Tolerance for diversity
    1—no effect
    2—positive
    3—negative
    8—not applicable

Server Finding 6: Satisfaction from serving
    1—no effect
    2—positive
    3—negative
    8—not applicable

Server Finding 7: Health
    1—no effect
    2—positive
    3—negative
    8—not applicable

Served Finding 1: Impacts on direct beneficiary
    1—no effect
    2—positive
    3—negative
    8—not applicable

Served Finding 2: Impacts on indirect beneficiary
    1—no effect
    2—positive
    3—negative
    8—not applicable

Served Finding 3:
    1—no effect
    2—positive
    3—negative
    8—not applicable

Institution Finding 1: Expand service
    1—no effect
    2—positive
    3—negative
    8—not applicable

Institution Finding 2: Improve quality of services
    1—no effect
    2—positive
    3—negative
    8—not applicable

Institution Finding 3: Create new institutions
    1—no effect
    2—positive
    3—negative
    8—not applicable

Community Finding 1: Community strengthening
    1—no effect
    2—positive
    3—negative
    8—not applicable

Community Finding 2: Benefit-cost
    1—no effect
    2—positive
    3—negative
    8—not applicable

Community Finding 3: Volunteer network/leveraging
    1—no effect
    2—positive
    3—negative
    8—not applicable

Notes:

Implementation

Implementation Issue 1: Program management
 1—yes
 2—no
\Implementation Issue 2: Executive leadership
 1—yes
 2—no

Implementation Issue 3: Training
 1—yes
 2—no

Implementation Issue 4: Program visibility/awareness
 1—yes
 2—no

Implementation Issue 5: Attrition/retention/recruitment
 1—yes
 2—no

Implementation Issue 6: Paperwork/administrative burdens
 1—yes
 2—no

Implementation Issue 7: Sponsoring agency
 1—yes
 2—no

Implementation Issue 8: Funding issues
 1—yes
 2—no

Notes:

Threats to Validity Scale

This is a count of threats to internal and statistical conclusion validity. The composite scale ranges from 0 to 10.

Table B.1

Threats to Validity Definitions

Threat to validity	Definition
History	External event between pretest and posttest that affects results
Maturation	Changes in subjects between pretest and posttest that affects results
Testing	Changes in posttest due to pretest
Instrumentation	Change in measure between pretest and posttest that affects results
Selection	Initial differences between treated and controls account for results
Ambiguity about the direction of causal inference	Inability to separate cause and effect common in cross-sectional and some retrospective studies
Low statistical power	Too few subjects to detect a difference
Violated assumptions of statistical tests	Inappropriate use of statistics
Fishing and error rate problem	Performing multiple analyses without adjusting the significance level or using sequential designs
Reliability of measures	Amount of error in the outcome or dependent measures

Appendix C

Civic Service Programs Included in the Synthesis

Civic service programs are incredibly diverse, encompassing a variety of time periods, programmatic goals, and identities. Because some of these programs may not be familiar to readers, brief descriptions of them are provided here, beginning with the oldest.

Civilian Conservation Corps

The Civilian Conservation Corps (CCC) was established in early 1933. Its mission was twofold: to reduce unemployment and to preserve natural resources. Projects focused on such activities as planting forests, creating flood control infrastructure, and preventing soil erosion. Within four months of its creation, the CCC enrolled 250,000 young men. At its peak in 1936, the CCC enrolled nearly 500,000.

The CCC administrative structure, created from existing departments, was complex. The U.S. Army ran the camps. The Departments of Interior and Agriculture were responsible for work projects and personnel to manage them. The Department of Labor selected enrollees with the help of local boards.

The CCC enrolled unemployed males between the ages of eighteen and twenty-five. The enrollment period was for six months with the opportunity to reenlist for another six months up to a maximum of two years. Each enrollee was paid $30 a month, of which $25 was sent to his family. The government provided room, board, clothing, and tools. The enrollee was expected to work a forty-hour week and to follow the camp rules. While serving in these camps, each enrollee was taught a new skill and could also attend classes to better his education.

American Friends Service Committee Work Camp

Riecken describes the work camp program of the American Friends Service Committee (AFSC) as "a society in microcosm—a group of assorted individuals who are gradually integrated in the course of a summer into a religiously centered community serving others."[1] Campers were typically college students or teachers who could devote two months to the experience. They received no pay and were required to cover their subsistence costs. Although the camps sought a heterogeneous group of volunteers, Riecken reports that the time commitments and costs confined participation largely to "middle and upper social classes, predominantly white Christian and Jewish groups."[2]

The activities of the work camps were a combination of physical labor and study and reflection about the conditions of the people and area where the camp was located. Among the projects pursued by the camps were installation of a water supply system near Greensburg, Pennsylvania, construction of Quonset huts on a Navajo reservation, repairing a school house in Crawford, Tennessee, and constructing and supervising playgrounds in racially diverse areas of Detroit and Chicago.

Volunteers in Service to America

Volunteers in Service to America (VISTA) was created in 1964 as part of the Johnson administration's "war on poverty" initiatives. Over the years, VISTA has had several organizational homes. It was originally part of the Office of Economic Opportunity. Later it was merged with the Peace Corps and other service programs in ACTION. In 1993, VISTA became part of the new Corporation for National and Community Service (CNCS) and is now known as AmeriCorps*VISTA.

VISTA's mission is to provide full-time volunteers for one year to local public and nonprofit organizations to assist them in alleviating poverty and poverty-related problems. Members work and live in the communities they serve. Projects are designed to create a working partnership among the project's sponsoring organization, the community, and the private sector. To sustain these projects, members focus on building community capacity, mobilizing private and public resources, and recruiting community volunteers.

Foster Grandparent Program

The Foster Grandparent Program (FGP) originated in 1965. It is a federally funded program authorized by the Domestic Volunteer Service Act of 1973 and reauthorized by the National and Community Service Act of 1993. Like other civic service programs originating in the 1960s, FGP has been housed in different parent organizations. CNCS now administers it as part of the National Senior Service Corps.

Foster grandparents must be age sixty or above and meet specified low-income requirements. The program provides opportunities for foster grandparents to develop ongoing relationships with children and youth who have exceptional or special needs. The FGP is designed to serve the dual purpose of being personally meaningful to the foster grandparents and providing support to the children served.

Senior Companion Program

The Senior Companion Program (SCP) has many parallels with the FGP. It, too, originated in the mid-1960s, was authorized as part of the Domestic Volunteer Service Act of 1973, and reauthorized by the National and Community Service Act of 1993. SCP, like FGP, is part of the National Senior Service Corps.

Where SCP differs from FGP is in its target population. The SCP is directed to providing support services to adults with special health, welfare, and social needs. Members help homebound clients with such tasks as paying bills and buying groceries. Senior companions serve twenty hours a week and receive the same stipend and insurance as foster grandparents.

Teacher Corps

The Teacher Corps evolved from separate bills introduced by Senators Gaylord Nelson of Wisconsin and Edward Kennedy of Massachusetts. It was subsequently authorized by the Higher Education Act of 1965 and administered through an affiliation of federal, state, and community agencies, universities, and public school systems. The Teacher Corps pursued an ambitious set of goals that sought to reform teacher development and engage the schools in urban communities.

The Teacher Corps program had two main components, divided between preservice and in-service activities. During preservice, interns took graduate education courses and observed schools and communities. The in-service component of the program consisted of university study, an internship in a poor school, and a service experience with poor children and their families.[3] The Teacher Corps was discontinued in 1982.

University Year for ACTION

In 1971, the newly created federal volunteer agency, ACTION, launched the University Year for ACTION (UYA) program. UYA provided grants to colleges and universities to permit students to serve full-time for a year in antipoverty projects. Students could simultaneously make normal progress toward a college degree. UYA members worked in diverse areas, among them health, criminal justice, education, and housing. One of the goals of UYA was to institutionalize service learning in university curricula. The program was discontinued in 1981.

Youth Community Service

The Youth Community Service (YCS) was a demonstration program initiated in 1978.[4] YCS was sponsored by ACTION through an interagency agreement with the U.S. Department of Labor. A local board of directors administered it. The demonstration lasted for two years, after which it was discontinued.

YCS offered unemployed out-of-school youth between sixteen and twenty-one an opportunity to spend a year as stipended community service volunteers, without regard to family income. Volunteers performed community service in projects that YCS staff developed with public agencies and nonprofit community organizations. YCS volunteers served in a wide variety of projects dealing with basic needs, such as health, education, conservation, recreation, community development, and housing.

Youth Conservation Corps

Congress authorized the Youth Conservation Corps (YCC) in 1970.[5] The first group of participants entered the YCC in summer 1971. The U.S. Departments of Agriculture and Interior administered YCC. YCC sought to increase participants' learning about the environment, complete conservation projects, and contribute to the personal development of participants.

Conservation camps were scattered throughout the United States and its territories. Most camps were structured as seven-day, residential experiences. Length of service varied from four to eight weeks. The size of camps also varied between eight and sixty corps members. Budget reductions in 1981 virtually eliminated YCC, but states picked up the idea.

Program for Local Service

The Program for Local Service (PLS) was an experimental volunteer program sponsored by ACTION. The program's primary attributes were that it recruited people from the general population and provided them with training and referral services for volunteer assignments at government or nonprofit antipoverty or social service agencies. Volunteers were paid a subsistence allowance for their full-time efforts for a period of a year. The program was discontinued but we are unable to identify exact dates.

California Conservation Corps

The most prominent conservation corps since the Depression is the California Conservation Corps. Governor Jerry Brown initiated it in 1976, and it has been supported by each of his successors. The program is state-funded.

The dual goals of the corps are to do useful work for the state of California and to provide service to the youth that enroll in it.[6] The useful-work goal is achieved primarily through natural resources and environment projects. Youth enrolled in the program receive meaningful education and work opportunities and on-the-job training. The corps imposes no means tests for enrollment, but high proportions of its members are educationally or economically disadvantaged.

Youth Conservation and Service Corps

This is actually a class of programs modeled after the Civilian Conservation Corps and the California Conservation Corps. They have been defined collectively as "a special class of social programs that promote the development of young people while they do useful work of real value to their communities."[7] Although the traditional corps engaged youth solely in physical work projects in rural or wilderness areas, the model has been transplanted to urban settings where corps members may do physical and human service work.

Among the more prominent urban variants of the conservation corps model are the San Francisco Conservation Corps (SFCC), the City Volunteer Corps (CVC), and the Marin Conservation Corps (MCC). The SFCC was the first urban, nonresidential youth corps.[8] The CVC, in New York City, pioneered adapting the corps model to human service work.[9] The Marin corps, which is also nonresidential, is unique in its twin emphasis on cost-reimbursable projects to fund the program and strong skills training for corps members.[10]

City Year

City Year is a team-based service program that operates in thirteen sites nationwide. It was founded as a privately funded corps in Boston in 1988. City Year's goals are to perform meaningful community service, break down barriers among races and classes, and inspire young people to become engaged civically.

Members serve forty hours a week in their communities, rehabilitating houses, staffing community centers, and working with elderly and homeless people. Members must adhere to standards of conduct, uniform dress, punctuality, attendance, and physical training. They are also required to participate in acts of citizenship—registering to vote, getting certified in first aid and cardiopulmonary resuscitation, and obtaining library cards. They receive a subsistence stipend during their service. Many also receive an education award if they complete their term of service.

Georgia Peach Corps

The Georgia Peach Corps was created through a national demonstration grant under the National and Community Service Act of 1990.[11] The program was designed to test the feasibility of a full-time, rural service program. The corps operated in two counties, responding to needs identified by a local steering committee. It used intergenerational crews that rotated through a variety of service sites. Service learning was an integral feature of the design. The program ended in 1994.

Public Allies

Public Allies is a national nonprofit operating in nine communities that combines community service with youth leadership development. Public Allies targets young people ages eighteen to thirty for intensive leadership training and apprenticeship in a community organization. Allies receive a living allowance, health and child care benefits, and an educational award. The leadership training emphasizes skills such as conflict resolution, identifying community assets, critical thinking, and personal responsibility and accountability.

AmeriCorps*State/National

AmeriCorps*State/National was authorized by the National and Community Service Trust Act of 1993.[12] It is community-based, designed to respond to local needs and concerns. AmeriCorps*State/National funding flows through several channels to support community service programs. State community service programs receive a third of the funds according to a population-based formula. At least another third of the funding goes to state commissions for programs that they submit to the federal agency CNSC for competitive consideration. National nonprofits are eligible for grants to programs operating in more than one state. In addition, 2 percent of AmeriCorps grant funds are set aside for Indian tribes and U.S. territories.

AmeriCorps*State/National provides full- and part-time opportunities for community service in four broad areas of activity: education, public safety, environment, and other human needs. Members receive an education award when they complete 1,700 hours of full-time service. Part-time members must complete 900 hours of service to receive half the amount of the education award. In addition to the education award, members receive a small living allowance and health insurance as well as child care assistance for those who qualify for such support.

AmeriCorps*National Civilian Community Corps

AmeriCorps*National Civilian Community Corps (NCCC), a full-time residential service program, was proposed by a bipartisan group of senators in 1991. It was enacted into law in 1993 and launched in 1994.

Members serve for ten months on a wide range of team-based service projects in collaboration with local sponsors. Projects focus on environmental activities, education, human needs, and disaster response, with many of them situated in low-income communities. Project sponsors include nonprofit community-based and national organizations, park services, educational institutions, and state and local governments. Service learning is integrated into the projects and member development.

Summer of Safety

The Summer of Safety (SOS) was a one-summer special program initiated in conjunction with the start-up of CNCS. CNCS allocated $10 million to support ninety-one local programs in which more than seven thousand people participated. Some of the programs were small, community-based efforts. Others were larger, sometimes involving an array of projects organized by a regional coalition.

SOS represented the spectrum of CNCS programs. Learn and Serve America sponsored eight programs involving youth from kindergarten through high school. Twenty of the programs were initiatives of National Senior Service Corps (the new umbrella designation for Foster Grandparents, Senior Companions, and the Retired and Senior Volunteer Program (RSVP), which had been founded many years earlier). The bulk of the ninety-one programs, sixty-two altogether, were AmeriCorps. They included thirty-one AmeriCorps*VISTA, seventeen national direct, fourteen youth corps grants for eighteen- to twenty-five-year-olds, and the National Civilian Community Corps for youth fourteen to seventeen.

Experience Corps

The Experience Corps began in early 1996 as an eighteen-month pilot to connect the talent and skills of older adults with the needs of low-income children in inner-city public elementary schools.[13] Twelve schools in five cities participated in the pilot: Philadelphia; Minneapolis; Portland, Oregon; Port Arthur, Texas; and the South Bronx in New York City. New public and private funds kept Experience Corps operating in all five sites at the conclusion of the pilot.

The program was created through a collaboration of Public/Private Ventures, a nonprofit whose mission is to develop disadvantaged children and youth; Johns Hopkins University; and CNCS. The Foster Grandparent Program and RSVP, both arms of the National Senior Service Corps in CNCS, ran the local programs.

Seniors for Schools

Seniors for Schools is a national demonstration conducted by CNCS.[14] Its goal, like that of Experience Corps, is to marshal the talents of older volunteers to help children to read independently by the end of the third grade. Nine Seniors for Schools sites operate around the nation, in Florida, Massachusetts, Missouri, New York, Ohio, Oregon, Pennsylvania, and Texas. Senior volunteers are recruited, trained, and placed in elementary schools to provide literacy services, including tutoring in reading to students in primary grades.

Notes

Notes to Introduction

1. President George W. Bush, inaugural address, January 20, 2001; available at www.2001inaugural.com/2001-inaugural-address.html (January 25, 2003).

2. Corporation for National and Community Service, "Press Release: July 16, 2002"; available at www.cns.gov/news/pr/071602.html (January 25, 2003).

3. Michael Sherraden, "Civic Service: Issues, Outlook, Institution Building" (paper presented at the Biennial Conference of the Inter-University Seminar on Armed Forces and Society, Baltimore, MD, October 19–21, 2001), p. 8.

4. Richard Danzig and Peter Szanton, *National Service: What Would It Mean?* (Lexington, MA: Lexington Books, D.C. Heath, 1986), p. 10.

5. Michael Sherraden and Donald Eberly, eds., *National Service: Social, Economic, and Military Impacts* (New York: Pergamon Press, 1982), p. 3.

6. Grantmaker Forum on Community and National Service, *The State of Service-Related Research* (Berkeley, CA: Grantmaker Forum on Community and National Service, 2000).

7. Ibid., pp. 15–16.

8. Nowhere is this more apparent than in the expansive statutory language of the National and Community Service Trust Act of 1993. National service is defined as a means to

(1) meet the unmet human, educational, environmental, and public safety needs of the United States. . . ;

(2) renew the ethic of civic responsibility and the spirit of community. . . ;

(3) expand educational opportunity by rewarding individuals who participate in national service with an increased ability to pursue higher education or job training;

(4) encourage citizens of the United States . . . to engage in full-time or part-time national service;

(5) reinvent government to eliminate duplication, support locally established initiatives, require measurable goals for performance, and offer flexibility in meeting those goals;

(6) expand and strengthen existing service programs . . . ;

(7) build on the existing organizational service infrastructure of Federal, State, and local programs and agencies to expand . . . service opportunities for all citizens; and

(8) provide tangible benefits to the communities in which national service is performed (see "Public Law 103–82: National and Community Service Trust Act of 1993" (107 Stat. 785; September 21, 1993). Text from: *United States Public Laws*. Available from LexisNexis Congressional (Bethesda, MD: Congressional Information Service).

9. Sherraden, "Civic Service," p. 5.

10. Sherraden and Eberly, *National Service*, p. 3.

11. This argument is not new to Sherraden. See also Charles C. Moskos, *A Call to Civic Service: National Service for Country and Community* (New York: Free Press, 1988).

12. Sherraden, "Civic Service," p. 5.

13. The Global Service Institute at the Center for Social Development, Washington University, St. Louis, Missouri, defines civic service as "an organized period of substantial engagement and contribution to the local, national, or world community, recognized and valued by society, with minimal monetary compensation to the participant" (available at www.gwbweb.wustl.edu/csd/gsi/ [January 25, 2003]). These key dimensions are also closely related to dimensions identified by earlier scholars in the field such as Charles Moskos, who defines national service as "the full-time undertaking of public duties by young people—whether as citizen soldiers or civilian servers—who are paid subsistence wages" (*A Call to Civic Service*, p. 1), and Richard Danzig and Peter Szanton, who conclude that "national service is a federally supported program in which, for a period of time, participants sacrifice some degree of personal advancement, income, or freedom to serve a public interest" (*National Service*, p. 10).

14. Danzig and Szanton, *National Service*, p. 7.

15. For an excellent discussion of the state of the national service field, see James L. Perry and Mark T. Imperial, "A Decade of Service-Related Research," *Nonprofit and Voluntary Sector Quarterly* 30, no. 3 (2001): 462–79; see also Grantmaker Forum on Community and National Service, *The State of Service-Related Research*, p. 16.

16. William James, "The Moral Equivalent of War," International Conciliation, no. 27 (1910): 3–20; Morris Janowitz, *The Reconstruction of Patriotism: Education for Civic Consciousness* (Chicago: University of Chicago Press, 1983); Charles C. Moskos, *A Call to Civic Service*; and William F. Buckley Jr., *Gratitude: Reflections on What We Owe to Our Country* (New York: Random House, 1990).

17. Danzig and Szanton, *National Service*.

18. Janowitz, *Reconstruction of Patriotism*.

19. Danzig and Szanton are forthright about the limitations of their policy scenario approach. They conclude: "[Our] answers to the questions we pose, like any assertions about the future, amount to no more than informed speculation" (*National Service*, p. xi).

20. Research synthesis is intended, in the words of one analyst, to "replace those papers that have been lost from sight behind the research front." Derek J. de Solla Price, "Networks of Scientific Papers," *Science* 149 (1965): 56–64, as quoted in Harris Cooper and Larry V. Hedges, "Research Synthesis as a Scientific Enterprise," in *The Handbook of Research Synthesis*, ed. Harris Cooper and Larry V. Hedges (New York: Russell Sage Foundation, 1994).

21. Perry and Imperial, "A Decade of Service-Related Research," p. 476.

22. Grantmaker Forum on Community and National Service, *State of Service-Related Research*, pp. 15–17.

23. Cooper and Hedges, "Introduction," in *The Handbook of Research Synthesis*, p. 5.

24. Thomas D. Cook et al., *Meta-Analysis for Explanation* (New York: Russell Sage Foundation, 1992), p. 3.

25. Jeffrey L. Pressman and Aaron Wildavsky, *Implementation: How Great Expectations Are Dashed in Oakland* (Berkeley: University of California Press, 1984).

26. Moskos, *A Call to Civic Service*, p. 2.

Part I. Ideological and Historical Context

Notes to Chapter 1

1. William James, "The Moral Equivalent of War" International Conciliation, no. 27, p. 15.

2. For an excellent discussion of the conceptual and theoretical perspectives on civic virtue, see David K. Hart, "The Virtuous Citizen, the Honorable Bureaucrat, and 'Public' Administration," *Public Administration Review* 47 (March 1984): 111–20.

3. Ibid., 113.

4. James A. Morone, *The Democratic Wish: Popular Participation and the Limits of American Government* (New Haven, CT: Yale University Press, 1990), p. 1.

5. For detailed description of these two perspectives, see Benjamin R. Barber, *Strong Democracy: Participatory Politics for a New Age* (Berkeley, CA: University of California Press, 1984), and Morone, *Democratic Wish*. "Classic liberal democracy" is meant to refer to a particular political system characterized by three dominant dispositions: anarchist, realist, and minimalist. "The American political system," writes Barber,

> is a remarkable example of the co-existence—sometimes harmonious, more often uncomfortable—of all three dispositions. Americans, we might say, are anarchists in their values (privacy, liberty, individualism, property, and rights); realists in their means (power, law, coercive mediation, and sovereign adjudication); and minimalists in their political temper (tolerance, wariness of government, pluralism, and such institutionalizations of caution as the separation of powers and judicial review). (*Strong Democracy*, p. 5)

Morone best explains classic republicanism. "In the republican view," he writes,

> the colonial and Revolutionary ideal lay, not in the pursuit of private matters, but in the shared public life of civic duty, in the subordination of individual interests to the *res publica*. Citizens were defined and fulfilled by participation in political community [which to the first American generation was] a single organic whole, binding each of its members into a civic body of shared interests that transcended individual concerns. [Rather] than institutions framed to harness self-interest, the [classic republicans] see a social vision that demanded (and fostered) virtue in its citizens. [Here] is an image of a virtuous, united people, bound together by a shared public good, active in civic affairs,

and populating rural communities outside historical time. (*Democratic Wish*, p. 16)

6. Morone, *Democratic Wish*, pp. 9–13.

7. In "The Virtuous Citizen," Hart identifies the following characteristics of the "virtuous citizen": the capacity for "doing" moral philosophy, belief in American regime values, individual moral responsibility, and civility (pp. 114–16).

8. Office of the Federal Register, "Remarks on National Service at Rutgers University in New Brunswick, March 1, 1993," in Weekly Compilation of President Presidential Documents, Monday, March 8, 1993, Volume 29–Number 9 (Washington, DC: National Achives and Records Administration, p. 341).

9. For a fascinating legislative history of the passage of the National and Community Trust Act of 1993, see Steven Waldman, *The Bill: How the Adventures of Clinton's National Service Bill Reveal What Is Corrupt, Comic, Cynical—and Noble—About Washington* (New York: Viking, 1995).

10. Hart, "Virtuous Citizen," p. 113.

11. Morris Janowitz "Sociological Theory and Social Control," *American Journal of Sociology* 81, Issue 1 (1975): 82, 86.

12. Morris Janowitz, *The Reconstruction of Patriotism: Education for Civic Consciousness* (Chicago: The University of Chicago Press, 1983) pp. xi–xii, 195, 203.

13. Charles C. Moskos, *A Call to Civic Service: National Service for Country and Community* (New York: Free Press, 1988), p. 181.

14. Ibid., p. 146.

15. Ibid., p. 181.

16. Ibid., p. 166.

17. Ibid., p. 181.

18. Richard Danzig and Peter Szanton, *National Service: What Would It Mean?* (Lexington, MA: Lexington Books, D.C. Heath, 1986), p. 9.

19. Morone, *Democratic Wish*.

20. Moskos, *A Call to Civic Service*, pp. 37–38.

21. In 1990, President George H.W. Bush signed into law the National and Community Service Act of 1990, which created the Commission on National and Community Service and provided funding for certain community-based programs and a national nonprofit organization, the Points of Light Foundation, whose purpose is to promote private voluntarism. This act set the stage for the commission's 1993 report, *What You Can Do For Your Country*, which helped in the development of the National and Community Service Trust Act of 1993 (P.L. 103–82), signed into law by President Clinton on September 21, 1993. Under this law, a new agency was created—the Corporation for National and Community Service—an umbrella agency that houses all domestic national service programs in the United States and Clinton's signature program, AmeriCorps.

22. Laurence J. O'Toole, "Treating Networks Seriously: Practical and Research-Based Agendas in Public Administration," *Public Administration Review* 57, no. 1 (1997): 45–52; see also Walter W. Powell, "Neither Market Nor Hierarchy: Network Forms of Organization," *Research in Organizational Behavior* 12 (1990): 295–336.

23. Horst W.J. Rittel and Melvin Webber coined this phrase in their article "Dilemmas in a General Theory of Planning," *Policy Sciences* 4 (June 1973): 155–69.

24. See Barber, *Strong Democracy*; Michael J. Sandel, *Democracy's Discontent: America in Search of a Public Philosophy* (Cambridge, MA: Harvard University Press, 1996); Amitai Etzioni, *An Immodest Agenda: Rebuilding America Before the 21st*

Century (New York: New Press, 1983); Michael W. Sherraden and Donald J. Eberly, eds., *National Service: Social, Economic, and Military Impacts* (New York: Pergamon Press, 1982); Morris Janowitz, *The Reconstruction of Patriotism: Education for Civic Consciousness* (Chicago: University of Chicago Press, 1983).

25. Morone, *Democratic Wish*, pp. 9, 13, 334.

Notes to Chapter 2

1. James A. Morone, *The Democratic Wish: Popular Participation and the Limits of American Government* (New Haven, CT: Yale University Press, 1990), p. 13.

2. Barry Checkoway, "Institutional Impacts of AmeriCorps on the University of Michigan," *Journal of Public Service and Outreach* 2, no. 1 (1997): 70–79.

3. For a thorough understanding of the CCC, see Edwin G. Hill, *In the Shadow of the Mountain: The Spirit of the CCC* (Pullman: Washington State University Press, 1990); see also Michael W. Sherraden, "The Civilian Conservation Corps: Effectiveness of the Camps" (Ph.D. diss., University of Michigan, 1979).

4. Hill, *In the Shadow of the Mountain.*

5. Ibid.

6. Sherraden, "The Civilian Conservation Corps."

7. Morris Janowitz, *The Reconstruction of Patriotism: Education for Civic Consciousness* (Chicago: University of Chicago Press, 1983), pp. 173, 176.

8. Booz Allen, Public Administration Services, Inc., *Cost-Benefit Study of the Foster Grandparent Program* (Washington, DC: ACTION 1972), p. 1.

9. Ronald G. Corwin, *Reform and Organizational Survival: The Teacher Corps as an Instrument of Educational Change* (New York: Wiley, 1973), p. 2.

10. Corwin, *Reform and Organizational Survival.*

11. For an interesting popular discussion of Earth Day, see the well-organized EnviroLink Resource Guide Web site www.envirolink.org (January 25, 2003); see also Senator Gaylord Nelson, "How the First Earth Day Came About"; available at earthday.envirolink.org/history.html (July 28, 2002).

12. "Public Law 91–378: Youth Conservation Corps, Establishment" (84 Stat. 794; August 13, 1970). Text from *Statutes at Large.* Available from LexisNexis Congressional (Bethesda, MD: Congressional Information Service).

13. Wendy C. Wolf, Sally Leiderman, and Richard Voith, *The California Conservation Corps: An Analysis of Short-Term Impacts on Participants* (Philadelphia: Public/Private Ventures, 1987).

14. Ibid., pp. 1, 7.

15. Ibid.

16. See National Association of Service and Conservation Corps, "History of the Youth Corps Movement"; available at www.nascc.org/history2.shtml (January 25, 2003).

17. Shirley Sagawa, *Ten Years of Youth in Service to America* (Washington, DC: American Youth Policy Forum, 1998), p. 2.

18. For a fascinating history and discussion of City Year, see City Year, "About City Year: History"; available at www.cityyear.org/about/history.cfm# (January 25, 2003); see also Suzanne Goldsmith, *A City Year: On the Streets and in the Neighborhoods with Twelve Young Community Service Volunteers* (New York: New Press, 1993).

19. Sagawa, *Ten Years of Youth in Service to America,* p. 3.

20. Ibid.

21. The Corporation for National and Community Service was envisioned as a model federal agency for the reinventing government movement. Early on, the corporation made a point of emphasizing its role as catalytic, innovative, entrepreneurial, and fostering partnerships; competition, decentralization, and results-oriented service were central to the corporation's mission. For a discussion of these issues, see Leslie Lenkowsky and James L. Perry, "Reinventing Government: The Case of National Service," *Public Administration Review* 60, no. 4 (2000): 298–307.

22. Shirley Sagawa and Eli Segal, *Common Interest, Common Good: Creating Value Through Business and Social Sector Partnerships* (Boston: Harvard Business School Press, 2000), p. i.

23. Steven Waldman, *The Bill: How the Adventures of Clinton's National Service Bill Reveal What Is Corrupt, Comic, Cynical—and Noble—About Washington* (New York: Viking, 1995), p. 11.

24. Corporation for National Service, *Principles for High Quality National Service Programs* (Washington, DC: Corporation for National Service, 1994), p. 1.

25. James L. Perry et al., "Inside a Swiss Army Knife: An Assessment of AmeriCorps," *Journal of Public Administration Research and Theory* 9, no. 2 (1999): 230.

26. For a detailed description of this new association, see American Association of State Service Commissions, "America's Service Commissions" available at www.asc-online.org (January 25, 2003).

27. For links to a large number of other organizations devoted to service, volunteerism, and research, see the CNCS Web site www.cns.gov (January 25, 2003).

28. This information was obtained through America's Service Commissions, "Legislative Alert," November 7, 2001, Distribution list (http://AskUs@ASC-online.org; accessed November 7, 2001).

29. The broad categories of reform addressed in the Citizen Service Act of 2002 are to: (1) support and encourage greater engagement of citizens in volunteering, (2) make federal funds more responsive to state and local needs, (3) make federal support more accountable and effective, and (4) provide greater assistance to secular and faith-based community organizations. For a detailed description of the principles and reforms instituted by the Citizen Service Act, see CNCS, "About Us: Principles" and "Reforms For a Citizen Service Act"; available at www.nationalservice.org/about/principles/principles_reforms.html (January 25, 2003).

30. Ibid.

31. For a complete description and history of the USA Freedom Corps, see USA Freedom Corps Annual Report 2002; available at www.usafreedomcorps.gov/pdfs/annual_report.pdf (January 2003).

32. For a detailed description of the civic service programs presented in this chapter, and many more also created during the four policy cycles, see Appendix C.

33. William F. Buckley Jr., *Gratitude: Reflections on What We Owe to Our Country* (New York: Random House, 1990), pp. 22, 25–26.

34. Ibid., p. 25.

Part II. Evidence and Methods

Notes to Chapter 3

1. Harris Cooper and Larry V. Hedges, "Research Synthesis as a Scientific Enterprise," in *The Handbook of Research Synthesis*, ed. Harris Cooper and Larry V. Hedges (New York: Russell Sage Foundation, 1994), p. 4.

2. Ibid.

3. J.A. Hall et al., "Hypotheses and Problems in Research Synthesis," in *The Handbook of Research Synthesis*, ed. Harris Cooper and Larry V. Hedges (New York: Russell Sage Foundation), p. 21.

4. Cooper and Hedges, "Research Synthesis as a Scientific Enterprise," p. 11.

5. Hall et al., "Hypotheses and Problems in Research Synthesis," p. 27.

6. See James L. Perry and Mark T. Imperial, "A Decade of Service-Related Research: A Map of the Field," *Nonprofit and Voluntary Sector Quarterly* 30, no. 3 (2001): 462–79; see also James L. Perry et al., *A Review of Service Related Research 1990–1999: A Report to the Grantmaker Forum Research Task Force* (Bloomington, IN: Indiana University, 1999). This *Review* includes more detailed and technical information than that contained in the report of the Grantmaker Forum on Community and National Service, *The State of Service-Related Research* (Berkeley, CA: Grantmaker Forum on Community and National Service, 2000).

7. On success bias in civic service research, Perry and Imperial write, "[This] success bias is understandable given the interests of program leaders in sharing success stories with others committed to service and of journals and other outlets in publishing research about successful interventions rather than failures, [but] often, more can be learned from examining programs that vary in their levels of success" ("A Decade of Service-Related Research," pp. 475–76).

8. James L. Perry and Ann Marie Thomson, *Building Communities Through AmeriCorps: Final Report* (Bloomington: Indiana University, August 26, 1997), p. 7.

9. Ibid.

10. Corporation for National Service, *Annual Performance Plan for Fiscal 1999* (Washington, DC: Corporation for National Service, 1998), p. 29.

11. For an excellent discussion on evaluating effectiveness, see Hal G. Rainey, *Understanding and Managing Public Organizations* (San Francisco: Jossey-Bass, 1991), pp. 207–22, p. 214, Table 9.1.

12. Laurence E. Lynn Jr., *Public Management as Art, Science, and Profession* (Chatham, NJ: Chatham House, 1996), p. 97.

13. Charles C. Ragin, *The Comparative Method: Moving Beyond Qualitative and Quantitative Strategies* (Berkeley: University of California Press, 1987), p. xiv.

14. Lynn, *Public Management as Art, Science, and Profession*, pp. 165, 164–65. At the end of this statement, Lynn cites Sam E. Overman and Kathy J. Boyd, "Best Practices Research and Post-Bureaucratic Reform," *Journal of Public Administration Research and Theory* 4, no. 1 (1994): 67–83.

15. Hall et al., "Hypotheses and Problems in Research Synthesis," p. 27.

16. Ibid., pp. 18–19.

Notes to Chapter 4

1. Harris Cooper and Larry V. Hedges, "Summary," in *The Handbook of Research Synthesis*, ed. Harris Cooper and Larry V. Hedges (New York: Russell Sage Foundation, 1994), p. 522.

2. Michael W. Sherraden and Donald J. Eberly, eds., *National Service: Social, Economic, and Military Impacts* (New York: Pergamon Press, 1982), p. 3.

3. Citing examples like the development of the public education system and the Civilian Conservation Corps, Sherraden argues that purposeful institutional change can occur not only when economic and social forces are right, but when individuals

take "it upon themselves to put something new in place." Michael W. Sherraden, "Civic Service: Issues, Outlook, Institution Building" (paper presented at the Biennial Conference of the Inter-University Seminar on Armed Forces and Society, Baltimore, MD, October 19–21, 2001), pp. 7–9.

4. Ibid., p. 8.

5. James L. Perry and Michael C. Katula, "Does Service Affect Citizenship?" *Administration & Society* 33, no. 3 (July 2001): 330–65; Shelley H. Billig, *Learning in Deed: The Impacts of Service Learning on Youth, Schools, and Communities: Research on K Through 12 School-Based Service Learning, 1990 to 1999* (Missoula: University of Montana–Volunteer Action Services Monograph, 1999); Susan M. Anderson, "Service Learning: A National Strategy for Youth Development" (New York: New York University, 1998). The last reference is to a position paper issued by the Education Policy Task Force, Institute for Communitarian Policy Studies, and George Washington University. It is based in part on the Task Force on Service Learning and Community Service, Conference on Character Building sponsored by the Communitarian Network, the White House, and Congress, June 12, 1997 (Chair, Susan M. Anderson), and on a related workshop conducted at the New England Conference on Community Service Learning, November 18, 1997 (co-led by Don Ernst, Association of Supervision and Curriculum Development).

6. Ram A. Cnaan, Femida Handy, and Margaret Wadsworth, "Defining Who Is a Volunteer: Conceptual and Empirical Considerations," *Nonprofit and Voluntary Sector Quarterly* 25, no. 3 (1996): 364–83.

7. William S. Trochim, "Guttman Scaling," in *Research Methods Knowledge Base*; available at http://trochim/human.cornell.edu/kb/scalgutt.htm (January 25, 2003). *The Research Methods Knowledge Base* is a Web-based social research methods textbook by William S. Trochim. See also Earl Babbie, *Survey Research Methods*, 2d ed. (Belmont, CA: Wadsworth, 1990), pp. 167–70. Babbie describes Guttman scaling in this way: "[Guttman] scaling is based on the fact that some items under consideration might prove to be 'harder' indicators of the variable than others. Respondents who accept a given hard item also accept the easier ones. If such a structure appears in the data under examination, we might say that the items form a Guttman Scale" (p. 167).

8. Linda Forsyth, personal communication, November 1999.

9. Charles C. Moskos, *A Call to Civic Service: National Service for Country and Community* (New York: Free Press, 1988), p. 2.

10. Ibid.

11. These attributes include and expand upon the five key dimensions we use to define civic service in the introduction of this book: (1) a substantial commitment beyond oneself, (2) with minimal monetary reward, (3) for a defined but prolonged length of time, (4) that contributes to the benefit of local, national, and/or global communities, (5) through formal organizational structures and programs.

12. Paul M. Wortman, "Judging Research Quality," in *The Handbook of Research Synthesis*, ed. Harris Cooper and Larry V. Hedges (New York: Russell Sage Foundation, 1994) pp. 97–109.

13. See, for example, Henry Riecken's *The Volunteer Work Camp: A Psychological Evaluation* (Cambridge, MA: Addison-Wesley, 1952).

14. Wortman, "Judging Research Quality."

15. Earl Babbie, *The Practice of Social Research*, 7th ed. (Belmont, CA: Wadsworth, 1995), p. 106.

16. Babbie, *Survey Research Methods*, p. 133.

17. For an in-depth discussion of threats to validity, Thomas Cook and Donald Campbell's 1979 book on quasi-experimentation still stands as one of the best. See Thomas D. Cook and Donald T. Campbell, *Quasi-Experimentation: Design and Analysis Issues for Field Settings* (Boston: Houghton Mifflin, 1979), pp. 37–91; see also George E. Matt and Thomas D. Cook, "Threats to the Validity of Research Synthesis," in *The Handbook of Research Synthesis*, ed. Harris Cooper and Larry V. Hedges (New York,: Russell Sage Foundation, 1994), pp. 503–20.

18. For more detailed description of the methodology, see Appendices A–C.

19. Wortman, "Judging Research Quality," pp. 101–2.

20. Cooper and Hedges, "Summary," p. 527.

21. Ibid, p. 528. Cooper and Hedges cite Kenneth Strike and George Posner, "Types of Syntheses and Their Criteria," in *Knowledge Structure and Use: Implications for Synthesis and Interpretation*, ed. Spencer Ward and Linda Reed (Philadelphia: Temple University Press, 1983), when they discuss criteria for determining what makes research synthesis valuable.

Part III. Research Synthesis Findings

Notes to Chapter 5

1. Henry W. Riecken, *The Volunteer Work Camp: A Psychological Evaluation* (Cambridge, MA: Addison-Wesley, 1952).

2. Macro International, *Evaluation of DC Reads Book Partners Program: Year 1 Final External Report* (Washington, DC: Macro International, 1998), and *Evaluation of DC Reads: Year Two Final Report* (Washington, DC: Macro International, 2000).

3. Susan Bartlett, Reva Gold, and Julie Masker, *Case Studies of Selected Summer Youth Corps Programs (Report 1 of 2)* (Washington, DC: Corporation for National Service, 1993); Alvia Branch, Sally Leiderman, and Thomas J. Smith, *Youth Conservation and Service Corps: Findings from a National Assessment* (Philadelphia: Public/Private Ventures, 1987); JoAnn Jastrzab et al., *Impacts of Service: Final Report on the Evaluation of American Conservation and Youth Service Corps* (Cambridge, MA: Abt Associates, 1996); and John C. Scott, B.L. Driver, and Robert W. Marans, *Toward Environmental Understanding: An Evaluation of the 1972 Youth Conservation Corps* (Ann Arbor, MI: Institute for Social Research, 1973).

4. Marc Freedman and Linda Fried, *Launching Experience Corps* (Oakland, CA: Civic Ventures, 1999).

5. ACTION, *An Evaluation Report on the Volunteers in Service to America Summer Associates Program* (Washington, DC: Corporation for National and Community Service and ACTION, 1993); and Development Associates, Inc., *An Evaluation Report on Volunteers in Service to America* (Washington, DC: ACTION, Office of Policy, Research and Evaluation, Program Analysis and Evaluation Division, 1993).

6. ACTION, *University Year for ACTION: An Evaluation* (Washington, DC: Office of Policy and Planning, Evaluation Division, 1973); and American University School of Education, *Evaluation of University Year for ACTION* (Washington, DC: ACTION, 1975).

7. Katheryn L. Volle and Jamie P. Merisotis, *Public Allies: An Alumni Survey* (Washington, DC: Institute for Higher Education Policy, 1997).

8. U.S. General Accounting Office, *Assessment of the Teacher Corps Program* (Washington, DC: General Accounting Office, 1972); *Assessment of the Teacher Corps Program at the University of Southern California and Participating Schools in Tulare County Serving Rural-Migrant Children* (Washington, DC: General Accounting Office, 1971); and Ronald B. Corwin, *Reform and Organizational Survival: The Teacher Corps as an Instrument of Educational Change* (New York: Wiley, 1973).

9. J.W. Frees et al., *Final Report: National Service Demonstration Programs (Subtitle D)* (Cambridge, MA: Abt Associates, 1995).

10. Colleen Yvette Griffiths, *The Impact of Service: An Exploration of the Characteristics of Volunteer Tutors in the AmeriCorps for Math and Literacy Program and the Benefits They Gained From Service* (Columbus: Ohio State University, 1998); Harder+Company Community Research, *Getting Good Things Done in Northern California: A Comprehensive Assessment of Northern California Grantmakers' National Service Task Force-Funded AmeriCorps Program* (San Francisco: Northern California Grantmakers, 1998); Catherine Paglin et al., *A Close Look at Four AmeriCorps Programs in the Pacific Northwest (Oregon, Washington, Montana, and Idaho)* (Portland, OR: Northwest Regional Educational Laboratory, 1999); Phillip David Sherwood, "The Development of At Risk Young Adults: The California Conservation Corps Experience 1987 to 1995" (D.P.A. diss., University of Southern California, 1996); Robert D. Shumer and Jane Maland Cady, *YouthWorks AmeriCorps Evaluation: Second Year Report 1995–1996* (Minneapolis: University of Minnesota, 1997); Robert D. Shumer and Kathryn Rentel, *YouthWorks AmeriCorps Evaluation: Third Year Report 1996–1997* (Minneapolis: University of Minnesota, 1998); Changhua Wang, *Montana AmeriCorps*State Programs 1996–1997* (Portland, OR: Northwest Regional Educational Laboratory, 1998), *Oregon AmeriCorps*State Programs 1996–1997* (Portland, OR: Northwest Regional Educational Laboratory, 1998), *Washington AmeriCorps*State Programs 1996–1997* (Portland, OR: Northwest Regional Educational Laboratory, 1998), and *Report on Results of Northwest Former AmeriCorps Members Survey* (Portland, OR: Northwest Regional Educational Laboratory, 1999).

11. Aguirre International, *AmeriCorps State/National Programs Impact Evaluation: First Year Report* (San Mateo, CA: Aguirre International, 1997), and *Making a Difference: Impact of AmeriCorps*State/National Direct on Members and Communities 1994–95 and 1995–96* (San Mateo, CA: Aguirre International, 1999).

12. Education for the Future, *AmeriCorps Watershed Project: Project Evaluation Summary Year End 1995–96* (Chico, CA: Education for the Future, n.d.); and Susan Alice Hicks, "AmeriCorps and the North Carolina Child Care Corps: A Mechanism for Addressing the Child Care Crisis" (Ph.D. diss., University of North Carolina at Greensboro, 1997).

13. Westat, *AmeriCorps*NCCC: Analysis of Responses to the Class Two Exit Survey* (Rockville, MD: Westat, 1996).

14. Corwin, *Reform and Organizational Survival*.

15. Aguirre International, *Making a Difference*.

16. Ibid.

17. Susan Bartlett and Erik Beecroft, *Educational Impacts of Summer 1993 Washington Service Teams* (Washington, DC: Corporation for National Service, 1995); Jean Grossman and Joseph P. Tierney, "The Fallibility of Comparison Groups," *Evaluation Review* 17, no. 5 (October 1993): 556–71; Robert W. Marans, B.L. Driver, and John C. Scott, *Youth and the Environment: An Evaluation of the 1971 Youth Conservation Corps* (Ann Arbor, MI: Institute for Social Research, 1972); Robert Austin

Pence, "Organizational Context and Young Adult Education in an Urban Service Corps" (Ph.D. diss., University of Wisconsin, Madison, 1996); and Wendy C. Wolf, Sally Leiderman, and Richard Voith, *The California Conservation Corps: An Analysis of Short-Term Impacts on Participants* (Philadelphia: Public/Private Ventures, 1987).

18. Pence, "Organizational Context and Young Adult Education."

19. Bartlett and Beecroft, *Educational Impacts*.

20. Grossman and Tierney, "Fallibility of Comparison Groups."

21. Wolf, Leiderman, and Voith, *California Conservation Corps*.

22. Scott, Driver, and Marans, *Toward Environmental Understanding*.

23. Wolf, Leiderman, and Voith, *California Conservation Corps*, p. iii.

24. Michael Sherraden, "The Civilian Conservation Corps: Effectiveness of the Camps" (Ph.D. diss., University of Michigan, 1979).

25. Bartlett and Beecroft, *Educational Impacts*.

26. Wolf, Leiderman, and Voith, *California Conservation Corps*.

27. Michael J. Sandel, *Democracy's Discontent: America in Search of a Public Philosophy* (Cambridge, MA: Harvard University Press, 1996).

28. Riecken, *Volunteer Work Camp*.

29. Aguirre International, *AmeriCorps State/National Programs Impact Evaluation* and *Making a Difference*.

30. Education for the Future, *AmeriCorps Watershed Project*; Harder+Company, *Getting Good Things Done in Northern California*; Paglin et al., *A Close Look*; Christopher A. Simon and Changhua Wang, *Impact of AmeriCorps on Members' Political and Social Efficacy, Social Trust, Institutional Confidence, and Values in Idaho, Montana, Oregon, and Washington* (Portland, OR: Northwest Regional Educational Laboratory, 1999); and Wang, *Report on Results*.

31. Development Associates, *An Evaluation Report on Volunteers in Service to America*.

32. Lynne Ford, *Youth Volunteer Corps of America Final Evaluation Report* (Charleston, SC: College of Charleston, 1994).

33. Westat, *AmeriCorps*NCCC*.

34. Volle and Merisotis, *Public Allies*.

35. Frees et al., *Final Report*.

36. Riecken, *Volunteer Work Camp*.

37. Ford, *Youth Volunteer Corps of America*.

38. Ford, *Youth Volunteer Corps of America*; and Harder+Company, *Getting Good Things Done in Northern California*.

39. Aguirre International, *AmeriCorps State/National Programs Impact Evaluation* and *Making a Difference*.

40. Development Associates, *An Evaluation Report on Volunteers in Service to America*.

41. David Fox and Louise Fox, *End of the Year Evaluation of the National School and Community Corps 1997–1998, Report 2: Impact of the NSCC on Participating Schools, Children and Communities and on Team Leaders and Corpsmembers* (Fox and Fox Associates, 1998); Daniel Hajdo, "Political Alienation, 'Liberal' and 'Communitarian' Citizenship, and the Potential of Participation in AmeriCorps" (paper presented at the Annual Meeting of the American Political Science Association, Boston, MA, 1998); Christina Helferich, *Getting Things Done in Richmond, Virginia: 1996–1997 VCU AmeriCorps Program Evaluation* (Richmond, VA: VCU AmeriCorps Program, Boston, MA: 1998); Jastrzab et al., *Impacts of Service*; and James L. Perry and Ann Marie

Thomson, *Building Communities through AmeriCorps: Final Report* (Bloomington: Indiana University School of Public and Environmental Affairs, 1997).

42. Jastrzab et al., *Impacts of Service*.

43. Fox and Fox, *End of the Year Evaluation*; Helferich, *Getting Things Done in Richmond, Virginia*; and Perry and Thomson, *Building Communities through AmeriCorps*.

44. Hajdo, "Political Alienation."

45. Jastrzab et al., *Impacts of Service*.

46. Aguirre International, *Making a Difference*.

47. Jastrzab et al., *Impacts of Service*.

48. Charles C. Moskos, *A Call to Civic Service: National Service for Country and Community* (New York: Free Press, 1988).

49. Harry C. Boyte and Nancy N. Kari, *Building America: The Democratic Promise of Public Work* (Philadelphia: Temple University Press, 1996).

50. Aguirre International, *AmeriCorps State/National Programs Impact Evaluation* and *Making a Difference*; and the four studies by the Northwest Regional Education Laboratory.

51. Jastrzab et al., *Impacts of Service*.

52. American University, *Evaluation of University Year for ACTION*; Aguirre International, *AmeriCorps State/National Programs Impact Evaluation* and *Making a Difference*; Frees et al., *Final Report*; Harder+Company, *Getting Good Things Done in Northern California*; David Karl Larson, "AmeriCorps: The Oregon Experience" (Ph.D. diss., University of Oregon, 1995); Marta Elisa Moret, *1997–1998 AmeriCorps*State Evaluation* (Hartford: Connecticut Commission on National and Community Service, 1998); Paglin et al., *A Close Look*; Volle and Merisotis, *Public Allies*; and Wang, *Report on Results*.

53. American University, *Evaluation of University Year for ACTION*, pp. iii–37.

54. Jastrzab et al., *Impacts of Service*.

55. See, for example, Ford, *Youth Volunteer Corps of America*.

56. ACTION, *Foster Grandparent Program: Impact Evaluation, Effects on the Foster Grandparents, Summary Report Year One* (Washington, DC: Office of Policy and Planning, Evaluation Division, 1981), and *An Evaluation Report on the Foster Grandparent Program* (Washington, DC: Corporation for National and Community Service and ACTION, 1994).

57. Riecken, *Volunteer Work Camp*.

58. ACTION, *Foster Grandparent Program*, and *An Evaluation Report on the Foster Grandparent Program*; Rosalyn Saltz, *Further Analyses of Data Gathered 1966–1968 by Merrill-Palmer Foster Grandparent Research Project* (Washington, DC: ACTION, 1968), and "Research Evaluation of a Foster Grandparent Program," *Journal of Children in Contemporary Society* 20 (1989): 205–15.

59. Bartlett, Gold, and Masker, *Case Studies of Selected Summer Youth Corps Programs*; and Ford, *Youth Volunteer Corps of America*.

60. Wolf, Leiderman, and Voith, *California Conservation Corps*.

61. Janet D. Griffith, *Evaluation of the SCP/AoA Joint Initiative for the Vulnerable Elderly Program* (Research Triangle Park, NC: Research Triangle Institute, 1994).

62. Riecken, *Volunteer Work Camp*.

63. Development Associates, *An Evaluation Report on the VISTA Literary Corps* (Washington, DC: ACTION, Office of Policy, Research and Evaluation, Program Analysis and Evaluation Division, 1991).

64. Perry and Thomson, *Building Communities through AmeriCorps*.

65. Morris Rosenberg, *Society and the Adolescent Self-Image* (Princeton, NJ: Princeton University Press), 1965.

66. Fox and Fox, *End of the Year Evaluation*.

67. Riecken, *Volunteer Work Camp*.

68. ACTION, *Evaluation Report on the Volunteers in Service to America Summer Associates Program*.

69. Frees et al., *Final Report*.

70. Harder+Company, *Getting Good Things Done in Northern California*.

71. Ford, *Youth Volunteer Corps of America*; Helferich, *Getting Things Done in Richmond, Virginia*; Macro International, *Study of Race, Class, and Ethnicity* (Macro International, 1997); Perry and Thomson, *Building Communities through AmeriCorps*; and Wolf, Leiderman, and Voith, *California Conservation Corps*.

72. Ford, *Youth Volunteer Corps of America*; Perry and Thomson, *Building Communities through AmeriCorps*; and Wolf, Leiderman, and Voith, *California Conservation Corps*.

73. Wolf, Leiderman, and Voith, *California Conservation Corps*.

74. Macro International, *Study of Race, Class, and Ethnicity*.

75. Frees et al., *Final Report*, p. 31.

76. Riecken, *Volunteer Work Camp*.

77. Ibid., p. 162.

78. Ibid., p. 162.

79. Macro International, *Study of Race, Class, and Ethnicity*.

80. Ibid., p. v.

81. ACTION, *University Year for ACTION, Foster Grandparent Program*, and *An Evaluation Report on the Foster Grandparent Program*; Susan Bartlett and Adrienne Gallant, *VISTA Goal Accomplishments and Community Effects Evaluation* (Washington, DC, ACTION Evaluation Division, 1988); Booz, Allen, Hamilton, *Senior Companion Program Study* (Washington, DC: ACTION, 1975); Corwin, *Reform and Organizational Survival*; Development Associates, *An Evaluation Report on Volunteers in Service to America*; Mary Dingwall and Tracy Flaherty, *Findings from the 1996 Survey of AmeriCorps Members* (Rockville, MD: Westat, 1997); Freedman and Fried, *Launching Experience Corps*; Fox and Fox, *End of the Year Evaluation*; Frees et al., *Final Report*; Griffith, *Evaluation of the SCP/AoA Joint Initiative*; Griffiths, *Impact of Service*; Harder+Company, *Getting Good Things Done in Northern California*; Jastrzab et al., *Impacts of Service*; Larson, "AmeriCorps: The Oregon Experience"; Macro International, *Description and Evaluation of the Summer Reads Initiative* (Calverton, MD Macro International, 1997); Marans, Driver, and Scott, *Youth and the Environment*; Paglin et al., *A Close Look*; Perry and Thomson, *Building Communities through AmeriCorps*; Project Star, *Seniors for Schools: Content Analysis of 1997–98 Project Evaluation Reports* (San Mateo, CA: Project Star, 1998); Saltz, *Further Analyses of Data* and "Research Evaluation of a Foster Grandparent Program"; Scott, Driver, and Marans, *Toward Environmental Understanding*; Henrietta Sherwin and Judith Whang, *Foster Grandparents Providing Care for New Populations of High Risk Children: A Research Study* (New York: New York City Department for the Aging, 1990); Shumer and Cady, *YouthWorks AmeriCorps Evaluation: Second Year Report*; Shumer and Rentel, *YouthWorks AmeriCorps Evaluation: Third Year Report*; Sociometrics, *An Evaluation of Family Caregiver Services* (Washington, DC: ACTION, 1988); Regina

Yudd et al., *Member Surveys for AmeriCorps*State/National, AmeriCorps*VISTA, and AmeriCorps*NCCC* (Rockville, MD: Westat, 1997); Regina Yudd, Isabelle Nguyen, and William Strang, *Member Surveys for AmeriCorps*State/National, AmeriCorps*VISTA, and AmeriCorps*NCCC* (Rockville, MD: Westat, 1999); Wang, *Montana AmeriCorps*State Programs, Oregon AmeriCorps*State Programs*, and *Washington AmeriCorps*State Programs*.

82. For example, see Jastrzab et al., *Impacts of Service*.

83. For example, see Booz, Allen, Hamilton, *Senior Companion Program Study*; and Freedman and Fried, *Launching Experience Corps*.

84. Corwin, *Reform and Organizational Survival*.

85. For example, see Bartlett and Gallant, *VISTA Goal Accomplishments*; and Development Associates, *An Evaluation Report on Volunteers in Service to America*.

86. For example, see Paglin et al., *A Close Look*.

87. Ibid.

88. Saltz, *Further Analyses of Data* and "Research Evaluation of a Foster Grandparent Program."

89. ACTION, *Foster Grandparent Program*.

90. Booz, Allen, Hamilton, *Senior Companion Program Study*; SRA Technologies, *Senior Companion Program Impact Evaluation* (Washington, DC: ACTION, 1985).

91. SRA Technologies, *Senior Companion Program Impact Evaluation*.

92. Arawak Consulting Corporation, *Volunteers as Care Givers: ACTION's National Long-Term Care Demonstration Research Project, Volume III, Final Impact Evaluation Report* (Washington, DC: ACTION, Office of Policy Research and Evaluation, 1990).

93. Although RSVP members participated in this demonstration, the vast majority of the 105 participants were enrolled in the SCP.

94. Aguirre International, *Making a Difference*; Christopher Capsambelis, *Evaluation of the AmeriCorps Pinellas Program: 1998 Calendar Year* (Tampa, FL: University of Tampa, 1998); Education for the Future, *AmeriCorps Watershed Project*; Moret, *1997–1998 AmeriCorps*State Evaluation*; Perry and Thomson, *Building Communities through AmeriCorps*; and Ann Zuvekas, Lea Scarpulla Nolan, and Carol Tumaylle, *Impact of Community Health Workers on Access, Use of Services and Patient Knowledge/Behavior* (Washington, DC: Center on Health Policy Research, George Washington University Medical Center, 1998).

95. Bartlett and Gallant, *VISTA Goal Accomplishments*; Development Associates, *Evaluation Report on Volunteers in Service to America*.

96. Frees et al., *Final Report*.

97. For example, see ACTION, *Evaluation Report on the Foster Grandparent Program*.

98. Only one of the ninety-nine studies specifically addressed public safety; eighteen were directed at education.

99. Mary Achatz and Amy Siler, *Evaluation of the Foster Grandparent Program: Final Report* (Rockville, MD: Westat, 1997); Fox and Fox, *End of the Year Evaluation*; Freedman and Fried, *Launching Experience Corps*; Susan Gabbard and Nicole Vicinanza, *An Analysis of 1996/97 AmeriCorps Tutoring Outcomes* (San Mateo, CA: Aguirre International, n.d.); Helferich, *Getting Things Done in Richmond, Virginia; Macro International, Description and Evaluation of the Summer Reads Initiative* (Calverton, MD: Macro International, 1997); Macro International, *Evaluation of DC*

Reads Book Partners Program: Year 1 and *Evaluation of DC Reads: Year 2*; Project Star, *Seniors for Schools: Content Analysis* and *Seniors for Schools Evaluation Results 1998–1999 School Year* (San Mateo, CA: Project Star, 2000); Mary E. Van Verst, *The Lower Yakima Valley Summer Reading Tutoring Project: A Case Study* (Washington State Commission for National and Community Service, 1997).

100. Corwin, *Reform and Organizational Survival.*

101. For example, see Macro International, *Evaluation of DC Reads Book Partners Program: Year 1* and *Evaluation of DC Reads: Year 2.*

102. Achatz and Siler, *Evaluation of the Foster Grandparent Program*; and Freedman and Fried, *Launching Experience Corps.*

103. Project Star, *Seniors for Schools: Content Analysis* and *Seniors for Schools Evaluation Results.*

104. Macro International, *Evaluation of DC Reads Book Partners Program: Year 1* and *Evaluation of DC Reads: Year 2.*

105. The other areas of improvement were letter identification, word attack, oral reading fluency, and comprehension.

106. Achatz and Siler, *Evaluation of the Foster Grandparent Program.*

107. Project Star, *Seniors for Schools: Content Analysis* and *Seniors for Schools Evaluation Results.*

108. Project Star, *Seniors for Schools Evaluation Results*, pp. 1–2.

109. Saltz, *Further Analyses of Data.*

110. Achatz and Siler, *Evaluation of the Foster Grandparent Program*; Booz, Allen, Hamilton, *Senior Companion Program Study*; Griffith, *Evaluation of the SCP/AoA Joint Initiative*; Saltz, "Research Evaluation of a Foster Grandparent Program"; Sociometrics, *An Evaluation of Family Caregiver Services*; SRA Technologies, *Senior Companion Program Impact Evaluation*; and Laura Wilson, *The Senior Companion Program and Visiting Nurse Association of America Public/Private Partnership Program: An Evaluation Report* (College Park: Center on Aging, University of Maryland, 1994).

111. Arawak Consulting, *Volunteers as Care Givers*; and Mary Tschirhart, "Understanding the Older Stipended Volunteer: Age-Related Differences among AmeriCorps Members," *Public Productivity and Management Review* 22, no. 1 (1998): 35–48.

112. Booz, Allen, Hamilton, *Senior Companion Program Study.*

113. Arawak Consulting, *Volunteers as Care Givers*; Booz, Allen, Hamilton, *Senior Companion Program Study*; and SRA Technologies, *Senior Companion Program Impact Evaluation.*

114. Saltz, "Research Evaluation of a Foster Grandparent Program."

115. Arawak Consulting, *Volunteers as Care Givers*; Booz, Allen, Hamilton, *Senior Companion Program Study*; and SRA Technologies, *Senior Companion Program Impact Evaluation.*

116. Jastrzab et al., *Impacts of Service*; Wolf, Leiderman, and Voith, *California Conservation Corps.*

117. Education for the Future, *AmeriCorps Watershed Project*; Freedman and Fried, *Launching Experience Corps*; Fox and Fox, *End of the Year Evaluation*; Project Star, *Seniors for Schools: Content Analysis* and *Seniors for Schools Evaluation Results*; and Sociometrics, *Evaluation of Family Caregiver Services.*

118. Fox and Fox, *End of the Year Evaluation*; Project Star, *Seniors for Schools: Content Analysis* and *Seniors for Schools Evaluation Results.*

119. Project Star, *Seniors for Schools: Content Analysis* and *Seniors for Schools Evaluation Results.*

120. Sociometrics, *Evaluation of Family Caregiver Services.*

121. Corwin, *Reform and Organizational Survival.*

122. Aguirre International, *AmeriCorps State/National Programs Impact Evaluation* and *Making a Difference*; Helferich, *Getting Things Done in Richmond, Virginia*; Perry and Thomson, *Building Communities through AmeriCorps*; Research Triangle Institute, *Assessment of the Value-Added Effect of National Service Programs on the Communities They Serve: Field Report* (Research Triangle Park, NC: Research Triangle Insititute, 1999); Shumer and Cady, *YouthWorks AmeriCorps Evaluation: Second Year Report*; Van Verst, *Lower Yakima Valley Summer Reading*; and Zuvekas, Nolan, and Tumaylle, *Impact of Community Health Workers.*

123. ACTION, *Evaluation Report on the Volunteers in Service to America Summer Associates Program*; Bartlett and Gallant, *VISTA Goal Accomplishments*; and Development Associates, *An Evaluation Report on Volunteers in Service to America.*

124. Booz, Allen, Hamilton, *Senior Companion Program Study*; Griffith, *Evaluation of the SCP/AoA Joint Initiative*; Sociometrics, *Evaluation of Family Caregiver Services*; and Wilson, *Senior Companion Program.*

125. Branch, Leiderman, and Smith, *Youth Conservation and Service Corps.*

126. Rehab Group, *University Year for ACTION (UYA) Effects Study: Final Report* (Falls Church, VA: Rehab Group, 1981).

127. Marans, Driver, and Scott, *Youth and the Environment.*

128. U.S. General Accounting Office, *Assessment of the Teacher Corps Program at the University of Southern California*, and *Assessment of the Teacher Corps Program.*

129. Freedman and Fried, *Launching Experience Corps*; Frees et al., *Final Report*; and Project Star, *Seniors for Schools Evaluation Results.*

130. Frees et al., *Final Report*, Appendix B.

131. Van Verst, *Lower Yakima Valley Summer Reading.*

132. The twenty-four studies are ACTION, *An Evaluation Report on the Volunteers in Service to America Summer Associates Program* and *An Evaluation Report on the Foster Grandparent Program*; Aguirre International, *AmeriCorps State/National Programs Impact Evaluation* and *Making a Difference*; Corwin, *Reform and Organizational Survival*; Development Associates, *Evaluation Report on Volunteers in Service to America*; Fox and Fox, *End of the Year Evaluation*; Freedman and Fried, *Launching Experience Corps*; Helferich, *Getting Things Done in Richmond, Virginia*; Hicks, "AmeriCorps and the North Carolina Child Care Corps"; Jastrzab et al., *Impacts of Service*; Macro International, *Description and Evaluation of the Summer Reads Initiative*, Macro International, *Evaluation of DC Reads Book Partners Program: Year 1* and *Evaluation of DC Reads: Year 2*; Paglin et al., *A Close Look*; Perry and Thomson, *Building Communities through AmeriCorps*; Research Triangle Institute, *Assessment of the Value-Added Effect of National Service Programs*; Sherwin and Whang, *Foster Grandparents Providing Care*; Shumer and Cady, *YouthWorks AmeriCorps Evaluation: Second Year Report*; Shumer and Rentel, *YouthWorks AmeriCorps Evaluation: Third Year Report*; U.S. General Accounting Office, *Assessment of the Teacher Corps Program at the University of Southern California* and *Assessment of the Teacher Corps Program*; Wilson, *The Senior Companion Program*; and Zuvekas, Nolan, and Tumaylle, *Impact of Community Health Workers.*

133. Macro International, *Evaluation of DC Reads: Year 2.*

134. Aguirre International, *AmeriCorps State/National Programs Impact Evaluation* and *Making a Difference*; American University, *Evaluation of University Year for ACTION*; Bartlett and Gallant, *VISTA Goal Accomplishments*; Barry Checkoway, "Institutional Impacts of AmeriCorps on the University of Michigan," *Journal of Public Service and Outreach* 2, no. 1 (1997): 70–79; Corwin, *Reform and Organizational Survival*; Perry and Thomson, *Building Communities through AmeriCorps*; John Rogard Tabori, I. Margarita Gordon, and Ron L. Martinez, *The Sustainability of AmeriCorps*VISTA Programs and Activities* (Los Angeles: People Works, 1997); U.S. General Accounting Office, *Assessment of the Teacher Corps Program at the University of Southern California* and *Assessment of the Teacher Corps Program*.

135. Aguirre International, *AmeriCorps State/National Programs Impact Evaluation* and *Making a Difference*.

136. Aguirre International, *Making a Difference*, p. 66.

137. Ibid., p. 69.

138. Checkoway, "Institutional Impacts of AmeriCorps on the University of Michigan."

139. Bartlett and Gallant, *VISTA Goal Accomplishments*.

140. In contrast to these results, a later report on VISTA was far more pessimistic about long-term project sustainability (see Development Associates, *Evaluation Report on the VISTA Literary Corps*). The report is not included among those whose results relate to institution creation because its conclusions were not a direct outgrowth of the research and are speculative in character.

141. American University, *Evaluation of University Year for ACTION*.

142. Beecroft and Gallant, 1988.

143. Corwin, *Reform and Organizational Survival*; U.S. General Accounting Office, *Assessment of the Teacher Corps Program at the University of Southern California* and *Assessment of the Teacher Corps Program*.

144. Corwin, *Reform and Organizational Survival*.

145. Ibid., p. 350.

146. Perry and Thomson, *Building Communities through AmeriCorps*.

147. Adrienne von Glatz, Crystal MacAllum, and William Strang, *Measuring AmeriCorps*VISTA's Impacts on the Communities and Organizations It Serves* (Rockville, MD: Westat, 1997), pp. 16–17.

148. Marilyn Gittel with Marguerite Beardsley, and Marsha Weissman, *Final Evaluation Report on Syracuse Youth Community Service* (Washington, DC: Aguirre International, 1981).

149. American University, *Evaluation of University Year for ACTION*.

150. Aguirre International, *AmeriCorps State/National Programs Impact Evaluation* and *Making a Difference*; Bartlett and Gallant, *VISTA Goal Accomplishments*; Branch, Leiderman, and Smith, *Youth Conservation and Service Corps*; Development Associates, *Evaluation Report on the VISTA Literary Corps* and *Evaluation Report on Volunteers in Service to America*; Paglin et al., *A Close Look*; Rehab Group, *University Year for ACTION (UYA) Effects Study*; Research Triangle Institute, *Assessment of the Value-Added Effect of National Service Programs*; Wang, *Montana AmeriCorps*State Program* and *Washington AmeriCorps*State Programs*.

151. Aguirre International, *Making a Difference*; and Development Associates, *Evaluation Report on the VISTA Literary Corps*.

152. Aguirre International, *Making a Difference*.

153. For example, see Paglin et al., *A Close Look*; Wang, *Montana AmeriCorps*State Programs* and *Washington AmeriCorps*State Programs*.

154. U.S. General Accounting Office, *Assessment of the Teacher Corps Program*.

155. Education for the Future, *AmeriCorps Watershed Project*; Fox and Fox, *End of the Year Evaluation*; and Perry and Thomson, *Building Communities through AmeriCorps*.

156. Education for the Future, *AmeriCorps Watershed Project*.

157. Perry and Thomson, *Building Communities through AmeriCorps*.

158. Fox and Fox, *End of the Year Evaluation*.

159. Edward M. Gramlich, *Benefit-Cost Analysis of Government Programs* (Englewood Cliffs, NJ: Prentice-Hall, 1981); U.S. General Accounting Office, *National Service Programs: AmeriCorps*USA Benefit-Cost Study* (Washington, DC: General Accounting Office, 1995).

160. Gramlich, *Benefit-Cost Analysis of Government Programs*.

161. Aguirre International, *Making a Difference*; George R. Neumann et al., *The Benefits and Costs of National Service Methods for Benefit Assessment with Application to Three AmeriCorps Programs* (Washington, DC: Corporation for National Service, 1995); Robert D. Shumer, *YouthWorks AmeriCorps Evaluation: A Cost-Benefit Analysis* (Minneapolis: University of Minnesota, 1995); Shumer and Cady, *YouthWorks AmeriCorps Evaluation: Second Year Report*; Shumer and Rentel, *YouthWorks AmeriCorps Evaluation: Third Year Report*; and Changhua Wang, Tom Owens, and Kyung-Sup Kim, *A Cost-and-Benefit Study of Two AmeriCorps Projects in the State of Washington* (Portland, OR: Northwest Regional Educational Laboratory, 1995).

162. California Conservation Corps, *California Conservation Corps, 1976–1979: Report to the Legislature* (Sacramento, CA: California Conservation Corps, 1979); Jastrzab et al., *Impacts of Service*; Public Interest Economics-West, "Economic Impact of California Conservation Corps Projects" (mimeograph) (San Francisco: Public Interest Economics-West, 1980); and Wolf, Leiderman, and Voith, *California Conservation Corps*.

163. Elaine Carlson and William Strang, *Volunteers in Service to America: An Analysis of the Benefits and Costs for Selected AmeriCorps*VISTA Projects* (Westat, 1996).

164. Booz, Allen Public Administration Services, *Cost-Benefit Study of the Foster Grandparent Program* (Washington, DC: ACTION, 1972).

165. Control Systems Research, *The Program for Local Service: Summary Findings* (Seattle: Control Systems Research, 1973); and Frees et al., *Final Report*.

166. Neumann et al., *Benefits and Costs of National Service Methods*, pp. 12, 21–38.

167. U.S. General Accounting Office, *National Service Programs*.

168. Wang, Owens, and Kim, *Cost-and-Benefit Study*.

169. Shumer, *YouthWorks AmeriCorps Evaluation: A Cost-Benefit Analysis*; Shumer and Cady, *YouthWorks AmeriCorps Evaluation: Second Year Report*; and Shumer and Rentel, *YouthWorks AmeriCorps Evaluation: Third Year Report*.

170. Aguirre International, *Making a Difference*.

171. Wolf, Leiderman, and Voith, *California Conservation Corps*.

172. California Conservation Corps, *California Conservation Corps, 1976–1979*; and Public Interest Economics-West, "Economic Impact of California Conservation Corps Projects."

173. Jastrzab, et al., *Impacts of Service*.

174. Carlson and Strang, *Volunteers in Service to America*.

175. Booz, Allen Public Administration Services, *Cost-Benefit Study of the Foster Grandparent Program*.

176. Frees et al., *Final Report*.

177. Control Systems Research, *Program for Local Service*.

178. Aguirre International, *Making a Difference*.

179. Development Associates, *Evaluation Report on Volunteers in Service to America*.

180. Aguirre International, *AmeriCorps State/National Programs Impact Evaluation*.

181. Perry and Thomson, *Building Communities through AmeriCorps*.

182. ACTION, *University Year for Action*; and American University, *Evaluation of University Year for ACTION*.

183. Freedman and Fried, *Launching Experience Corps*; and Sociometrics, *Evaluation of Family Caregiver Services*.

184. Macro International, *Evaluation of DC Reads Book Partners Program: Year 1* and *Evaluation of DC Reads: Year 2*.

185. Moret, *1997–1998 AmeriCorps*State Evaluation*.

186. Perry and Thomson, *Building Communities through AmeriCorps*.

187. Ibid., p. 49.

188. Research Triangle Institute, *Assessment of the Value-Added Effect of National Service Programs*; Perry and Thomson, *Building Communities through AmeriCorps*.

Notes to Chapter 6

1. The counts represent the number of times an implementation issue was referred to in the studies synthesized. Because many of the studies synthesized were impact-oriented, the evidence about implementation tends to be scattered and indirect. The authors of many of the studies gave little attention to implementation, while others provided substantial detail about what worked and what did not. Rather than scoring studies on what they noted about favorable or unfavorable implementation, each study was coded whether it addressed some facet of implementation. If inadequate training was observed to detract from civic service, it was scored with a "yes." A study that identified training as an exemplar received the same "yes" code.

2. Aguirre International, *Making a Difference: Impact of AmeriCorps*State/National Direct on Members and Communities 1994–95 and 1995–96* (San Mateo, CA: Aguirre International, 1999); Susan Bartlett and Adrienne Gallant, *VISTA Goal Accomplishments and Community Effects Evaluation* (Washington, D.C., ACTION Evaluation Division, 1988); Susan Bartlett, Reva Gold, and Julie Masker, *Case Studies of Selected Summer Youth Corps Programs (Report 1 of 2)* (Washington, DC: Corporation for National Service, 1993); Alvia Branch and Marc Freedman, *YouthCorps Case Studies: The New York City Volunteer Corps* (Philadelphia: Public/Private Ventures, 1986); Ronald Corwin, *Reform and Organizational Survival: The Teacher Corps as an Instrument of Educational Change* (New York: Wiley, 1973); Development Associates, *An Evaluation Report on Volunteers in Service to America* (Washington, DC: ACTION, Office of Policy, Research and Evaluation, Program Analysis and Evaluation Division, 1993); Mary Dingwall and Tracy Flaherty, *Findings from the 1996 Survey of AmeriCorps Members* (Rockville, MD: Westat, 1997); Timothy Emmett

Dolan, *The Politics of Life Cycles: Service as a Rite of Passage to Adult Citizenship* (Ph.D. diss., University of Hawaii, 1991); Nicole Driebe, *The Devolution Challenge: A Case Study of AmeriCorps* (Ph.D. diss., Cornell University, 2000); Lynne Ford, *Youth Volunteer Corps of America Final Evaluation Report* (Charleston, SC: College of Charleston, 1994); Marc Freedman and Linda Fried, *Launching Experience Corps* (Oakland, CA: Civic Ventures, 1999); J.W. Frees et al., *Final Report: National Service Demonstration Programs* (Subtitle D) (Cambridge, MA: Abt Associates, 1995); Marilyn Gittel with Marguerite Beardsley, and Marsha Weissman, *Final Evaluation Report on Syracuse Youth Community Service* (Washington, DC: Aguirre International, 1981); Harder+Company Community Research, *Getting Good Things Done in Northern California: A Comprehensive Assessment of Northern California Grantmakers' National Service Task Force-Funded AmeriCorps Program* (San Francisco: Northern California Grantmakers, 1998); Susan Alice Hicks, "AmeriCorps and the North Carolina Child Care Corps: A Mechanism for Addressing the Child Care Crisis" (Ph.D. diss., University of North Carolina at Greensboro, 1997); Keith Jamtgaard, Charles Schwartz, and Carol Youngner, *National VISTA Study FY 1977* (Washington, DC: ACTION, Office of Policy and Planning, 1978); David Lah, Wendy Wolf, and Sally Leiderman, *YouthCorps Case Studies: The Marin Conservation Corps* (Philadelphia: Public/Private Ventures, 1985); Macro International, *Study of Race, Class, and Ethnicity* (Washington, DC: Macro International, 1997), *Evaluation of DC Reads Book Partners Program: Year 1 Final External Report* (Washington, DC: Macro International, 1998), and *Evaluation of DC Reads: Year 2 Final Report* (Washington, DC: Macro International, 2000); Robert W. Marans, B.L. Driver, and John C. Scott, *Youth and the Environment: An Evaluation of the 1971 Youth Conservation Corps* (Ann Arbor, MI: Institute for Social Research, 1972); Marta Elisa Moret, *1997–1998 AmeriCorps*State Evaluation* (Hartford: Connecticut Commission on National and Community Service, 1998); Robert Austin Pence, "Organizational Context and Young Adult Education in an Urban Service Corps" (Ph.D. diss., University of Wisconsin, Madison, 1996); James L. Perry and Ann Marie Thomson, *Building Communities through AmeriCorps: Final Report* (Bloomington: Indiana University School of Public and Environmental Affairs, 1997); Project Star, *Seniors for Schools Evaluation Results 1998–1999 School Year* {San Mateo, CA: Project Star, 2000); Henrietta Sherwin and Judith Whang, *Foster Grandparents Providing Care for New Populations of High Risk Children: A Research Study* (New York: New York City Department for the Aging, 1990); Phillip David Sherwood, "The Development of At Risk Young Adults: The California Conservation Corps Experience 1987 to 1995" (D.P.A. diss., University of Southern California, 1996); Robert D. Shumer and Jane Maland Cady, *YouthWorks AmeriCorps Evaluation: Second Year Report 1995–1996* (Minneapolis: University of Minnesota, 1997); Mary Tschirhart, "Understanding the Older Stipended Volunteer: Age-Related Differences among AmeriCorps Members," *Public Productivity and Management Review* 22, no. 1 (1998): 35–48; Changhua Wang, *Montana AmeriCorps*State Programs 1996–1997* (Portland, OR: Northwest Regional Educational Laboratory, 1998), *Oregon AmeriCorps*State Programs 1996–1997* (Portland, OR: Northwest Regional Educational Laboratory, 1998), and *Washington AmeriCorps*State Programs 1996–1997* (Portland, OR: Northwest Regional Educational Laboratory, 1998); Westat, *AmeriCorps*NCCC: Analysis of Responses to the Class Two Exit Survey* (Rockville, MD: Westat, 1996); Wendy Wolf and Alvia Branch, *Youth Corps Profiles* (Philadelphia: Public/Private Ventures, 1986); and

Ann Zuvekas, Lea Scarpulla Nolan and Carol Tumaylle, *Impact of Community Health Workers on Access, Use of Services and Patient Knowledge/Behavior* (Washington, DC: Center on Health Policy Research, George Washington University Medical Center, 1998).

3. Aguirre International, *Making a Difference*; and Perry and Thomson, *Building Communities through AmeriCorps*.

4. Perry and Thomson, *Building Communities through AmeriCorps*.

5. Susan Bartlett and Erik Beecroft, *Educational Impacts of Summer 1993 Washington Service Teams* (Washington, DC: Corporation for National Service, 1995).

6. Macro International, *Description and Evaluation of the Summer Reads Initiative* (Calverton, MD: Macro International, 1997).

7. Hicks, "AmeriCorps and the North Carolina Child Care Corps"; and Wang, *Montana AmeriCorps*State Programs 1996–1997*.

8. Development Associates, *An Evaluation Report on the VISTA Literary Corps* (Washington, DC: ACTION, Office of Policy, Research and Evaluation, Program Analysis and Evaluation Division, 1991).

9. Paul Sabatier and Daniel Mazmanian, "The Conditions of Effective Implementation: A Guide to Accomplishing Policy Objectives," *Policy Analysis* 5, no. 4 (1979): 481–525; and Carson K. Eoyang and Peter D. Spencer, "Designing Effective Programs," in *Handbook of Public Administration*, 2d. ed., ed. James L. Perry (San Francisco: Jossey-Bass, 1996), pp. 232–49.

10. M.A. Moss, J. Hiller, and Douglas Moore, *Descriptive Study of AmeriCorps Literacy Programs* (Cambridge, MA: Abt Associates, 1999).

11. See Wang, *Washington AmeriCorps*State Programs*; and Westat, *AmeriCorps*NCCC*.

12. ACTION, *University Year for ACTION: An Evaluation* (Washington, DC: Office of Policy and Planning, Evaluation Division, 1973).

13. Bartlett, Gold, and Masker, *Case Studies of Selected Summer Youth Corps Programs*.

14. For example, see Branch and Freedman, *YouthCorps Case Studies*; Bartlett, Gold, and Masker, *Case Studies of Selected Summer Youth Corps Programs*; Pence, "Organizational Context and Young Adult Education"; and Sherwood, "Development of At Risk Young Adults."

15. Perry and Thomson, *Building Communities through AmeriCorps*.

16. Lah, Wolf, and Leiderman, *YouthCorps Case Studies*.

17. Branch and Freedman, *YouthCorps Case Studies*; and Sherwood, "The Development of At Risk Young Adults."

18. Bartlett, Gold, and Masker, *Case Studies of Selected Summer Youth Corps Programs*; Pence, "Organizational Context and Young Adult Education"; and Sherwood, "Development of At Risk Young Adults."

19. Marans, Driver, and Scott, *Youth and the Environment*.

20. Sherwood, "Development of At Risk Young Adults," p. 204.

21. Jamtgaard, Schwartz, and Youngner, *National VISTA Study FY 1977*.

22. Macro International, *Study of Race, Class, and Ethnicity*.

23. Catherine Paglin et al., *A Close Look at Four AmeriCorps Programs in the Pacific Northwest (Oregon, Washington, Montana, and Idaho)* (Portland, OR: Northwest Regional Educational Laboratory, 1999).

24. Macro International, *Evaluation of DC Reads Book Partners Program: Year 1*, pp. iv–6.

25. Hicks, "AmeriCorps and the North Carolina Child Care Corps"; and Macro International, *Description and Evaluation of the Summer Reads Initiative*.

26. Macro International, *Description and Evaluation of the Summer Reads Initiative*, pp. iv–6.

27. Ibid., pp. iv–6.

28. Jamtgaard, Schwartz, and Youngner, *National VISTA Study FY 1977*.

29. Shumer and Cady, *YouthWorks AmeriCorps Evaluation: Second Year Report*.

30. Robert D. Herman, *Handbook of Nonprofit Management and Leadership* (San Francisco: Jossey-Bass, 1994).

31. Mary Achatz and Amy Siler, *Evaluation of the Foster Grandparent Program: Final Report* (Rockville, MD: Westat, 1997); ACTION, *An Evaluation Report on the Volunteers in Service to America Summer Associates Program* (Washington, DC: Corporation for National and Community Service and ACTION, 1993), and *An Evaluation Report on the Foster Grandparent Program* (Washington, DC: Corporation for National and Community Service and ACTION, 1994); Aguirre International, *AmeriCorps State/National Programs Impact Evaluation: First Year Report* (San Mateo, CA: Aguirre International, 1997), and *Making a Difference*; Bartlett, Gold, and Masker, *Case Studies of Selected Summer Youth Corps Programs*; Booz, Allen, Hamilton, *Senior Companion Program Study* (Washington, DC: ACTION, 1975); Branch and Freedman, *YouthCorps Case Studies*; California Conservation Corps, *California Conservation Corps, 1976–1979: Report to the Legislature* (Sacramento, CA: California Conservation Corps, 1979); Corwin, *Reform and Organizational Survival*; Development Associates, *Evaluation Report on the VISTA Literary Corps*, and *Evaluation Report on Volunteers in Service to America*; Dolan, *Politics of Life Cycles*; Freedman and Fried, *Launching Experience Corps*; J.W. Frees et al., *Final Report: National Service Demonstration Programs (Subtitle D)* (Cambridge: Abt Associates, 1995); Gittel, Beardsley, and Weissman, *Final Evaluation Report on Syracuse Youth Community Service*; Colleen Yvette Griffiths, *The Impact of Service: An Exploration of the Characteristics of Volunteer Tutors in the AmeriCorps For Math and Literacy Program and the Benefits They Gained From Service* (Columbus: Ohio State University, 1998); Hicks, "AmeriCorps and the North Carolina Child Care Corps"; Lah, Wolf, and Leiderman, *YouthCorps Case Studies*; Crystal MacAllum et al., *Evaluation of the First Year of the AmeriCorps Education Awards Program* (Rockville, MD: Westat, 1999); Marans, Driver, and Scott, *Youth and the Environment*; Macro International, *Description and Evaluation of the Summer Reads Initiative, Study of Race, Class, and Ethnicity, Evaluation of DC Reads Book Partners Program: Year 1*, and *Evaluation of DC Reads: Year 2*; Moret, *1997–1998 AmeriCorps*State Evaluation*; Pence, "Organizational Context and Young Adult Education"; Project Star, *Seniors for Schools: Content Analysis of 1997–98 Project Evaluation Reports* (San Mateo, CA: Project Star, 1998), and *Seniors for Schools Evaluation Results*; Public Interest Economics-West, "Economic Impact of California Conservation Corps Projects" (mimeograph) (San Francisco: Public Interest Economics-West, 1980); Sheila Rosenblum and Sally Leiderman, *Youth Corps Case Studies: The San Francisco Conservation Corps* (Philadelphia: Public/Private Ventures, 1986); Henrietta Sherwin and Judith Whang, *Foster Grandparents Providing Care*; Sherwood, "Development of At Risk Young Adults"; Shumer and Cady, *YouthWorks AmeriCorps Evaluation: Second Year Report*; Mary E. Van Verst, *The Lower Yakima Valley Summer Reading Tutoring Project: A Case Study* (Washington State Commission for National and Community Service, 1997); Katheryn L. Volle and Jamie P. Merisotis, *Public Allies: An Alumni*

Survey (Washington, DC: Institute for Higher Education Policy, 1997); Wang, *Montana AmeriCorps*State Programs*; Westat, *AmeriCorps*NCCC*; Laura Wilson, *The Senior Companion Program and Visiting Nurse Association of America Public/Private Partnership Program: An Evaluation Report* (College Park: Center on Aging, University of Maryland, 1994); Wolf and Branch, *Youth Corps Profiles*; Wendy C. Wolf, Sally Leiderman, and Richard Voith, *The California Conservation Corps: An Analysis of Short-Term Impacts on Participants* (Philadelphia: Public/Private Ventures, 1987); and Zuvekas, Nolan, and Tumaylle, *Impact of Community Health Workers*.

32. Tschirhart, "Understanding the Older Stipended Volunteer."

33. Sherwin and Whang, *Foster Grandparents Providing Care*; Wilson, *Senior Companion Program*.

34. Macro International, *Description and Evaluation of the Summer Reads Initiative*, *Evaluation of DC Reads Book Partners Program: Year 1*, and *Evaluation of DC Reads: Year 2*.

35. Wang, *Montana AmeriCorps*State Programs*.

36. Macro International, *Description and Evaluation of the Summer Reads Initiative*.

37. ACTION, *An Evaluation Report on the Volunteers in Service to America*; and Freedman and Fried, *Launching Experience Corps*.

38. Freedman and Fried, *Launching Experience Corps*.

39. California Conservation Corps, *California Conservation Corps*; Lah, Wolf, and Leiderman, *YouthCorps Case Studies*; Marans, Driver, and Scott, *Youth and the Environment*; Pence, "Organizational Context and Young Adult Education"; Rosenblum and Leiderman, *Youth Corps Case Studies*; Wolf, Leiderman, and Voith, *California Conservation Corps*.

40. Shumer and Cady, *YouthWorks AmeriCorps Evaluation: Second Year Report*.

41. Gittel, Beardsley, and Weissman, *Final Evaluation Report on Syracuse Youth Community Service*.

42. Griffiths, *Impact of Service*.

43. Bartlett, Gold, and Masker, *Case Studies of Selected Summer Youth Corps Programs*.

44. Public Interest Economics-West, "Economic Impact of California Conservation Corps Projects."

45. Macro International, *Description and Evaluation of the Summer Reads Initiative*.

46. ACTION, *Evaluation Report on the Volunteers in Service to America*, and *An Evaluation Report on the Foster Grandparent Program*; Aguirre International, *Making a Difference*; American University, *Evaluation of University Year for ACTION*; Bartlett and Gallant, *VISTA Goal Accomplishments*; Bartlett, Gold, and Masker, *Case Studies of Selected Summer Youth Corps Programs*; Booz, Allen, Hamilton, *Senior Companion Program Study*; Branch and Freedman, *YouthCorps Case Studies*; Michael Sherraden, "The Civilian Conservation Corps: Effectiveness of the Camps" (Ph.D. diss., University of Michigan, 1979); Development Associates, *Evaluation Report on Volunteers in Service to America*; Dingwall and Flaherty, *Findings from the 1996 Survey of AmeriCorps Members*; Dolan, *Politics of Life Cycles*; Alexa Fraser and Mary Madigan, *Effect of Living Allowances and Educational Awards on AmeriCorps Members' Ability to Serve and on Fostering Socio-Economic Diversity* (Rockville, MD: Westat, 1995); Freedman and Fried, *Launching Experience Corps*; Frees et al., *Final Report*; Griffiths, *Impact of Service*; Harder+Company, *Getting Good Things Done in Northern California*; Hicks, "AmeriCorps and the North Carolina Child Care Corps"; JoAnn Jastrzab et al., *Impacts of Service: Final Report on the Evaluation of*

American Conservation and Youth Service Corps (Cambridge: Abt Associates, 1996); Lah, Wolf, and Leiderman, *YouthCorps Case Studies*; MacAllum et al., *Evaluation of the First Year of the AmeriCorps Education Awards Program*; Macro International, *Description and Evaluation of the Summer Reads Initiative, Study of Race, Class, and Ethnicity, Evaluation of DC Reads Book Partners Program: Year 1*, and *Evaluation of DC Reads: Year 2*; Paglin et al., *A Close Look*; Pence, "Organizational Context and Young Adult Education"; Perry and Thomson, *Building Communities through AmeriCorps*; Rehab Group, *University Year for ACTION (UYA) Effects Study: Final Report* (Falls Church, VA: Rehab Group, 1981); Rosenblum and Leiderman, *Youth Corps Case Studies*; Sherwin and Whang, *Foster Grandparents Providing Care*; Shumer and Cady, *YouthWorks AmeriCorps Evaluation: Second Year Report*; Tschirhart, "Understanding the Older Stipended Volunteer"; Wilson, *Senior Companion Program*; Wolf and Branch, *Youth Corps Profiles*; Wolf, Leiderman, and Voith, *The California Conservation Corps*; and Zuvekas, Nolan, and Tumaylle, *Impact of Community Health Workers*.

47. Macro International, *Study of Race, Class, and Ethnicity*.

48. Wolf, Leiderman, and Voith, *California Conservation Corps*.

49. Pence, "Organizational Context and Young Adult Education"; Jastrzab et al., *Impacts of Service*.

50. Zuvekas, Nolan, and Tumaylle, *Impact of Community Health Workers*; Perry and Thomson, *Building Communities through AmeriCorps*.

51. Branch and Freedman, *YouthCorps Case Studies*.

52. Zuvekas, Nolan, and Tumaylle, *Impact of Community Health Workers*.

53. Tschirhart, "Understanding the Older Stipended Volunteer."

54. Gittel, Beardsley, and Weissman, *Final Evaluation Report on Syracuse Youth Community Service*.

55. Fraser and Madigan, *Effect of Living Allowances and Educational Awards*; David Karl Larson, "AmeriCorps: The Oregon Experience" (Ph.D. diss., University of Oregon, 1995). Fraser and Madigan report that 31 percent of AmeriCorps members in a stratified random sample of 850 indicated they could afford to be a member if they were not paid. About 40 percent of this group held additional part-time or full-time employment. Thirty-eight percent of the sample indicated that the stipend was not enough to live on and another 32 percent responded that it was barely enough to live on. See *Effect of Living Allowances and Educational Awards*.

56. Larson, "AmeriCorps: The Oregon Experience."

57. American University School of Education, *Evaluation of University Year for ACTION* (Washington, DC: ACTION, 1975).

58. MacAllum et al., *Evaluation of the First Year of the AmeriCorps Education Awards Program*, p. ix.

59. Griffiths, *Impact of Service*.

60. Freedman and Fried, *Launching Experience Corps*.

61. ACTION, *Evaluation Report on the Volunteers in Service to America Summer Associates Program*.

62. Macro International, *Evaluation of DC Reads Book Partners Program: Year 1*.

63. Tschirhart, "Understanding the Older Stipended Volunteer."

64. Ibid., p. 45, 47.

65. Lah, Wolf, and Leiderman, *YouthCorps Case Studies*; Pence, "Organizational Context and Young Adult Education"; Wolf and Branch, *Youth Corps Profiles*.

66. Westat, *AmeriCorps*NCCC*.

67. Rosenblum and Leiderman, *Youth Corps Case Studies*, p. vi.

68. Bartlett and Gallant, *VISTA Goal Accomplishments*.

69. ACTION, *An Evaluation Report on the Foster Grandparent Program*; Aguirre International, *Making a Difference*; American University, *Evaluation of University Year for ACTION*; Bartlett and Gallant, *VISTA Goal Accomplishments*; Bartlett, Gold, and Masker, *Case Studies of Selected Summer Youth Corps Programs*; Branch and Freedman, *YouthCorps Case Studies*; Corwin, *Reform and Organizational Survival*; Development Associates, *Evaluation Report on the VISTA Literary Corps*, and *Evaluation Report on Volunteers in Service to America*; Janet D. Griffith, *Evaluation of the SCP/AoA Joint Initiative for the Vulnerable Elderly Program* (Research Triangle Park, NC: Research Triangle Institute, 1994); Lah, Wolf, and Leiderman, *YouthCorps Case Studies*; MacAllum et al., *Evaluation of the First Year of the AmeriCorps Education Awards Program*; Paglin et al., *A Close Look*; Perry and Thomson, *Building Communities through AmeriCorps*; Project Star, *Seniors for Schools Evaluation Results*; U.S. General Accounting Office, *National Service Programs: AmeriCorps*USA Benefit-Cost Study* (Washington, DC: General Accounting Office, 1995), *National Service Programs: Role of State Commissions in Implementing the AmeriCorps Program* (Washington, DC: General Accounting Office, 1997), *National Service Programs: Status of AmeriCorps Reform Efforts* (Washington, DC: General Accounting Office, 1997), *National Service Programs: Two AmeriCorps Programs' Finding and Benefits* (Washington, DC: General Accounting Office, 2000); Wang, *Oregon AmeriCorps*State Programs*, and *Washington AmeriCorps*State Programs*; Wolf and Branch, *Youth Corps Profiles*; and Zuvekas, Nolan, and Tumaylle, *Impact of Community Health Workers*.

70. Barry Checkoway, "Institutional Impacts of AmeriCorps on the University of Michigan," *Journal of Public Service and Outreach* 2, no. 1 (1997): 79.

71. Development Associates, *Evaluation Report on Volunteers in Service to America*.

72. U.S. General Accounting Office, *AmeriCorps*USA Benefit-Cost Study* and *National Service Programs: Two AmeriCorps Programs' Finding and Benefits*, 2000.

73. Development Associates, *Evaluation Report on Volunteers in Service to America*; and Zuvekas, Nolan, and Tumaylle, *Impact of Community Health Workers*.

74. Branch and Freedman, *YouthCorps Case Studies*.

75. William F. Buckley Jr., *Gratitude: Reflections on What We Owe to Our Country* (New York: Random House, 1990); and Charles C. Moskos, *A Call to Civic Service: National Service for Country and Community* (New York: Free Press, 1988).

76. Sherraden, "Civilian Conservation Corps."

77. U.S. General Accounting Office, *AmeriCorps*USA Benefit-Cost Study* and *National Service Programs: Two AmeriCorps Programs' Finding and Benefits*, 2000.

78. Zuvekas, Nolan, and Tumaylle, *Impact of Community Health Workers*.

79. Griffith, *Evaluation of the SCP/AoA Joint Initiative*.

80. SCP projected volunteer service years (VSYs), which includes stipend and administrative costs, at $3,600. Using this estimate, the median nonfederal funds of $15,400 could support 4.3 VSY.

81. Lah, Wolf, and Leiderman, *YouthCorps Case Studies*.

82. Sherwood, "Development of At Risk Young Adults."

83. Corwin, *Reform and Organizational Survival*.

84. Ibid.

85. Richard Graham, cited in Corwin, *Reform and Organizational Survival*, p. 335.

86. Corwin, *Reform and Organizational Survival*.

87. Grantmaker Forum on Community and National Service, "National Service in the Next Century: Taking It to Scale" (a summary of proceedings, Cleveland, Ohio, June 3, 1998).

88. Paglin et al., *A Close Look*, p. 12.

89. ACTION, *Evaluation Report on the Foster Grandparent Program*.

99. American University, *Evaluation of University Year for ACTION*; Booz, Allen Public Administration Services, *Cost-Benefit Study of the Foster Grandparent Program* (Washington, DC: ACTION, 1972); Corwin, *Reform and Organizational Survival*; Development Associates, *An Evaluation Report on the VISTA Literary Corps*; Dolan, *Politics of Life Cycles*; Ford, *Youth Volunteer Corps of America Final Evaluation Report*; Frees et al., *Final Report*; Gittel, Beardsley, and Weissman, *Final Evaluation Report on Syracuse Youth Community Service*; Griffith, *Evaluation of the SCP/ AoA Joint Initiative*; Linda Z. Jucovy and Kathryn L. Furano, *Public Allies at Work: Examining Allies' Impacts on Communities and Organizations* (Philadelphia: Jucovy, 1998); Macro International, *Study of Race, Class, and Ethnicity*; Marans, Driver, and Scott, *Youth and the Environment*; Perry and Thomson, *Building Communities through AmeriCorps*; Mitchell Ratner, *Kick Starting National Service: Ethnographic Studies of the Summer of Safety* (Washington, DC: Corporation for National Service, 1994); Rehab Group, *University Year for ACTION (UYA) Effects Study*; Rosenblum and Leiderman, *Youth Corps Case Studies*; Sherraden, "Civilian Conservation Corps"; Thomas J. Smith and Linda Z. Jucovy, *AmeriCorps in the Field: Implementation of the National and Community Service Trust Act in Nine Study States* (Philadelphia: Public/Private Ventures, 1996); U.S. General Accounting Office, *AmeriCorps*USA Benefit-Cost Study*; and Wolf and Branch, *Youth Corps Profiles*.

91. Smith and Jucovy, *AmeriCorps in the Field*.

92. Ibid.

93. Gittel, Beardsley, and Weissman, *Final Evaluation Report on Syracuse Youth Community Service*, p. 6.

94. Rosenblum and Leiderman, *Youth Corps Case Studies*, p. iv.

95. Wolf and Branch, *Youth Corps Profiles*.

96. Frees et al., *Final Report*.

97. Perry and Thomson, *Building Communities through AmeriCorps*.

98. Griffith, *Evaluation of the SCP/AoA Joint Initiative*.

99. Jucovy and Furano, *Public Allies at Work*; and Perry and Thomson, *Building Communities through AmeriCorps*.

100. Jucovy and Furano, *Public Allies at Work*.

101. Griffith, *Evaluation of the SCP/AoA Joint Initiative*.

102. Frees et al., *Final Report*.

103. Marans, Driver, and Scott, *Youth and the Environment*, pp. viii–5.

104. Ford, *Youth Volunteer Corps of America Final Evaluation Report*.

105. For example, see Booz, Allen Public Administration Services, *Cost-Benefit Study of the Foster Grandparent Program*.

106. Ford, *Youth Volunteer Corps of America Final Evaluation Report*, pp. ii–iii.

107. Booz, Allen Public Administration Services, *Cost-Benefit Study of the Foster Grandparent Program*.

108. Aguirre International, *Making a Difference*; Bartlett, Gold, and Masker, *Case Studies of Selected Summer Youth Corps Programs*; Branch and Freedman, *YouthCorps Case Studies*; Driebe, *Devolution Challenge*; Moret, *1997–1998 AmeriCorps*State*

Evaluation; Pence, "Organizational Context and Young Adult Education"; Perry and Thomson, *Building Communities through AmeriCorps*; Ratner, *Kick Starting National Service*; Henry W. Riecken, *The Volunteer Work Camp: A Psychological Evaluation* (Cambridge: Addison-Wesley, 1952); Sherraden, "Civilian Conservation Corps"; Sherwood, "Development of At Risk Young Adults"; Smith and Jucovy, *AmeriCorps in the Field*; and Wang, *Montana AmeriCorps*State Programs*.

109. Sherraden, "Civilian Conservation Corps."

110. Riecken, *Volunteer Work Camp*, p. 168.

111. Moret, *1997–1998 AmeriCorps*State Evaluation*.

112. Aguirre International, *Making a Difference*.

113. Bartlett, Gold, and Masker, *Case Studies of Selected Summer Youth Corps Programs*; and Ratner, *Kick Starting National Service*.

114. Driebe, *Devolution Challenge*.

115. Smith and Jucovy, *AmeriCorps in the Field*.

116. Aguirre International, *Making a Difference*; Christopher Capsambelis, *Evaluation of the AmeriCorps Pinellas Program: 1998 Calendar Year* (Tampa, FL: University of Tampa, 1998); Driebe, *Devolution Challenge*; Freedman and Fried, *Launching Experience Corps*; MacAllum et al., *Evaluation of the First Year of the AmeriCorps Education Awards Program*; Paglin et al., *A Close Look*; Perry and Thomson, *Building Communities through AmeriCorps*; and U.S. General Accounting Office, *National Service Programs: Role of State Commissions*.

117. Capsambelis, *Evaluation of the AmeriCorps Pinellas Program*.

118. Paglin et al., *A Close Look*, p. 12.

119. Driebe, *Devolution Challenge*.

120. Ibid., p. 3.

121. Aguirre International, *Making a Difference*.

122. Ibid., p. 176.

123. Perry and Thomson, *Building Communities through AmeriCorps*.

124. Ibid., p. 52.

125. MacAllum et al., *Evaluation of the First Year of the AmeriCorps Education Awards Program*.

126. Driebe, *Devolution Challenge*; Frank Fear et al., *Environmental Problem Solving in Lansing: Michigan's AmeriCorps* (East Lansing: Michigan State University, 1996); Macro International, *Description and Evaluation of the Summer Reads Initiative*; Perry and Thomson, *Building Communities through AmeriCorps*; Project Star, *Seniors for Schools Evaluation Results*; and Wang, *Montana AmeriCorps*State Programs, Oregon AmeriCorps*State Programs*, and *Washington AmeriCorps*State Programs*.

127. Fear et al., *Environmental Problem Solving in Lansing*; Perry and Thomson, *Building Communities through AmeriCorps*; and Wang, *Montana AmeriCorps*State Programs, Oregon AmeriCorps*State Programs*, and *Washington AmeriCorps*State Programs*.

128. Wang, *Montana AmeriCorps*State Programs, Oregon AmeriCorps*State Programs*, and *Washington AmeriCorps*State Programs*.

129. Driebe, *The Devolution Challenge*, p. 2.

130. Perry and Thomson, *Building Communities through AmeriCorps*.

131. Macro International, *Description and Evaluation of the Summer Reads Initiative*.

132. Project Star, *Seniors for Schools Evaluation Results*.

133. Fear et al., *Environmental Problem Solving in Lansing*, pp. 66–67.

Part IV. Summing Up and Taking Stock

Notes to Chapter 7

1. Harris Cooper and Larry V. Hedges, "Research Synthesis as a Scientific Enterprise," in *The Handbook of Research Synthesis*, ed. Harris Cooper and Larry V. Hedges (New York: Russell Sage Foundation, 1994), p. 5.

2. Judith A. Hall et al., "Hypotheses and Problems in Research Synthesis," in *The Handbook of Research Synthesis*, p. 19.

3. Two statistical tests were performed to assess the stability of findings over time. T-tests were conducted comparing the proportions of positive findings pre-1990 and post-1990. There were no significant differences comparing pre-1990 to post-1990 studies. An analysis of positive, negative, and no effect findings across six periods (1950s, 1960s, 1970s, 1980s, 1990s, and 2000) also identified no significant differences.

4. Leslie Lenkowsky and James L. Perry, "Reinventing Government: The Case of National Service," *Public Administration Review* 60, no. 4 (2000): 298–306.

5. AmeriCorps's scale also figures into the scrutiny accorded it. AmeriCorps*State and National, which enrolled more than 20,000 members in its first year, eclipsed the size of its 1960s predecessors, the Peace Corps and VISTA, which together never had more than 20,000 members in their thirty years of operation. Plans to increase AmeriCorps membership by several times its first-year membership assured close scrutiny.

6. In 1997, the General Accounting Office also conducted an investigation of twenty-four AmeriCorps projects from seven different states and found that, together, AmeriCorps members "organized food programs that served 2500 children; assisted with totally rehabilitating 16 vacant public housing units; operated a 7–week summer reading camp for 36 children; planted trees, removed debris, and created gardens improving 32 urban neighborhoods; and provided parenting classes to low-income families" (U.S. General Accounting Office, *National Service Programs: Role of State Commissions in Implementing the AmeriCorps Program* [U.S. General Accounting Office, 1997, p. 13]).

7. See James L. Perry et al., "Inside a Swiss Army Knife: An Assessment of AmeriCorps," *Journal of Public Administration Research and Theory* 9, no. 2 (1999): 225–50, for an interesting discussion on the early years of civic service policy implementation.

8. Grantmaker Forum on Community and National Service, *The State of Service-Related Research* (Berkeley, CA: Grantmaker Forum on Community and National Service, 2000).

9. Lynne Ford, *Youth Volunteer Corps of America Final Evaluation Report* (Charleston, SC: College of Charleston, 1994).

10. Charles C. Moskos, *A Call to Civic Service: National Service for Country and Community* (New York: Free Press, 1988).

11. For a more in-depth discussion of these two schools of thought (labeled by Moskos as *instrumental* and *civic content*), see Moskos, *Call to Civic Service*, p. 2.

12. "Public Law 103–82: National and Community Service Trust Act of 1993" (107 Stat. 785; September 21, 1993). Text from *United States Public Laws*. Available from LexisNexis Congressional (Bethesda, MD: Congressional Information Service). For the list of eight goals, see endnote 8 in the Introduction. For a discussion of how they sometimes conflict, see James L. Perry et al., "Inside a Swiss Army Knife." (Accessed January 26, 2003)

13. Steven Waldman, *The Bill: How the Adventures of Clinton's National Service Bill Reveal What Is Corrupt, Comic, Cynical—and Noble—About Washington* (New York: Viking, 1995), p. 20.

14. Michael W. Sherraden, "The Civilian Conservation Corps: Effectiveness of the Camps" (Ph.D. diss., University of Michigan, 1979).

15. Jeffrey L. Pressman and Aaron Wildavsky, *Implementation: How Great Expectations Are Dashed in Oakland* (Berkeley: University of California Press, 1984); see also Carson K. Eoyang and Peter D. Spencer, "Designing Effective Programs," in *Handbook of Public Administration*, 2d ed., ed. James L. Perry (San Francisco: Jossey-Bass, 1996), pp. 232–49.

16. We know, for example, that low member skills at entry and low member educational attainment and socioeconomic status (creating the potential for misunderstanding of service as employment) negatively affect the service intensity–outcome relationship.

17. For a more detailed discussion of interorganizational, intersectoral partnerships, see James L. Perry and Ann Marie Thomson, "Can AmeriCorps Build Communities?" *Nonprofit and Voluntary Sector Quarterly* 27, no. 4 (1998): 399–419; see also Ann Marie Thomson, *AmeriCorps Organizational Networks on the Ground: Six Case Studies of Indiana AmeriCorps Programs* (Washington, DC: Corporation for National and Community Service, 1999).

18. Cooper and Hedges. "Research Synthesis as a Scientific Enterprise," in *The Handbook of Research Synthesis*, p. 5.

19. James L. Perry and Michael C. Katula, "Does Service Affect Citizenship?" *Administration and Society* 33, no. 3 (July 2001): 360.

20. Harris Wofford, Testimony before a U.S. Senate Hearing of the Sub-Committee of the Committee on Appropriations, Departments of Veterans Affairs and Housing and Urban Development and Independent Agencies Appropriations for Fiscal Year 1998, March 4, 1997, p. 108.

21. Moskos, *A Call to Civic Service*, p. 2.

22. Harry C. Boyte, "Community Service and Civic Education," *Phi Delta Kappan*, June 1991, pp. 766–67.

23. Miranda Yates and James Youniss, "Community Service and Political-Moral Identity in Adolescents," *Journal of Research on Adolescents* 6, no. 3 (1996): 271–84.

24. Perry and Katula, "Does Service Affect Citizenship?"

25. Robin Garr, *Reinvesting in America* (Reading, MA: Addison-Wesley, 1995); Shirley Sagawa and Eli Segal, *Common Interest, Common Good: Creating Value Through Business and Social Sector Partnerships* (Boston: Harvard Business School Press, 2000); and William Shore, *The Cathedral Within: Transforming Your Life by Giving Something Back* (New York: Random House, 1999).

26. William James, "The Moral Equivalent of War," *International Conciliation*, no. 27 (1910): 3–20.

27. Harris Cooper and Larry V. Hedges, "Potentials and Limitations of Research

Synthesis," in *The Handbook of Research Synthesis*, ed. Harris Cooper and Larry V. Hedges (New York: Research Sage Foundation, 1994), p. 524.

28. Perry et al., "Inside a Swiss Army Knife," p. 246.

Notes to Chapter 8

1. The term *objective function* is used here in the same way that it is used by operations researchers to denote the set of goals that are pursued in a program.

2. Wendy Kopp, *One Day, All Children: The Unlikely Triumph of Teach for America and What I Learned Along the Way* (New York: Public Affairs, 2001), p. 20.

3. The figures are from a 1999 survey conducted by the research firm of Kane, Parsons, and Associates. Reported in Kopp, *One Day, All Children*, pp. 151–52.

4. Ronald G. Corwin, *Reform and Organizational Survival: The Teacher Corps as an Instrument of Educational Change* (New York: Wiley, 1973).

5. Ibid.

6. Leslie Lenkowsky, "Funding the Faithful: Why Bush Is Right," *Commentary* 111 (2001): 19.

7. Charles C. Moskos, *A Call to Civic Service: National Service for Country and Community* (New York: Free Press, 1988), p. 1.

8. William F. Buckley Jr., *Gratitude: Reflections on What We Owe to Our Country* (New York: Random House, 1990), pp. 136–52.

9. Ibid., and Moskos, *Call to Civic Service*.

10. Suzanne Goldsmith-Hirsch, *Leveraged Grantmaking: Challenging Funders and Programs to Sustain National Service* (Washington, DC: Points of Light Foundation, 2000); Grantmaker Forum on Community and National Service, "Service as a National Movement NOT Just Another Federal Program," 1997; available at www.gfcns.org/pubs/GFCNS_NationalMovement.pdf (December 24, 2002), "National Service in the Next Century: Taking It to Scale," 1998; available at www.gfcns.org/pubs/GFCNS_NextCentury.pdf (December 24, 2002).

11. Shirley Sagawa and Eli Segal, *Common Interest, Common Good: Creating Value through Business and Social Sector Partnerships* (Boston: Harvard Business School Press, 2000).

12. Arthur C. Brooks, "Public Subsidies and Charitable Giving: Crowding Out, Crowding In, or Both?" *Journal of Policy Analysis and Management* 19 (2000): 451–64, "Is There a Dark Side to Government Support for Nonprofits?" *Public Administration Review* 60 (2000): 211–18, and "Do Public Subsidies Leverage Private Philanthropy for the Arts? Empirical Evidence on Symphony Orchestras," *Nonprofit and Voluntary Sector Quarterly* 28, no. 1 (1999): 32–45.

13. Robert Bellah et al., *Habits of the Heart: Individualism and Commitment in American Life* (Berkeley: University of California Press, 1985).

14. Robert D. Putnam, *Bowling Alone: The Collapse and Revival of American Community* (New York: Simon and Schuster, 2000).

15. Robert D. Putnam, "Bowling Together," *The American Prospect* 13, no. 3 (February 11, 2002); available at www.prospect.org/print/V13/3/putnam-r.html (January 25, 2003).

16. Buckley, *Gratitude*, especially Chapter 9.

17. Alexis de Tocqueville, *Democracy in America* [The Henry Reeve Text] (New York: Alfred A. Knopf, 1945), pp. 114–18.

Appendices

Notes to Appendix A

1. James L. Perry et al., *A Review of Service Related Research 1990–1999: A Report to the Grantmaker Forum Research Task Force* (Bloomington: Indiana University, 1999).

2. Harris Cooper and Larry V. Hedges, "Research Synthesis as a Scientific Enterprise," in *The Handbook of Research Synthesis*, ed. Harris Cooper and Larry V. Hedges (New York: Russell Sage Foundation, 1994), p. 11.

3. Corporation for National and Community Service, "About Us: History of National Service"; available at www.nationalservice.org/about/history.html (January 26, 2003).

4. Library of Congress, "Library of Congress Online Catalog"; available at http://catalog.loc.gov (January 26, 2003).

5. More details about the database are available at www.gfcns.org/pubs/GFCNS_ResearchMonograph.pdf.

6. Gary Kowalczyk, National Service: Meeting Its Goal (internal document) (Washington, DC: Corporation for National Service, November, 1999); and Lance Potter, Five-Year Summary for Corporation for National Service Board of Directors (internal document) (Washington, DC: 1999).

7. Richard Danzig and Peter Szanton, *National Service: What Would It Mean?* (Lexington, MA: Lexington Books, D.C. Heath, 1986).

8. Charles C. Moskos, *A Call to Civic Service: National Service for Country and Community* (New York: Free Press, 1988).

Notes to Appendix B

1. Harris Cooper and Larry V. Hedges, "Introduction," in *The Handbook of Research Synthesis*, ed. Harris Cooper and Larry V. Hedges (New York: Russell Sage Foundation, 1994), p. 8.

Notes to Appendix C

1. Henry W. Riecken, *The Volunteer Work Camp: A Psychological Evaluation* (Cambridge, MA: Addison-Wesley, 1952), p. 49; Riecken cites David Henly, "Work Camps," *Quaker Education Considered* (Guildford, NC: Guilford College, 1946) when talking about the AFSC.

2. Riecken, *The Volunteer Work Camp*, p. 50.

3. Ronald B. Corwin, *Reform and Organizational Survival: The Teacher Corps as an Instrument of Educational Change* (New York: Wiley, 1973).

4. Marilyn Gittel with Marguerite Beardsley, and Marsha Weissman, *Final Evaluation Report on Syracuse Youth Community Service* (Washington, DC: Aguirre International, 1981).

5. Robert W. Marans, B.L. Driver, and John C. Scott, *Youth and the Environment: An Evaluation of the 1971 Youth Conservation Corps* (Ann Arbor, MI: Institute for Social Research, 1972); and John C. Scott, B.L. Driver, and Robert W. Marans, *To-*

ward Environmental Understanding: An Evaluation of the 1972 Youth Conservation Corps (Ann Arbor, MI: Institute for Social Research, 1973).

6. Wendy C. Wolf, Sally Leiderman, and Richard Voith, *The California Conservation Corps: An Analysis of Short-Term Impacts on Participants* (Philadelphia: Public/Private Ventures, 1987).

7. Alvia Branch, Sally Leiderman, and Thomas J. Smith, *Youth Conservation and Service Corps: Findings from a National Assessment* (Philadelphia: Public/Private Ventures, 1987), p. i.

8. Sheila Rosenblum and Sally Leiderman, *Youth Corps Case Studies: The San Francisco Conservation Corps* (Philadelphia: Public/Private Ventures, 1986).

9. Alvia Branch and Marc Freedman, *YouthCorps Case Studies: The New York City Volunteer Corps* (Philadelphia: Public/Private Ventures, 1986).

10. David Lah, Wendy Wolf, and Sally Leiderman, *YouthCorps Case Studies: The Marin Conservation Corps* (Philadelphia: Public/Private Ventures, 1985).

11. Mary Anne Lahey, Jeffrey L. Brudney, and William H. Newbolt, "Implementing the Goals of the Corporation for National and Community Service: Lessons Learned in the State of Georgia" (paper prepared for presentation at the Independent Sector Spring Research Forum, Alexandria, VA, March 23–24, 1995).

12. "Public Law 103–82: National and Community Service Trust Act of 1993" (107 Stat. 785; September 21, 1993). Text from *United States Public Laws*. Available from LexisNexis Congressional Online Service (Bethesda, MD: Congressional Information Service).

13. Marc Freedman and Linda Fried, *Launching Experience Corps* (Oakland, CA: Civic Ventures, 1999).

14. Project Star, *Seniors for Schools: Content Analysis of 1997–98 Project Evaluation Reports* (San Mateo, CA: Project Star, 1998), and *Seniors for Schools Evaluation Results 1998–1999 School Year* (San Mateo, CA: Project Star, 2000).

Name Index

Subject Index

About the Authors

James L. Perry is associate dean and chancellor's professor in the School of Public and Environmental Affairs (SPEA) at Indiana University-Purdue University Indianapolis. He has also held faculty appointments at the University of California, Irvine; the Chinese University of Hong Kong; the University of Wisconsin, Madison; and Indiana University, Bloomington. He received M.P.A. and Ph.D. degrees from the Maxwell School of Citizenship and Public Affairs at Syracuse University. Perry has twice served in federal agencies, most recently in the Corporation for National and Community Service. He is vice chair of the Indiana Commission on Community Service and Volunteerism and consultant for the Points of Light Foundation.

Ann Marie Thomson is adjunct assistant professor in the School of Public and Environmental Affairs, Indiana University. Her research focuses on civic service, policy implementation through interorganizational networks, and the nonprofit and voluntary sector (U.S. and international). She received a B.A. in international relations from North Park University in 1978, an associate degree in nursing, with registered nurse licensure in 1982, a master's in public affairs in 1992, and a Ph.D. in public policy in 2001. She is a member of the Indiana Commission on Community Service and Volunteerism.